Building Blocs

Building Blocs

HOW PARTIES ORGANIZE SOCIETY

Edited by Cedric de Leon, Manali Desai,

and Cihan Tuğal

Stanford University Press
Stanford, California

Stanford University Press
Stanford, California

Printed in the United States of America on acid-free, archival-quality paper

Library of Congress Cataloging-in-Publication Data

   Building blocs : how parties organize society / edited by Cedric de Leon, Manali Desai,
and Cihan Tuğal.
      pages cm
   Includes bibliographical references and index.
   ISBN 978-0-8047-9390-2 (cloth : alk. paper) —
   ISBN 978-0-8047-9492-3 (pbk. : alk. paper)
   1. Political parties—Social aspects. 2. Social conflict—Political aspects. 3. Social
structure—Political aspects. 4. Political sociology. 5. Comparative government.
I. Leon, Cedric de, editor. II. Desai, Manali, 1966– editor. III. Tuğal, Cihan, editor.
   JF2051B82 2015
   324.2—dc23

                                                                         2014041550

ISBN 978-0-8047-9498-5 (electronic)

Typeset by Thompson Type in 10/14 Minion

CONTENTS

TABLES, MAPS, AND FIGURES

ACKNOWLEDGMENTS

This project began as an article manuscript in 2007. Instead of dismissing us for studying something as marginal to sociology as political parties, Howard Kimeldorf introduced us to each other and assisted in forming the nucleus of what would become a wider and vibrant intellectual community.

Much has transpired in the ensuing seven years, and we have accumulated many debts along the way. The 2007 manuscript became a 2009 journal article. Julia Adams, who was then coeditor of *Sociological Theory*, worked closely with us during the revision process to sharpen our ideas. The program committee of the American Sociological Association (ASA) saw fit to turn our article into a thematic session at the 2009 annual meeting in San Francisco. We are thankful to them and to Isaac Martin, Dan Slater, and Dylan Riley, who were our copanelists. Conspicuous in the audience were three scholars who would become our advocates and most thoughtful critics in the years to come: Julia Adams, Lis Clemens, and Ann Orloff.

ASA 2009 was a rare treat, for it was the only time the three of us have ever been in the same room together: Our collaboration has been almost completely through e-mail. One near exception to that rule was our 2011 book conference in Chicago, where all of us except for Manali and Dylan sat in a boardroom for a day with Julia, Lis, Ann, and several talented University of Chicago graduate students, including Sofia Fenner, Mary Akchurin, and Jose Antonio Hernandez. We must thank Dan for placing his considerable resources at U of C at our disposal (incidentally, it was Dan who proposed the title, *Building Blocs*). Ann and Lis read every draft chapter for that conference, and their feedback greatly shaped what you are about to read. We would also like to thank our colleagues and students at the LSE, Cambridge University, UC Berkeley, and Providence College for their insightful comments along the way. They have helped shape the volume in innumerable ways. The perceptive criticisms of Loïc Wacquant, as well as the insights of Peter Evans and Michael Burawoy, were crucial in our rethinking of the entire project.

The board, editorial staff, and anonymous reviewers of Stanford University Press (SUP) have been extraordinarily generous and enthusiastic. We wish to thank our acquisitions editor, Frances Malcolm, for her commitment to the project; SUP Editor-in-Chief Kate Wahl, for seeing it through to fruition; and editorial assistant James Holt, for helping us in the final stages.

We end on a personal note, for something else happened on the way to writing this book: the three of us became parents. Our children have probably conspired to extend this project a year or two beyond what it would have taken had we been footloose and fancy free, but then this achievement would not have been as sweet, nor our lives as complete. This book is dedicated to them.

Building Blocs

INTRODUCTION
POLITICAL ARTICULATION
The Structured Creativity of Parties

Cedric de Leon, Manali Desai, and Cihan Tuğal

ALEXANDRE AUGUSTE LEDRU-ROLLIN WAS an unlikely leader of the Revolution of 1848 in France. His political allegiance shifted with the wind: from the Socialist Party on the left to the right-wing Party of Order. Rollin's indecision was so complete that it became the stuff of legend. Rollin, or so the story goes, saw a mass of workers marching through the streets of Paris and said, "I am their chief; I must follow them" (Calman 1922, 374). The story, however humorous, advances a serious analytical claim, one reminiscent of the so-called sociological approach to political behavior: that party politicians follow the lead of society and that society, furthermore, is the principal agent of social change.

Though this approach has become more sophisticated over time, its bedrock assumption has remained largely unchanged since the 1940s. Many scholars (and members of the educated public) assume that social cleavages like class and ethnicity best explain "individual vote choice" (that is, why a person votes for one party but not another) and, in turn, the behavior of political parties seeking to mobilize the sum of such choices to their electoral advantage. Thus, parties above all express social divisions in the electorate.

That view is broadly in line with the notion that parties are democratic organizations that represent the will of the electorate. Some critical scholarship, by contrast, envisions parties and indeed politics as a whole as an extension of the state or of the individual careers of politicians. On this account, leaders are thieves or usurpers of popular power. They form an oligarchy that serves only them and other elites and enhances the power of the state. The historical figures that come to mind are leaders like Jospin and Stalin, not Ledru-Rollin.

This book is the result of our growing dissatisfaction with both mainstream and critical approaches because, in our own work, we have found that parties do more than simply reflect social divisions or extend the influence of political leaders and the state. How would our perception of the state and society change, we came to ask, if we took politics as constitutive (rather than derivative) of both? As we pursued this question, we realized that such a perspective had even broader implications for how we understand history, social and political structure, and human action.

This book offers an alternative programmatic statement for a new generation of scholars, one that does not define political parties as the organizational reflection of voters, states, or ambitious politicians but as *usually the most influential agencies that structure social cleavages.* Parties politicize or "articulate" such divisions to build powerful blocs of supporters in whose name they attempt to remake states and societies. A key assumption of our approach, which we call "political articulation," is that ethnoreligious, economic, and gender differences, among others, have no natural political valence of their own and thus do not, on their own steam, predispose mass electorates to do anything. Nor do certain kinds of crisis (such as economic) have an elective affinity for certain parties (for example, socialist, fascist, or religious). Whether variation in religious affiliation becomes politically salient in times of war or recession, for instance, depends in part on whether parties articulate it as a matter of contention. Moreover, crises are themselves articulated politically: A war does not become a "quagmire" without it being framed in those terms, and likewise "an economic crisis" may be the result of too much social spending according to some and too little such spending according to others.

By this we are not suggesting that parties articulate social cleavages through rhetoric alone. Nor do we suggest that parties can articulate cleavages at will; as we discuss later, some parties are simply unable to carry out articulation projects, whereas others may experience failure at one time and success at another. Our broad claim is that we cannot understand cleavages without parties.

We define political articulation as the process by which parties "suture" together coherent blocs and cleavages from a disparate set of constituencies and individuals, who, even by virtue of sharing circumstances, may not necessarily share the same political identity. Articulation is both a process and a mechanism of bringing together the constituents of the social through specific tools that we call the "means of articulation." It is the *creative potential* of parties that is crucial to understanding the political articulation approach, for though parties have many tools at their disposal, these tools have to prompt individuals to "nominate"[1] themselves as members of social groups. Party politics is thus more than just a chess game or, in journalistic parlance, a matter of arithmetic; to succeed at articulation, target constituents must identify, say, as workers and therefore socialist, as Muslims and therefore Islamist, or as ethnic Russians and therefore nationalist. There is nothing automatic about this process of self-identification or about the process by which self-identification builds to bloc or cleavage formation.

It follows that not all attempts at articulation are successful. As Dan Slater discusses in Chapter 4 of this volume, the two major cleavages in Indonesian politics from the 1990s, regime and religious, have been disarticulated, and in the vacuum the major parties have sought to collude in promiscuous power-sharing. Disarticulation occurs when there is a deterioration in the ideological linkages between parties and their social base and a consequent collapse in existing political blocs. Likewise, articulations may be weak—as Manali Desai shows in Chapter 5, the articulations attempted by Congress and the Bharatiya Janata Party (BJP), as well as regional ethnic articulations have been marked by their inability to take hold and become hegemonic. Such articulations are vulnerable to instability and perpetual challenge, blocking any real attempt at the transformation of the political economy toward development. In both cases parties are constrained by factors external to them, but, as we show in this volume, some parties can be very creative in turning existing circumstances into opportunities for transformation.

The "means of articulation" that parties employ in their projects consist of state and nonstate mechanisms that they *uniquely* possess to politicize social differences that might not otherwise be politically salient. These include rhetoric; public policy; official state and paramilitary violence; co-optation (for example, appointing the head of an insurgent movement to high office or incorporating professional politicians from competing camps via shifts in policy and rhetoric); the provision of social services and infrastructure (as in patronage or public works projects); constitutional rules (for example, granting or changing voting, linguistic, worship, broadcasting, and other rights, or the structure of representation); peace commissions and other civic groups that mediate between different factions of the state, a divided society, and military and paramilitary groups; and electoral mobilization, including the recruitment (and possibly transformation) of powerful civil society organizations (for example, church, union, and newspaper endorsements).[2] We will clarify further in the following discussion why many of these means have usually been conceptualized simply (and reductively) as activities of the state.

These means are available primarily to parties, because in both democratic and nondemocratic societies alike parties usually control the system of nominations, appointments, and elections to political office and, as a consequence, control the resources and prerogatives of state power (for example, the right to make war, tax, allocate public moneys). Few other institutions are better positioned to structure social cleavages and usher new social orders into being.

Thus, an emphasis on the socially creative role of parties does not just clarify the relationship between political elites and their constituents. The implications of political articulation are more sweeping than that. As Talcott Parsons once wrote, sociology aims to solve the original "Hobbesian" puzzle, namely, how is social order possible (1951, 36)? Parsons, however, like Emile Durkheim before him, misperceived society as a self-propelling "system" or organism instead of an effect of political articulation, a suturing together of heterogeneous demands, people, and institutions into a seemingly integrated whole (in Parsons's case, the Cold War Keynesian order). Conversely, we hold that the state of purposelessness and unbridled heterogeneity envisioned by the classical concept of "anomie" obtains in the absence of an articulating agent. In such instances, previously revered (and reified) social categories such as "the common man," "the welfare state," and "the nation" threaten to come apart. Undoubtedly, the social is not merely the reflection of the political: We are not interested in replacing one form of reductionism with another. Nevertheless, we propose to examine the *partisan* sources of social organization, focusing first on the ways in which parties integrate collective identities, coalitions, and institutions into taken-for-granted social orders, and second on the ways in which the social thus constituted threatens to come apart when parties fail to do the work of articulation or when formerly dominant articulations are supplanted by others.

As such, our focus is not on "traditional" parties that orient toward minor questions, the resolution of which tends to maintain the existing social order (for example, "Which of us has the expertise to manage the government?" and "Will we extend conditional cash transfers to the next income bracket that is not covered under the prevailing welfare legislation?"). Rather, our focus here is on what we call "integral" parties that orient to transformational questions (for example, "Shall we prohibit slavery?" and "Are we a secular or a religious society?").

The distinction between traditional and integral parties requires clarification up front before we delve into greater theoretical detail. First, the term *integral* does not carry a positive valuation. The parties we examine in this volume are not necessarily or even typically parties whose politics we endorse. We employ this term with a critical edge. Second, one might ask whether integralness is a categorical variable (that is, either a party is integral or it isn't) or a continuous variable (for instance, 0 = traditional, 1 = somewhat traditional, . . . 6 = integral). For us, integralness is a categorical variable, but integral parties have (a) different capacities for realizing their transformational goals (for example, smaller or larger memberships) and (b) different orientations to transformational questions (for example, immediatist versus gradualist, electoral versus revolutionary). These variations are a function of several factors, including the origins of parties, degrees of monopolization of the political field, the influence of founding intellectuals and thinkers, and degrees of professionalism, among others. Finally, as we stated earlier, integral parties cannot transform social orders at will. Some conditions help bloc building, whereas others hinder it. Success depends on conditions that greatly enhance the ability of parties to take advantage of their unique resources, the means of articulation, whereas failure is caused by conditions that drastically curtail such ability. Parties that seek to employ means of articulation based on state resources may find it difficult to sustain during economic downturns—think of welfare programs, for instance. On the other hand, success for one party may mean failure for another. Thus, economic depressions increase an integral party's chances of success (especially if it is in the opposition), because the depression badly compromises the incumbent party's ability to maintain their blocs through, say, tax cuts or patronage. Wars can also cut both ways. A governing party's access to military power places at its disposal war making as a means of politicizing social divisions such as nationality or religion. On the other hand, depending on the length and conduct of the war, a putative defense of national sovereignty can greatly tax a country's economy, turn off the spigot of government largesse, and, in turn, undermine the idealistic rhetoric that helped to hold the party's bloc together.

This last point clarifies the position of parties vis-à-vis the state in our theoretical framework. Broadly speaking, the present volume aligns itself with studies of the state in arguing for the relative autonomy of the political, where politics are not reducible to social relations like competing class interests. Unlike some sociologists of the state, however, we do not see the state as the prime mover of social organization. Nor do we see parties as agents or residues of the state. Instead we envision a more collaborative relationship. For example, if we assume as Carl Schmitt ([1922] 2005) does that the most conspicuous feature of state power is the ability to declare an exception to the rules, then it bears mentioning that a party, once in power, assumes the prerogative to suspend civil liberties and, in an atmosphere of paranoia, further expand their base by ostentatiously routing out an alleged fifth column in their midst. The Nazi Party is the classic example of this, but there are many others, some of them contemporary to our time. Beyond deploying state power, parties may also give coherence and identity to the state. Characterizations such as the "totalitarian," "nanny," "socialist," or "bourgeois" state are not exclusively the work of government bureaucrats or other state managers; they may also be artifacts of the struggle among parties to interpret state actions for political advantage, expand and divert state power, or occasionally create new states.

Traditional parties also engage in many of the activities we call the means of articulation. What differentiates the integral party is that it subordinates these activities to its overall mission. For instance, a traditional party might pay lip service to social justice rhetoric if there are serious challenges to, say, the inegalitarian structures of the polity. An integral party, by contrast, revamps its policy orientations when the polity is faced by such challenges and thereby not only changes its rhetoric and policy but also draws to itself many cadres otherwise suspicious of party politics. It also seeks to reshape civil society organizations under its control along the lines of its new policies and rhetoric, even though the degree to which it can do this should be taken as a variable.

Institutional tools, too, can be turned into means of articulation. For instance, patronage is one of the core tools of traditional party building. But in the hands of a political party with integral orientations, it can go beyond simply serving a means–ends calculation (based on exchange of votes for benefits) and become the basis of a mobilizing identity. That is, some parties distribute coal and clothing not simply to get votes but to breed deeper identification with the ideological stance of the party. This orientation to politics, then, is what occasionally renders patronage and other activities (which some scholars have classified as state formation tools) means of articulation.

The rest of this introductory essay will press the foregoing claims in four parts. The first is a brief, critical assessment of the existing literature, much of which tends to view political parties as expressing or at most mediating other supposedly more important social actors and processes (for a more elaborate discussion of the theories discussed in this section, see de Leon 2014). In the second part, we review theoretical traditions similar to our own, acknowledging our shared intellectual debts but also clarifying where we depart from our predecessors. Next, we explain the political articulation framework in greater detail, with special attention to the analytical gaps identified by our colleagues in the years since we introduced the approach. Finally, we end by explaining our case selection rationale, outlining the chapter structure of the book and identifying the ways in which each piece contributes to a fresh party-centered approach to social organization.

THE REFLECTION HYPOTHESIS: SOCIAL, PARTISAN, ISSUE, AND VALUES VOTERS

The three dominant approaches to individual vote choice and political behavior more generally are the sociological or Columbia model, the social psychological or Michigan model, and the rational choice model. Though these are competing approaches, we read them as making a similar analytical move, namely, to employ *metaphors* (for example, interests, preferences, predispositions) for relating cleavages to parties at specific historical conjunctures. Metaphors are not causal mechanisms, however. If individual survey respondents appeared to be motivated by class during the New Deal, party identification in the 1950s, issues in the 1960s, and values in the 1980s, as these successive models suggest, then it remains unclear why this is so. Is it because one model is better than the other? Have we developed better survey techniques over time that reveal previously undiscovered voter motivations? Are different generations of voters simply motivated by different things: one by class, another by party, and still others by injustice or values? After our critical review of the literature, we will submit that these incommensurate findings are artifacts of successive political projects to remake society, or, in more theoretical language, competing modes of political articulation.

The Social Voter

Intellectual histories of the field (for example, Bartels 2008; Carmines and Huckfeldt 1996; Converse 2006; de Leon 2014) tend to begin with the first modern voting studies, which were conducted at Columbia University's

Bureau of Applied Social Research under the direction of sociologist Paul Lazarsfeld.

Lazarsfeld's research design was a "panel study" of vote choice in Erie County, Pennsylvania, in which he and his team interviewed individual voters at regular intervals leading up to, and immediately after, the 1940 U.S. presidential election. The entire study, including the questionnaire, was designed to capture campaign effects on the voter. Lazarsfeld found little support for his hypothesis. First, the overwhelming majority of voters did not change their minds from the first interview (when they identified their preferred candidate) to the last (when the respondents reported their vote). Evidently, the campaign had minimal effect. Second, the "background questions," asked routinely at the beginning of surveys to establish the respondent's basic biographical information, turned out to have the highest correlation with vote choice.[3]

Having found that campaigns had minimal impact on vote choice, Columbia sociologists resolved to do a follow-up study (this time under the leadership of Bernard Berelson and in Elmira, New York, for the 1948 U.S. presidential election) to uncover the reasons that social relations had been so decisive in explaining political differences. Their data confirmed once again that class, ethnic, and ecological (that is, residential) divisions continued to provide "the most durable social bases for political cleavage" (Berelson et al. 1954, 75). The *reason* that class, ethnicity, and residence were so important, however, was not that they could trigger an automatic response in the voter's psyche.[4] Concrete social relations guide vote choice by way of three mechanisms. First, social differences in the population such as religious affiliation are a condition for disagreement in a community, but they are not sufficient to *maintain* political differences. So, second, the "transmission" of those differences through the generations via the family and other social groups (such as churches, unions, and social clubs) is a condition for the persistence of political loyalties. Finally, there must be physical "contact" among people who are socially and politically alike to maintain consensus within the group (Berelson et al. 1954, 74). Because these conditions are best met in class (for example, workplace), ethnic (such as church), and residential (such as neighborhood) settings, they account for most of the variation in vote choice.

Lipset and the Functionalist Turn

Although the Bureau's work was avant garde for the time, it was nevertheless quickly eclipsed by four waves of scholars. The first was a new generation of sociologists led by a former Columbia graduate student, Seymour Martin Lipset. As Lipset himself wrote (Lipset [1959] 1965), because the unit of analysis in *The People's Choice* and *Voting* was the individual voter instead of society as a whole, the early voting studies were social psychological rather than sociological per se. To correct for this, Lipset sought to infuse the early interest in electoral politics with a "functionalist" sensibility. His central preoccupation in those early years was to identify the conditions enabling a stable democracy. His more mature work in this direction, however, and undoubtedly the last truly original programmatic statement in the sociology of political behavior, was his introduction (with Stein Rokkan) to an edited volume called *Party Systems and Voter Alignments* (1967). In a work of grand comparative and historical sweep, Lipset and Rokkan delineated the functions of political parties in a democratic order and theorized the social origins of party systems in Western Europe. Parties, they wrote, serve an *"expressive* function" in that "they develop a rhetoric for the translation of contrasts in the social and the cultural structure into demands and pressures for action or inaction." They also possess *"instrumental* and *representative* functions" in that parties force the leaders of competing interest groups to bargain with each other, stagger their demands over time, and occasionally join forces to exert the maximum pressure on the state (1967, 5) [emphasis in original]. Lipset and Rokkan traced the origins of these competing interest groups to two types of "critical juncture" in Western Europe: national revolution and industrial revolution.

Borrowing Parson's method for analyzing societies with conceptual polarities, they identified four types of partisan cleavage: majority versus minority ethnic groups, nation-state versus church, land owning versus industrial elites, and eventually the overriding one, elites versus nonelites (1967, 14–15). Linked to this account of European cleavage formation is Lipset and Rokkan's "freezing hypothesis," according to which revolutionary era cleavages became institutionalized in the party system beginning in the 1920s. Thus, they write, *"the party systems of the 1960s reflect, with few but significant exceptions, the cleavage structures of the 1920s . . . the party alternatives, and in remarkably many cases the party organizations, are older than the majorities of the national electorates"* (1967, 50) [emphasis in original]. The idea is that cleavages, once entrenched in the party system, narrow the electoral "support market" so much that no other causes or issues can gain traction (1967, 51).[5] It is important for Lipset that this is a desirable result, for it checks the emergence of extreme left- and right-wing parties seeking to undermine the democratic order.

Partisan Voter, Issue Voter, and Values Voter

But Lipset and his associates were not the only ones to distance themselves from the Columbia model. A group of social psychologists (Angus Campbell and Gerald Gurin) and political scientists (Warren Miller, Donald Stokes, and Philip Converse) at the University of Michigan would found the "social psychological" approach to vote choice. The canonical work in this literature is Campbell et al.'s (1960) *The American Voter*. Briefly, the latter held (and contemporary practitioners reassert) that social cleavages such as class and ethnicity do not correlate well with individual vote choice. A superior explanatory variable, which they gleaned from *national* surveys of voting behavior (Columbia's were community studies), was party identification, or "party ID." The variable is a misnomer in that it has little to do with parties; it is a political identity transmitted through family socialization. Rather than loyalty to social group, the Michigan model privileged loyalty to political group, a loyalty anchored in affective attachments to one's parents' or grandparents' partisan commitments.[6]

A challenge to the social psychological approach, which thereby opened up a second front against the Columbia model, was the body of work on "issue voting." This literature might meaningfully be divided into two camps: those who borrowed heavily from the Michigan tradition and those who did not. The former consists of the so-called revisionist and realignment traditions. Revisionists held that although uncritical adherence to one's partisan identity may have accurately described American voters during the New Deal era, it did not hold true for new voters who came of age during the 1960s as the issues of civil rights and the Vietnam War came to the fore. This new cohort of voters, whose parents were the children of Depression-era voters, were not only emotionally removed from the cleavages of the past but also more educated than the previous two cohorts of voters. They were, in other words, more open to political persuasion in the context of short-term "stimuli" such as events and new issues (Beck 1974; Carmines et al. 1987; Key 1966; Nie et al. [1976] 1979). Closely tied to revisionism is the realignment tradition, which holds that the advent of new issues among the mass electorate has the power to disrupt existing patterns of party dominance (see, for example, Abramson et al. 2010; Brady 1988; Burnham 1970; Carmines and Stimson 1989; Key 1955, 1959; Sundquist 1983).

Rational choice theory incited a clearer break with the Michigan tradition. Unlike the revisionists, proponents of "spatial theory" (Black [1958] 1963;

Downs 1957; Hotelling 1929; Smithies 1941) assume that voters are always rational actors. They are not blind partisans or oversocialized voters for a generation only to become rational in the next, as the revisionists imply. Voters have issue preferences or interests (for example, prochoice or prolife) and choose the candidates whose own stated preferences are closest to their own.

A related set of literatures on what might be called "values voting" cast further doubt on the sociological approach, which was seen as privileging the effect of social class on political behavior. The election of Ronald Reagan in 1980 occasioned a raft of fresh postmortems on the New Deal, centered on the conservative racial and moral values of white working- and middle-class American voters (see, for example, Frank 2004; Fraser and Gerstle 1989; Wattenberg 1995). Margaret Thatcher's ascendancy spurred similar studies in Britain (Franklin 1985; McAllister and Rose 1986), wheras Inglehart (1990) provided the empirical support for this "culture shift" in much of the Western industrialized world. With few exceptions, the decline of class voting is attributed to bottom-up socioeconomic processes. Inglehart's thesis is typical of these accounts: The narrative begins with the claim that the welfare state blunted the cruelest dislocations of laissez-faire capitalism; the resulting physical and economic security, in turn, allowed voters to turn to quality-of-life or "postmaterialist" issues like environmentalism.

Reasserting the Sociological Approach

It was in the context of the foregoing critiques that the two major restatements of the sociological approach emerged. The first was David Knoke's (1976) *Change and Continuity in American Politics*. In that piece, Knoke conceded the importance of party ID and the declining significance of class but insisted that religion, race, and residence remained important determinants of vote choice (1976, 36, 58, 89, 109). The reason for the persistence of social cleavages in general, he argued, was that political parties are diffuse "secondary" groups with whom voters have very little contact; it is only through the "penetration" of political sentiment in nonpolitical primary (family) and secondary social groups (for example, unions) that party loyalties can become and remain viable (1976, 11).

The second restatement was Manza and Brooks's (1999) *Social Cleavages and Political Change*. Like Knoke, they found that race, religion, and region remain important cleavages in American politics but add that gender and class are also decisive. Their theoretical framework, which they adapt from Bartolini and Mair (1990), aims to account for not only long-term shifts in voter loyalties but also short-term shifts, which sociology's attention to stable social characteristics is famously hard pressed to explain. Like Berelson et al. (1954), Manza and Brooks argue that cleavages must operate at three levels for them to have significant effects on vote choice and party-voter alignment. The first is voters' objective structural position (for example, immigrant status) because cleavage has an "'empirical' component rooted in social structure." But one's objective position is not enough to exert a political impact, so the second level, "group identification and conflict," suggests that "social groups making up a cleavage field" must "adopt conflicting forms of consciousness." People must, in other words, think differently about a given issue, say, immigration reform, such that poorer native-born white voters oppose such reform, for example, whereas more affluent whites and foreign-born voters of color favor it. But conflicting consciousness cannot lurk beneath the surface if a cleavage is to shape political behavior—it must be "expressed" through "individual interactions, institutions, and organizations, such as political parties, which develop as part of the cleavage" (1999, 33–35).

· · ·

The political articulation approach is at variance with the dominant theories of political behavior. Much of the foregoing literature is interested primarily in individual vote choice and secondarily on the ways in which the sea of heterogeneous choices add up to short-term electoral outcomes (that is, the winner of a single election) and long-term alignments between parties and mass electorates (that is, the dominance of one party for a generation). All politics is an expression of the individual's social relationships, interests, or values. This is clear from the field's methodological impulses: Lipset was correct to make hay out of the obvious point that the unit of analysis in survey research is the individual, not society. Any broader implications turn on the assumption that individual responses to survey questions coalesce into an accurate picture of the social. We, however, are skeptical of that assumption. For us, survey answers are mediated through political articulation, so that expressed interests, values, and social relations cannot be taken at face value as these scholars insist. More than this, we suggest that if voters appear motivated by class in the New Deal data, uncritically partisan in the 1950s data, rational in the 1960s data, and then motivated by values in the 1980s data, it is because parties emerged (or refashioned themselves) in each period to shape the very logic of political right-mindedness; they offered the "correct basis" for political judgment in their struggle for power. By contrast, in the realignment tradition, for example, the role of parties is unclear: One gets the sense that political organizations are at the mercy of voters' shifting policy preferences, as if those preferences are not themselves shaped by the myriad practices of political parties.

There are of course limited exceptions to our broad characterization of the existing literature. It was V. O. Key who, in 1961, wrote, "If a democracy tends toward indecision, decay, and disaster," then "the responsibility rests" with "the influentials, the opinion-leaders, the political activists in the order" and not with "the mass of the people" ([1961] 1964, 558). We do not endorse the exhortation to "responsible parties" implied here, but there is at least some healthy skepticism about the notion that the mass electorate determines the ethos of the social order. More recent practitioners of spatial theory point out, in our view correctly, that "in the Michigan model, the conceptualization of candidates is passive . . . [they] . . . are conceived as fixed parameters in the voter's force field" (Enelow and Hinich 1984, 6). Their critique of the Michigan model notwithstanding, in spatial theory American parties are assumed to act like firms, "modifying their behavior" (for example, fine-tuning their "message") so as to capture the middle-of-the-road or "median" voter. Although Manza and Brooks cannot reasonably be called "socially deterministic," neither can they be said to posit a distinct party-centered alternative to the Columbia model. Cleavages in the social structure scale up to shape voter consciousness and are "expressed," not just by parties (which, in any case, "develop as part of the cleavage") but also through myriad institutional, organizational, and interpersonal encounters. This is vaguely reminiscent of other multilevel theories in the social sciences. Katznelson and Zolberg (1986), for example, suggest that social class operates at four layers of history and theory: structure, ways of life, dispositions, and collective action. The distinction among structure, disposition, and collective action is also an important feature of Bourdieu's work on class. If these prominent social scientists are any indication, then we are not simply tangling with the ghosts of Lazarsfeld and Lipset: Newer society-driven approaches, although certainly more sophisticated than their forbears, nevertheless comprise a major and influential mode of contemporary sociological thinking about social cleavages.

ELITE THEORY AND ITS ANTECEDENTS

Though the works discussed in the preceding section comprise the dominant theories of political behavior, they are by no means the first or the only intellectual lineages in the field. Sociological analysis of parties has a long tradition deriving from Weber's theory of bureaucratic authority, which for him was key to understanding the structure and operation of modern institutions. Whereas the party was the necessary organizational counterpart to mass democracy, the inevitability of bureaucratic domination meant that the relationship between the party and democracy was in fact contradictory. Michels ([1911] 1962) took this idea and formed a devastating critique of parties, particularly of the radical left, whose social transformation projects he viewed as "inevitably" hindered by the hierarchy of party officialdom. For Michels, the "iron law" was that, regardless of programmatic ideology, party oligarchies tended to develop an independent interest in concentrating organizational power in their leadership. Since then, elite theory has treated the party and the state as simply concentrations of organizational power among leaders who possess specific intellectual capabilities (Mosca 1939; Pareto 1984). Strands of Michels's theory of parties have filtered into social movements scholarship, where the explicit or implicit assumption is that parties largely inhibit radical transformation and generally have little constructive role in the generation of movements.[7] However, some scholars have questioned the lawlike nature of Michels's proposition. For instance, Voss and Sherman (2000) and Stepan-Norris and Zeitlin (1989) have shown that when labor leaders challenge organizational hierarchies or when specific ideological currents necessitate less hierarchical structures, the iron law does not hold true (see also Clemens and Minkoff 2004 and Martin 2007). Likewise, Kitschelt (1989) argued that the German Green Party followed a "logic of constituency representation" (as opposed to Michels's "logic of electoral competition") that reflected the ecological movement's mobilizing strategies, including their lack of cohesion (1989, 2, 3, 5, 277). Parties, in other words, are themselves constructs of specific ideological and democratic practices, rather than reified organizations (Panebianco 1988).

·   ·   ·

Although Weber's work informs this long and influential strand of research on parties, it is important to bear in mind that his notion that bureaucratic domination was an inescapable fact of modern life was deeply influenced by the legacy of the Prussian state and its notion of *staatsraison*. The idea of the rational and impersonal state standing above society was a historically specific outcome of German state history, and despite Weber's interest in comparative enquiry there has as yet been a relatively weak acknowledgment of this facet of his writings in political sociology. Indeed, in Weber's (1946) less frequently cited writings, not least *Politics as a Vocation*, he emphasized that leadership and charismatic authority could be strong countervailing forces to bureaucratic domination. In this important lecture Weber dwelled at length on the qualities of leadership—the passion, responsibility, and sense of distance "to things and men" that would characterize the ideal leader. One could argue that, despite Weber's own pessimism about modern organization, his writings reveal a more subtle approach specifying a *contradiction* between the charismatic aspects of party leadership (the "necessity to woo and organize the masses" [Weber 1946, 102]), and the party as a "machine." This aspect has not been seriously developed in later appropriations of Weber's work in state theory and gesture toward an opening for the articulatory practices of political parties.

THE STATE AS POLITICS: ITS AUTONOMY AND FORMATION

The landmark edited volume *Bringing the State Back In* (Evans et al. 1985) was the first to outline a theory of state autonomy based on a clear distinction between state and society. The volume ignited a rich field of cross-disciplinary scholarship in which the state was viewed as an autonomous organization, located at the intersection of class structures and the international system of states, where it maneuvers to extract resources and build administrative capacities (Evans 1995; Skocpol 1979). Rather than classes or other groups constituting themselves in struggle as Marxists and pluralists held, it was institutions and organizations that penetrated to the core of society, organizing social groups accordingly. Yet, within this attempt to delineate an autonomous role for politics, parties remained curiously ancillary to the process (Ertman 1997; Mann 1986; Skocpol 1979). Instead, parties appear as institutions that carry out or reinforce these "Weberian" tasks.

When state autonomy explanations have integrated political parties as causal factors, they have tended to look at the way parties respond to the timing of bureaucratization, legacies of state capacity, and social pressures, rather than analyzing how political parties are formative of the social and the state itself (Finegold and Skocpol 1995; Orloff and Skocpol 1984; Shefter 1977; Skocpol 1980).[8] In Ann Orloff's work, which offers the most party-centered account from this perspective, the political actors (their constitution as subjects, their rhetoric, their orientations) are not central. The causal mechanism is their response to institutional context (here, mostly electoral competition and bureaucratic capacity and autonomy).[9]

The increasing attention to the state within political sociology was further refined in literature emerging during the 1990s centered on "state formation" (Ertman 1997; Gorski 2003; Corrigan and Sayer1985; Steinmetz 1999). In a more nuanced and less static approach to the state, sociologists largely working within the comparative-historical tradition sought to historicize the state itself, treating it not as a single, solid, and unified entity but as a process or mechanism that was imbricated in society (Hansen and Steputtat 2001). State formation includes rules and policy making, bureaucratic growth, legal codes, electoral rules, and, fundamentally, the "nature and location of boundaries between state and society" (Steinmetz 1999, 9). In this sense state activities such as the census, for example, organize groups such as castes in India. Thus, Bernard Cohn's (1987) work showed how important the British colonial census was to creating castes as political entities in India. This was only possible because individuals were grouped together in specific ways, and these groups were identified, named, and counted, that is, objectified. Likewise the strict separation of Hutu and Tutsi and the objectification of such differences are attributed to the use of identity cards by Belgian colonizers in Rwanda (Kertzer and Arel 2002; Mamdani 1996).

Although we will go on to outline some affinities with this approach, we disagree with the ontology of the state that is implicit in the "state autonomy" project. First, drawing on Timothy Mitchell (1999), we posit that the neo-Weberian analytical separation of the state from society underestimates the degree to which the very idea of the state is a contextual construct.[10] The line separating the state from society is not given; the ingredients of both the state and society are redefined in each political context. Moreover, as Jessop notes, "the unity of the state" is itself a "project" that results from the promotion of a party spirit that links the state to the national popular imagination (1990, 364).

SOCIAL MOVEMENTS

Scholarly approaches to social movements have developed more nuanced ways of exploring the remaking of the social through political processes. In the "political opportunities" approach, the central mechanisms that explain change are divisions within the state elite, the emergence of elite factions sympathetic to activists, and the willingness of the state to resort to violence against mobilization (McAdam 1982; Tarrow 1998). Although it has since been recognized that political opportunity structures must be recognized by activists as such, the burden of explanation of the success or failure of movements rests on an interaction between these structural breaks and the actions of movement activists (McAdam et al 2001). Parties are given a less central role relative to elite resilience, strategy, and failure in explaining social movements (McAdam 1982). In another strand of the social movements literature, resource mobilization theorists explain social change based on the capacity of activists to accumulate resources. They therefore focus more on the resources that party elites might grant to movement activists (Oberschall 1973), when they do not marginalize parties in their explanations altogether (see, for example, McCarthy and Zald 1977). In such accounts, party elites are the resources of social movements rather than central to explaining their direction, outcome, and timing. Put differently, there is an implicit bias in the emphasis on resources and opportunities in the social movements literature (Goodwin and Jasper 1999).

Among scholars who focus on political process there has been a greater acknowledgment of the independent role of parties in generating and organizing social movements (Costain and McFarland 1998; Burstein 1998; Goldstone 2003). Yet, because the focus of the scholarship is the movements themselves, parties remain secondary to the explanation of specific political outcomes. Furthermore, these works do not bring into focus the role of parties in structuring cleavages, which form the central objective of our project (for an exception, see Veugelers 1999). Piven and Cloward's work, with its special focus on the interactions between movements and parties, epitomizes some key theoretical differences between the movements literature and our approach. In *Poor People's Movements*, Piven and Cloward draw on Michels's classical framework (1979, xvi, 159) to argue that political parties have no positive role to play in social change. These organizations, rather, suck up the positive bottom-up energy of the people, with the unintended help of reformist or revolutionary organizations on the ground (1979, 72–82). The protestors are the real inciters of change through their disruptive capacities, not the establishment parties or their institutional challengers (1979, xxi–xxii, 27–32). Political parties ultimately co-opt and absorb the forces of social change, rather than foster them. Since then, Piven and Cloward (2000) have come to the conclusion that, although political parties are still less dependable than popular movements, they can be reformed to incorporate the energy of the grassroots. On that account, parties do not have quite the same chilling effect on social change because they can be prevented from obstructing change and can even channel popular discontent in ways that encourage change. We, however, suggest that, beyond merely absorbing or rechanneling popular pressure, parties have the capacity to construct grievances and mobilize the grassroots around them.

A related tendency in some earlier strands of the social movements scholarship takes grievances to be ubiquitous and available to be tapped (Hafez 2003; Olson 1965; McCarthy and Zald 1977; Tilly 1978). More recent approaches within the social movements literature have acknowledged the importance of "framing" such that, when projected movement frames align with popular grievance frames, the ensuing resonance can enable a movement's success (Snow and Benford 1988). Our theoretical focus is slightly different: Although we agree that framing is important, we do not take popular grievances as given and waiting to be tapped. In this, we follow Laclau and Mouffe to the degree that parties articulate grievances in specific ways through the construction of "chains of equivalence." For example, a given party may link unfulfilled demands in housing, employment, and schools; establish a bond among the victims in each area as if they were members of the same group (for example, a class or ethnic group); and thus construct a stable system of signification, whereby all those who favor meeting those demands are "the people" and all those against are "the elite." This view of the formation of political demands begins not with the individual or collective grievance but with its constitution into something stable that can be articulated and represented in the political domain. This way of thinking about grievances refutes the idea that "popular grievances" merely need representing through movement frames; rather, there is a crucial mediating practice that party leaders or movement activists perform in constituting them as antagonisms. As we clarify in the following section, however, we disagree with both the framing perspective *and* Laclau and Mouffe in the sense that rhetoric is only one of several means of articulation available to parties.

INTELLECTUAL DEBTS

The Construction of Interest and Identity

Our work dovetails with others that, in a general way, question the givenness of interests and cleavages. Perhaps the classic work in political science is Giovanni Sartori's (1969) essay, "From the Sociology of Politics to Political

Sociology." Sartori's target is Lipset's claim in *Political Man* (1960) that parties represent the democratic translation of the class struggle into electoral politics. He begins by asking whether voters can be said to have a class identity when they themselves are unaware of that identity (71, 73–74).

As an alternative to such imputations, Sartori's approach is to test what he calls an "organizational variable" that would map the "influence of party and trade union control" on voting behavior. In doing so, one might be able to confirm whether political parties organize workers to see themselves as a class or merely reflect what workers already realize based, say, on their experience of factory life. For instance, if an analyst finds that workers vote for the labor party in the absence of any local organizational influence (such as a labor party chapter), then we might say that parties have little to no influence on the inculcation of class identity and that therefore it is workers who exert upward pressure on parties to represent them (Sartori 1969, 84).

Once social scientists test the organizational variable, however, Sartori suspects that the data will contradict Lipset's findings. For Sartori, a worker's position in the economic system only makes it easier or at least possible that workers will see themselves as a class.[11] It is up to the parties to do the rest. Thus, Sartori wrote famously,

> To put it bluntly, it is not the "objective" class (class conditions) that creates the party, but the party that creates the "subjective" class (class consciousness). More carefully put, whenever parties reflect social classes, this signifies *more* about the party end than about the class end of the interaction. The party is not a "consequence" of the class. Rather, and before, it is the class that receives its identity from the party. Hence class behavior presupposes a party that not only feeds, incessantly, the "class image," but also a party that provides the structural cement of "class reality." (Sartori 1969, 84)

Class therefore has no objective existence outside of party politics. Class is only ever an "image," "reality," and "identity" that is constructed by parties. It follows, then, that class is not the only way that society may be divided; a party may also use religion to divide people. Whether the people embrace one identity or another depends on which party wins the "belief battle." He explains, "Whenever the class appeal outweighs the religious appeal, this is not because class is an 'objective reality'; rather, this is because the ideology of class wins the 'belief battle,' in conjunction with the prevalence of a new organizer, the mass party" (Sartori 1969, 87).

Sartori's analytical move finds a strong echo in the "political construc-tionist" literature, which holds that racialization occurs in the political arena (Gerteis 2003, 2007; Marx 1998; Redding 2003). A favorite case in point is the populist revolt of the late-nineteenth-century United States, in which white and black farmers joined forces to take over the political system. Rather than assume that these interracial farmer coalitions failed because whites and blacks had fundamentally conflicting interests, Gerteis demonstrates that black Republicans and white Democrats constructed "narratives of interest" that initially led farmers of different backgrounds to see each other as a class. It was only after organizing problems surfaced that the two parties came to view the meaning of the coalition differently and dissolved it (Gerteis 2003, 199, 202).

Redding (2003) uses a similar approach to explain the disfranchisement of blacks and poor whites in North Carolina after the populist revolt. Dis-satisfied with accounts that suggest that racial prejudice was its root cause, Redding argues that racism itself does not clarify how disfranchisement was actually accomplished. Thus, he writes (and we agree), "Motive is not a mecha-nism," an explanation for what happened and why (2003, 6). As an alternative, Redding explains that the contraction of democratic rights at the turn of the twentieth century originated with the way in which political elites *made* race and power.

That process occurred in three phases. In the immediate post–Civil War period, Democratic Party elites in North Carolina forged a "vertical organiza-tion of power" that tied different sectors of the community together through a system of mutual obligations and benefits that kept wealthy whites on top and poor whites and blacks on the bottom. But, in 1894 and 1896, a fusion of Republicans and Populists defeated the Democratic Party with a "horizontal organization of power" by "stressing equality and denying the significance of hierarchy within the group." Finally, Democratic Party elites borrowed from their opponents' strategies by building horizontal camaraderie among whites through the rhetoric of "white supremacy" in 1898 and 1900. "Once back in power," Redding observes, "elite Democrats used the state to disfranchise, and therefore demobilize, their opponents" (Redding 2003, 14–16). In this, Red-ding joins Gerteis by questioning the explanatory power of objective racial interests and differences. He writes,

> The absolute political relevance of certain categories of people (such as "class,"
> "farmer," or even "race")—and the attendant interests that are lumped to-

gether with them—cannot be assumed. Instead, the analysis must trace how certain identities came to be thoroughly politicized . . . [and] came to be essential mechanisms of mobilization. (2003, 11)

Social identities and interests may therefore exist, but parties have the potential to "make" them at certain historical conjunctures and remake them at others, thereby making power. To find the origins of political outcomes such as disfranchisement, then, one need look no further than the sphere of politics itself. "Political traditions and rules as well as party structures and activists," Redding argues, "are the primary organizers of political action" (ibid.). In this, parties have more than rhetoric at their disposal: Because of the system of party government, white supremacist Democrats "used the state" to undermine the interracial coalition of Republicans and Populists by disfranchising their base.

This approach resonates very much with our own, but it does not go as far as we would like. Although the challenge to interest-based theories is an important intellectual project, political construction stopped at the water's edge, namely with the critique that interest is not a causal mechanism and in any case has no objective value. This is a necessary first step, but it cannot be the only one. What remains is to craft a theoretical framework that can explain why and by what means some parties make metaphors like "interest," "class," and "values" into the shibboleths of appropriate state and policy making, whereas other parties do not.

Neo- and Post-Marxist Lineages

Lenin ([1902] 1973) was one of the first Marxists to conceptualize the role of the party as an organization that is formative, and not simply reflective, of social consciousness and mass struggles, though Marx ([1852] 1992) himself had studied how states and parties shape, divert, rechannel, and mediate economic forces. To arrive at the concept of political articulation, however, we follow the path of Antonio Gramsci, who initially took the centrality of class in Marxist theories as given and subsequently reformulated this centrality as ultimately a construct of political struggles. In this sense, our approach may be thought of as "neo-Gramscian."

The historical backdrop of Gramsci's approach was the "organic crisis" of interwar Italy in which parties proliferated and none recognized the authority of the others to rule. In this moment of frightening possibility, which eventuated in the rise of fascism, Gramsci (1921) wrote a piece titled "Parties and Masses," in which he observed, "The masses don't exist politically, if they are not framed in political parties." While in prison, Gramsci continued to write about the role of political parties in articulating the social world. In a note on "The Modern Prince" (his prison code word for the Communist Party), Gramsci wrote,

> Ideas and opinions are not spontaneously "born" in each individual brain: they have a centre of formation, of irradiation, of dissemination, of persuasion— a group of men ... which has developed them and presented them in the political form of current reality. The counting of votes is the final ceremony of a long process. (Gramsci 1971, 192)

Those who generate and shape ideas and opinions are the leaders and intellectuals of political parties. Gramsci is thus suspicious of economic determinists who insist that so-called objective conditions or interests naturally give rise to a certain kind of politics. For Gramsci, socioeconomic change in and of itself has no natural political valence that springs "spontaneously" to our consciousness. It is up to parties to interpret the socioeconomic "in the political form."

Later politics-centered revisions of Marxism focused on the social backgrounds of rulers or reduced each political organization (including political parties) to an apparatus of the state, even when the autonomy of the latter was recognized (Miliband 1969; Poulantzas [1968] 1973, 1974, 325). Bob Jessop (1982) has granted a more central role to parties and underlined how they coordinate conflicting particular interests and articulate them to a general interest. However, he has mostly emphasized economic interests, whereas our cases necessitate looking at how parties articulate these with noneconomic interests. Although Block (1987) and Przeworski (1985) have recentered the role of politicians and political parties, we go beyond both by pointing out the ideologically structuring power of parties—that is, their power to define the very terms in which rationality, interests, and incentives (which these authors sometimes take for granted)[12] are discussed and evaluated.

We point out that these important neo-Marxist contributions to political sociology (from Miliband to Jessop) have sidestepped one important issue Gramsci had raised: the sociologically constitutive role of the political party. This volume takes up the task of revisiting his insights, as well as revising and expanding them.

Gramsci ([1930–1932] 2007, 246) draws attention to the potential role of the party as the organizer of "collective will" (out of dispersed wills) through the arousal of passions and the circulation of myths. Classes are frequently not well-formed groups, so what parties are sometimes faced with is a set of dispersed wills (of economic groups, intellectuals, soldiers, and bureaucrats), rather than classes ready to be represented politically. Moreover, the party brings all of these subgroups together not by following a predetermined rational logic (of either the calculating individual actor of rational choice theory, or of the state builder as in most of recent political sociology); it operates through the logic of myths.

The party is *creative* in this process of organization. Indeed, the will it organizes has the potential to create or recreate states, but its creativity rests on historical conditions such as economic structures, the social balance of power (whether of classes or other groups), the formation of intellectuals, and the administrative legacies of states. That is, political parties may work to establish, say, a communist, theocratic, or apartheid state, but they do not do so under conditions of their own choosing. Whether and how such practices unfold depend, for example, on whether the state the party hopes to refashion is an authoritarian state, a constitutional monarchy, and so on. As intellectuals affiliated or sympathetic with the party work to discredit the intellectual basis of preceding regimes, it matters whether such regimes were based, say, in liberalism, socialism, or Social Darwinism.

Nevertheless, we maintain that the politician can be "a creator . . . [who] bases himself on . . . a relation of forces in continuous shifts of equilibrium . . . for the purpose of mastering and superseding it" (Gramsci 2007, 283). If historical conditions matter, they do not necessarily dictate the political outcome, as the political party can transform the intellectual makeup of the nation by infiltrating schools, unions, media organizations, religious institutions, and other pillars of existing civil society (and this infiltration we take as one of core means of articulation). It can also work to actively improve the economic conditions of multiple sectors, an improvement without which moral reform would be unsustainable.[13] For instance, contemporary socialist parties in agrarian Latin American countries enact policies that redistribute land and other resources to indigenous populations. When this occurs, it is not without the potential of profound changes to the mental outlook of people on the ground. Notions of good and evil, of what is just and unjust, may change throughout this process (Gramsci 2007, 246–249). Political parties thus have the potential to create a new civilization, an alternative morality, and a new state by cultivating leaders, who in turn organize, mobilize, and educate those whom they hope will become their "natural" constituency (2007, 266–267).[14]

Even though we draw on Gramsci's conceptualization of the political party, we would like to underline some differences between our approach and his. Critics of Gramsci, especially Laclau and Mouffe ([1985] 2001), have pointed out that for him hegemony amounts to class power. Laclau has also criticized classical as well as contemporary Marxists for not understanding how the "economy" and "classes" are discursively constructed (Laclau 1990; Laclau 2000, 290–293). Laclau brings to the fore the very activity of articulation that Gramsci dances around throughout his writings but never extensively theorizes. Laclau asks the question of how politics work to carve out "privileged" identities[15] from an ocean of mere differences (2005, 69, 73). For him, the process by which different identities and demands congeal into a popular bloc requires a series of steps. First, many unmet demands accumulate. These demands are then added onto others in a way that differentiates certain sectors of the population from others.[16] Laclau calls this process the creation of a "chain of equivalence" out of demands that would otherwise have remained isolated from each other (either by remaining mere differences or through their institutional incorporation). Finally, these demands, which have now become the common demands of a bloc, are stabilized into a system of signification (2005, 74–75, 77–78, 93). The process of stabilization cannot follow logically from the demands themselves; it can only happen when a discourse external to the demands harnesses them to a powerfully symbolic but vague word such as *freedom* or *justice*, in his words an "empty signifier" (2005, 96–98).

Seen from this angle, political activity is not exclusively the drafting of policies and their implementation (factors that the state formation literature focuses on, through concepts such as "state capacity" and "infrastructural power"). Nor is it just about securing votes and public support (that is, legitimate representation, which is the core focus of voting behavior scholars and some cultural analysts of the state). Rather, it is first and foremost the articulation of isolated demands and sectors into one's camp (148, 150–151) as well as the disarticulation of certain demands and sectors from the rival camp and their rearticulation into one's own camp (2005, 131–132).

Adapting some of this framework, we agree with Laclau that there are too many demands and identities that do not necessarily translate into class-based grievances and identities. Where we differ from Laclau is in our emphasis on the institutional and organizational elements of articulation, especially the role of political parties. For, in addition to dropping Gramsci's assumption that hegemonic blocs amount to class coalitions, Laclau also dispenses with the party as the organizer of such blocs. In other words, the process by which certain signifiers come to be these "privileged" articulating symbols gets a short shrift.[17] We point out that organizational histories and the making of professional party cadres and leaders[18] (who become experts in the manipulation of symbols and the uses of state power) is the missing mechanism in Laclau. Analytical narratives must, in our view, focus on the ensemble of structures and institutions that favor or prevent the gradual cultivation of such experts; Laclau's discourse analysis must be supplemented by political sociology; that is, by structural and institutional analyses.[19]

This analytical difference is based on our overall philosophical position, which draws on poststructuralism but is not poststructuralist. Though, like Laclau, we use linguistic metaphors and analyses, we do not reduce all elements of the social (including contradictions between classes) to linguistic equations (see Laclau 2005, 149, for an example of this).[20] Likewise, even though we perceive most social struggles as political struggles (compare Laclau 2005, 153–154), our notion of the political is ultimately not about fights over or between discourses. This is what also differentiates our position from others who have previously used the concept, "political articulation" (for example, Stallybrass 1990).

In addition, we see striking parallels and important differences between our discussion of political articulation and Bourdieu's analysis of classification struggles. For Bourdieu, what or whom is coded as classy or trashy, art or kitsch—in short, good or bad—is not given by objective criteria: Such classifications are the effects of struggles in fields largely removed from ordinary people, to define the yardstick against which all others must measure themselves. Like Bourdieu (1984, 479–81), we point out that social classes or groups are constructed by struggles. However, whereas Bourdieu holds that such struggles occur at some remove from the average citizen (1991a, 9; 1991b, 176–177, 196–197), we hold that parties, although relatively autonomous from the social, are effective only insofar as they are able link their "experts" to the populace. Moreover, we take issue with Bourdieu's idea that different fields (such as art, education, civil rights, labor) align because of similar structuring logics (1991a, 26–27; 1991b, 182–183, 187–188) or "homologies," as our discussion highlights that politicians articulate initially dissimilar arenas, groups, interests, and fields into a seemingly integrated whole. Finally, Bourdieu emphasizes parties insofar as they are engaged in the practice of representation. The act of conferring power, particularly from more dominated groups to their elected representatives, results in what he calls "political fetishism," a process by which groups come "into their own" as a force to be reckoned with (for example, workers during the Industrial Revolution, Latino immigrants in the contemporary United States), yet relinquish control over the group to their representatives (1991b, 204). Though we agree with parts of Bourdieu's analysis in this regard, we draw attention to the historical variation in the character and success of political fetishism. For example, despite the existence of relatively well-formed village communities in early-twentieth-century Russia, the Social Revolutionaries, the party that spoke in the name of the peasantry, was not able to organize them as a national class. By contrast, the Chinese Communists, acting under more favorable political circumstances and a radically reinterpreted Leninist model of organization, were able to forge a class out of the much more dispersed and disorganized Chinese peasantry.[21]

In sum, we see strong parallels between Bourdieu's dialectic of group formation and representation and our concept of articulation. Nevertheless, in our approach parties play a more autonomous role than Bourdieu appears to acknowledge. We combine Bourdieu's classification struggles and Laclau and Mouffe's more flexible theorization regarding the open nature of the social (that is, where social differences are not given and are thus open to articulation) with Gramsci's concrete focus on institutions, world-historical contexts, and conjunctures. Seen in this neo-Gramscian light, Bourdieu's symbolic power or what he calls, following Nelson Goodman, "worldmaking" (the power to transform "a serial collection of juxtaposed individuals" into collectivities)[22] becomes a capacity that fluctuates depending on the impact of historical forces. For all these reasons, we theorize the work of political parties in the next section as "structured creativity."

POLITICAL ARTICULATION: THE STRUCTURED CREATIVITY OF PARTIES

Political parties bring together the constituents of the social, which would otherwise come apart. We perceive societies as composed of numerous and dissimilar elements. And none of these elements—whether a class, religious community, ethnic group, or something else—has an internal self-reproducing logic that would automatically bind its so-called members together (Brubaker

2006; Jones 1983). Similarly, there is no natural link between any of these social groups and the state that claims to represent them.

The heterogeneity of most any society could render grand narratives (such
as the history and destiny of a nation) meaningless. However, unlike post-
modern analysis, which views heterogeneity as a virtue in and of itself (and as
a hodgepodge that does not add up to any meaning), we argue that political
activity may—and frequently does—forge unity out of disparity. Grand narratives become effective forces in history when they are politically circulated.
Society, then, is not a self-propelling entity, organism, or system but a result of
the contingent work of integration. We follow other thinkers in calling such
work "articulation" (Gramsci 1921; Hall 1986, 1987; Laclau 1977; Omi and
Winant 1994, chapters 5 and 6).[23]

It is frequently the incessant "suturing" activity of parties in cultural, parliamentary, and nonparliamentary arenas that "holds" class, religious, sexual,
and ethnic formations together and refashions them as constitutive elements
of hegemony. Classically defined by Gramsci as the acquisition of mass consent to rule, our view of hegemony is slightly more complex: For us, it is the
active participation of the broadest strata in the making of their own subordi-
nation by accepting select inequalities (for example, economic, gender, racial,
and the like) and institutions (such as the party, the state, welfare, the market)
as natural or common sense.[24] This process of interpellation, the "hailing of
individuals into these entities," produces the self-identification that we referred to at the beginning of this Introduction. We emphasize that this active
consent is not spontaneous (though it is frequently *experienced* as such): It is
produced. It is this structuring work of integration and the interpellation of
individuals into larger entities that the dominant theories tend to neglect.

Political activity articulates different sectors and demands into blocs;
blocs, in turn, provide the mass impetus for the (re-)formation of states and
other institutions. They employ particular "means" or tools for articulating
and disarticulating hitherto either unaffiliated or rival demands, identities, and sectors to one's own side. For example, a party that campaigns for
a constitutional amendment to enfranchise property-less citizens over the
objections of the political establishment would bring into the electorate a
ready-made constituency of its own. Such tools are available uniquely to party
organizations because with few exceptions they are the preeminent wielders
of formal state power; their leaders, once in power, are heads of state or the ex-
ecutives of subnational polities. Thus, the leading political party of a minority

government may exercise the state prerogative to make war against another state to expand its base from a relatively narrow nativist bloc to a majoritarian nationalist bloc.

This last example gestures to another implication of our approach: Neither parties nor the blocs they mobilize are static. In the process of articulation, disarticulation, and rearticulation, demands, identities, and sectors may change content and form (at times subtly, at times in straightforward ways). The organizations and networks that carry out the work of articulation also undergo changes during these processes. Both the articulating actors and the articulated sectors risk thorough mutation or even dissolution, though the strength of both paradoxically depends on articulation (hence, they avoid the game of articulation only at their own peril). This makes the game radically contingent: It is not inevitable that a self-identified Hindu, for example, will support a Hindu nationalist party; that would depend on historical context and on whether the struggle among competing parties makes, say, Hindu victimization a matter of contention.

Further, an "integral" party is able to politicize hitherto apolitical social identities, not because that is its function but because it orients to transformational questions. Such questions provoke the polity to make weighty choices such as whether their society should be laissez-faire or state regulated, slave or free, religious or secular, authoritarian or democratic. In contrast, "traditional" parties by definition orient to minor questions, the resolution of which leave the status quo unperturbed. The questions of traditional politics often turn on questions of management (that is, whether one's party or another is better suited to manage the economy) or small changes in policy (such as whether social benefits might be extended to cover the next income bracket).

An example of a traditional party is the post–New Deal Democratic Party, which first restricted its politics to minor moves within liberal welfarism and a few decades later succumbed to play within the conservative-neoliberal logic institutionalized by the conservatives. An example of an integral party is the Democratic Party of the New Deal itself, which set new terms and conditions of policy and state formation for a generation. Reaganite and Thatcherite conservatism comprise other examples, though the ascendancy of the Republican Party turned in part on the promise to preserve the racial privileges of the New Deal's white suburban middle-class power base (de Leon, Desai, and Tuğal 2009; de Leon 2011). A similar observation can be made regarding the Hindu nationalist Bharatiya Janata Party in India, which moved from a marginalized position to the center of Indian politics in the 1990s, largely because it set the terms of the debate over secularism and Nehruvian socialism and thereby shifted politics to the right. As an integral party, it went beyond the confines of the agenda that the Congress party had prosecuted for decades, forcing the latter to adopt many of its positions. The BJP did so through a complex process of articulating and rearticulating sectors ranging from the middle classes to subaltern groups (Desai 2012).

To repeat, integralness for us is a categorical variable, not a continuous one: A party either is or is not an integral party. However, as we noted earlier, integral parties have (a) different capacities for realizing their transformational goals and (b) different orientations to transformational questions. This variation is a function of various factors, including the history and intellectual basis of parties as well as the degree of professionalization among party operatives. For example, although ("moderate") Islamic parties are generally seen as being cut from the same cloth, they in fact differ organizationally and programmatically. The Turkish Justice and Development Party (Adalet ve Kalkınma Partisi, or AKP)—with its ability to forge cultural conservatism, economic liberalism, and an original blend of political liberalism and authoritarianism against secular authoritarianism and remnants of corporatism—is the leading example of an integral Islamic party (Tuğal 2009). Its innovative moves have led intellectuals and liberals to merge with conservatives, most Islamists and religious nationalists in their fight against leftists and Kemalists. Though the organizational structure of the historical Egyptian Muslim Brotherhood had acted as a model for the integralism of the AKP (and its Turkish predecessors), its uneven institutionalization (more specifically, its lower degrees of professionalism and of monopolization of the Islamic field) has eventuated in the failure to articulate a hegemonic bloc.

As the contrast between the AKP and the Brotherhood makes clear, our approach does not offer a voluntaristic conception of politics in which parties can organize constituencies as they please. Still, to speak (in the discourse of social science) of "conditions enabling or constraining bloc building" is tricky, as a constraint to one party may be an enabler to others. This paradox can be resolved through a focus on the means of articulation previously enumerated. Conditions that limit the ability of parties to exploit the resources uniquely at their disposal tend to cut against bloc building, whereas conditions that enhance such ability are favorable to bloc building. Depressions and recessions comprise one such condition, because they place constraints on the capacity of, say, an incumbent party to direct the economic means of articulation like patronage, social spending, and tax cuts toward constituencies in their coalition. Downturns therefore simultaneously enable bloc building by opposition parties because governing parties have less access to the economic resources that once helped to hold their blocs together.

War is another condition. Exercising the war-making prerogative of the state may allow a governing party to build blocs by stoking the fires of nationalism or ethnic pride, for instance, while stigmatizing the opponents of war as weaklings, traitors, or apathetic minorities. Using war as a means of articulation carries risks, however. A war that goes badly, is costly, and/or drags on may invite international sanctions and thereby shrink the aforementioned economic means of articulation that a party may use to maintain its governing bloc. Such a war could also discredit the government's nationalist rhetoric as impetuous and deleterious to the country's international reputation.

Still another condition is social transformation. Regardless of its source (that is, whether it is the project of a political party), the transition from a rural to an industrial economy or from a regulated to a market economy, for example, tends to boost the heterogeneity of social life: New demands, sectors, and identities have a tendency to proliferate in such contexts. Accordingly, traditional rhetoric, public policy, constitutional rules, and sources of taxation—in short, the means of articulation with their existing content—become less relevant, making the constituents of existing blocs available for recruitment. Political struggles to win them over to one's side intensify. Conversely, in the absence of social transformation, current rhetoric and policy suffice to maintain existing blocs, such that urging new demands or identities feels purposeless and emergent movements and identities simply fade.

The relative ability to exploit the means of articulation matters because previously articulated social cleavages and social orders shape the possibilities of, and limits to, hegemony. Parties do not conduct their creative work in an unarticulated vacuum—a tabula rasa. They must creatively dispense with or repurpose the discursive and institutional manifestations of articulations past. When the latter are weakened by war, depression, or social transformation, the articulative potential of integral parties increases; without these destabilizing influences, previous articulations remain salient and taken for granted as common sense, making it difficult for elites and constituents alike to imagine an alternative social order.

Of course, the foregoing conditions are not neatly applicable in cases where political organizations are weak and do not have decisive influence over the state and civil society. In such situations, factions within the state and civil society (or sometimes even prominent intellectuals and charismatic figures) act as quasi-parties to articulate social formations and cleavages. This was indeed the situation in Gramsci's native Italy, where intellectuals like Croce, more than organized parties, offered integrating logics. Nevertheless, such political disorganization invites crises, leading possibly to perpetual instability, overbearing charismatic figures, and turmoil (for example, fascism and eventually civil war in Italy).

Moreover, we assume in positing these conditions that political leaders are in contact with the led. We seek to avoid a political determinism that attributes creativity exclusively to political leaders. The latter generate new strategies and ways of thinking about the social precisely in their interaction with possible and actual constituencies. If leaders are completely cut off from the latter, they cannot craft strategies that will speak to the shifting needs and demands of the populace.[25] They become either useless and irrelevant or dictatorial.

In sum, our research program calls for a study of how and why integral parties emerge. This larger programmatic question may be asked in different ways. What kind of historical formations and crises make this emergence more likely? When do they succeed or fail? Which type of civil societies and states are more likely to produce integral parties? Can institutional parties evolve into integral parties? And is movement in the reverse reaction also possible? Under what circumstances?

The proposed research program also draws attention to the variegated social significance of the process of articulation. When do demands and sectors lose their distinguishing characteristics in the process of articulation? When do they, by contrast, radicalize the vision of the articulating actor? What types of articulating activity lead to the disintegration of the articulated elements and/or the articulating actor, and in which kinds of political contexts?

CASE SELECTION AND CHAPTER ORGANIZATION

To begin addressing these vexing programmatic questions, the contributors to this volume draw on their combined expertise on Indonesia, India, the United States, Canada, Egypt, and Turkey. The chapters offer examples of successful, failed, and weak articulation, as well as of disarticulation.

At this point one might reasonably inquire into the rationale for including these cases but not others. The first and most compelling reason in our view is the sheer variety of cases and outcomes. The cases span an ambitious range that is unusual for its lack of exclusive focus on Europe or the United States. Moreover, in each instance the authors show that outcomes such as American exceptionalism, neoliberalization in Turkey, and the cartelization of parties in Indonesia must be explained by attention to the capacity of political parties to structure social cleavages or build blocs. If political articulation is relevant in the oldest and newest democracies, on three continents, and for every kind of economic and political conjuncture, then we should expect to see those processes almost everywhere in the modern world. The cases therefore demonstrate that political articulation is (not an isolated, but) a general, phenomenon in need of systematic analysis.

Secondly, our cases also allow us to bring a party-centered approach to bear on classical and contemporary puzzles in political sociology. For example, the chapters on the United States and Canada address at least two long-standing research questions: Sombart's now century-old question, "Why is there no socialism in the United States?" and "What are the origins of working-class formation?" The chapters on India, Indonesia, Turkey, and Egypt address foundational debates on the sources of capitalist development and democratic reform; the chapter on Turkey and Egypt also theorizes the conditions enabling the success and failure of political Islam.

Having addressed our case selection rationale, we turn now to the individual chapters themselves. In Chapter 1, Cedric de Leon employs the articulation model to explain workers' shifting identity in Chicago from the Jacksonian era beginning in 1828 to the Haymarket Affair of 1886. He argues that the formation of American working-class identity took place in part in the arena of partisan struggle. For example, whereas early Democrats articulated Chicago workers to their party as members of an aggrieved class of producers together with farmers, Republicans articulated them as northerners together with employers and farmers in their section during the political crisis over slavery. Chicago workers began to identify as a class only after the Civil War in defiance of the political establishment, which reframed the wage contract as a metaphor for freedom instead of as a form of slavery, as it had previously been understood. Here the primary means of articulation were rhetoric, economic and territorial policy, and war. The first half of the empirical section turns on two relatively successful articulatory projects, whereas the second half explores the failure of the postbellum party system to articulate workers to their respective coalitions.

In Chapter 2, Barry Eidlin uses the articulation framework to address why the Canadian Cooperative Commonwealth Federation (CCF), precursor to the New Democratic Party, was able to establish itself as one of Canada's main political parties. Though debate on various aspects of the CCF has been hotly contested, the idea that the CCF or a similar party would take root in Canada is taken for granted. The argument is that Canada's parliamentary system, its political culture suffused with a "Tory-touched" liberalism, and a small but significant preexisting left tradition created a political terrain that was relatively favorable to independent left parties. Yet, despite these potential advantages, what is surprising is that no left party was able to establish a major and durable electoral presence prior to the CCF. Why then did the CCF succeed where previous left party efforts failed, and why did it succeed when it did? To explain this, Eidlin shows that the CCF was able to succeed when it did because the ruling Liberal and Conservative parties' responses to labor and agrarian protest during the Great Depression left these constituencies politically excluded, allowing the CCF to articulate an independent farmer–labor alliance that had eluded previous Canadian left parties. Unlike previous left party challenges, the CCF was ideologically and organizationally coherent enough to avoid co-optation while also being flexible enough to unite previously fragmented left constituencies. Repressive ruling party policies created a "common foe" that broke farmer and labor groups away from previous allegiances, while CCF ideology and practice forged a new independent coalition.

Cihan Tuğal's Chapter 3 on Islamist parties in Egypt and Turkey demonstrates the autonomous role of politics in crystallizing and prioritizing certain social differences or cleavages and rebuilding society around them. It first focuses on the Republic of Turkey, with its complex political scene and multiple cleavages, to demonstrate this claim. Divisions between Kurds and Turks, secular and pious sectors, upper and lower classes, and ultimately the ruling elite and the people have had an impact on the political scene for decades. These divisions seemed to naturally find their expression in the opposition of the center-left and the center-right until the late 1980s, but after that point Islamist leaders worked to revise these divisions. By redefining the normal citizen as a *mağdur* (wronged, mistreated), yet hard-working and entrepreneurial Muslim, they attacked the secular ruling elite and thereby rendered free market identity "popular" and built mass support around it. As evidence of this claim, the chapter discusses how the lack of a legal, professionalized, unified, mobilizing Islamic party has restricted (though not completely undermined) the process of Islamic neoliberalization in Egypt.

In Chapter 4, Dan Slater explores what happens when parties fail to do the work of political articulation. When Indonesia democratized in the late 1990s, it appeared that party competition would be characterized by two primary cleavages that had been incubated under Suharto's "New Order": a regime cleavage pitting reformist opponents of the recently fallen dictatorship against its holdovers and a religious cleavage distinguishing parties by their views on the proper political role for Islam. Yet some fifteen years later, neither a reformist nor a religious bloc exists in Indonesian politics. This is not because reformist and religious themes lack resonance among voters—it is because Indonesia's party elites effectively abandoned cleavage politics by promiscuously sharing power in an all-encompassing party cartel. This chapter argues that parties and their presumptive support blocs in Indonesia have become increasingly disarticulated, leaving reformist and religious social forces without the party champions necessary to secure collective expression in national politics. The origins of this disarticulation process can be traced to constitutional reform and the subsequent elite deal making that accompanied the formation of Indonesia's first democratic governing coalitions in 1999 and 2001. By promiscuously sharing power across cleavage lines, politicians disrupted the old party–voter alignments in the 2004 and 2009 elections. This has undermined Indonesia's initially robust party system and ominously opened the door to populist and antisystem challengers striving to rebuild the political blocs that party elites have actively unbuilt.

If Slater's chapter centers on the dynamics of outright disarticulation, Manali Desai's Chapter 5 turns to the related but distinct phenomenon of weak articulation in India. It does so by examining the paradox of growing interparty consensus on market liberalization on the one hand and increasing participation among lower castes and other "subaltern" groups on the other. The two dominant parties—BJP and Congress—have mobilized across class and caste lines since the eclipse of socialism, thereby undermining the salience of these older cleavages and replacing them with a series of novel oppositions (for example, religious nationalist versus secular, progovernance versus antipoor). However, these same articulations have been unable to either contain emerging claims to citizenship among the formerly disfranchised or thicken the latter's rather thin political commitments. The resulting electoral volatility and regional fragmentation have not exactly threatened the market transition, but neither do they provide the kind of full-throated mass support necessary for a truly robust economic development agenda.

The final chapter, Chapter 6 by Dylan Riley, pulls together the dominant themes of the volume by reflecting on Antonio Gramsci's vision of the relationship between party hegemony and democracy, particularly as it applies to contemporary neoliberal democracy. It argues that Gramsci rightly viewed the role of political parties in the construction of hegemony as differing depending on overall historical circumstances; that is, on whether parties operated under conditions of revolutionary or normal politics. In doing so, Riley does not simply reiterate the contributions of the chapters but raises a series of additional questions that would underpin a new research program on sociohistorical transformations across the globe. Under what conditions do parties suppress or create the possibilities for large-scale social transformations? Why are parties unable to do so in some cases (for example, India or Egypt), while playing such a critical role in redefining the cleavages and ideological fault lines of an era (such as the nineteenth-century United States, Canada, Turkey)? The importance of such a perspective in the context of the Arab Spring and other contemporary movements cannot be emphasized enough.

ONE THE POLITICAL ORIGINS OF WORKING CLASS FORMATION IN THE UNITED STATES

Chicago, 1844–1886

Cedric de Leon

THIS CHAPTER SEEKS TO EXPLAIN THE TWISTS and turns in the formation of working-class political identity in Chicago from the Jacksonian era (1828–1844) to the Haymarket Affair of 1886. The two main schools of thought in the literature on working-class formation correspond to what Pierre Bourdieu (1989) has called the "objectivist" and "subjectivist" moments of class. Objectivists claim that class formation results from the structural location of workers and their employers in the system of production. Subjectivists by contrast insist that workers come to identify as a class as opposed to another class in contexts such as labor disputes with their employers.

Yet the trajectory of class formation in mid-nineteenth-century Chicago does not fit either of these frameworks neatly. Chicago workers' first political organization was a land reform league established in 1848 to protest the expansion of slavery into the western territories. Workers organized the city's first trade unions as the slavery issue subsided in the early 1850s, but organizing dropped off as the controversy over slavery extension reemerged. Unions resurfaced midway through the U.S. Civil War. It was at this time that workers began increasingly to refer to themselves as a class. Moreover, although workers' analyses of their deteriorating conditions in the postbellum period referenced unscrupulous employers, they reserved a singular animosity for the major political parties, whom they accused of abandoning the republicanism of the American Revolution (which favored independent farming and artisanry over wage dependency) in support of free market liberalism (which viewed the individual wage contract as the ultimate source of freedom).

This trajectory bears out the broad subjectivist claim that workers come to recognize themselves as a class organically, in their own way and time, but adds that class formation may take place in contexts beyond workplace struggles, namely, in the political arena, where parties compete to articulate coalitions or "blocs" by naturalizing and denaturalizing social divisions such as race and class. Whereas Chicago workers saw themselves as an aggrieved class of producers together with farmers in the early years of the Democratic Party, and then as northern "free labor" during the political crisis over slavery, they began to identify as the working class when the major parties reframed the wage contract as a metaphor for freedom in the post–Civil War era. The city's workingmen viewed this discursive shift and the antilabor violence it permitted as a betrayal of their military service and the promise of the war, which they understood to be nothing less than the emancipation of white workers from wage dependency. In other words, whereas the antebellum period was marked by the successful articulation of workers to political parties, the postbellum period was marked by profound *disarticulation*.

The interlocking dynamics of articulation and disarticulation in turn helped to set the stage for the monumental clashes between capital and labor during Reconstruction and the Gilded Age, not least in the Haymarket Affair of 1886, in which leading Chicago anarchists were hanged for allegedly bombing a rally that they themselves had organized. On the one hand, because of their victory in the late war, Chicago political elites claimed the coercive prerogative of the state to protect industrial capital from labor as it did from the South. Accordingly, the major parties often equated the Chicago labor movement's criticisms of capitalism with proslavery rhetoric. On the other hand, the end of the war limited the Chicago party system's ability to articulate northern workers together with their employers as partners in the Grand Army of the Republic, thereby creating room for a new mode of articulation in which trade unionists and socialists, among others, began to hail workers into a "workingman's party." The convergence of a triumphant and still belligerent northern political elite and a double-crossed working class therefore comprised the real Haymarket bomb, but its fuse, as I seek to demonstrate, had been set well before 1886.

Accordingly, this chapter is not only about the capacity of parties to articulate novel identities and forms of social organization but also about the ways in which the dissolution of previous articulations may give rise to alternative sociopolitical blocs. The postbellum eclipse of the slavery question and the major parties' failure to articulate workers with a contractual vision of a free society cleared the way for the incipient organized Left to articulate workers as a class.

CLASS FORMATION AND POLITICAL ARTICULATION

The debate over the origins of working class formation proceeds in large part from Marx's own enigmatic distinction in the *Communist Manifesto* between the class-in-itself (*an sich*) and the class-for-itself (*für sich*). Marx states that the goal of communism is "the formation of the proletariat into a class"; that is, from a group of workers who share the same structural position as non-owners of the means of production to a "self-conscious" revolutionary movement (Marx and Engels [1848] 1998, 51). The distinction is enigmatic, because it is unclear whether working-class formation follows inexorably from workers' structural location at the bottom of the capitalist system or if a working class can be said to exist only when workers actually identify as a class through their experience of struggle against another class.

Objectivists claim that class formation is a matter of structural position. Thus, Dahrendorf writes, "Classes are based on the differences in legitimate power associated with certain positions, i.e., on the structure of social roles." As such, an individual "belongs to a class because he occupies a position in a social organization; i.e., class membership is derived from the incumbency of a social role" (Dahrendorf 1959, 148–149). Perry Anderson likewise argued against the subjectivist notion that "class consciousness" is the "very hallmark of class formation." "Classes have frequently existed whose members did not 'identify their antagonistic interests' in any process of common clarification or struggle," Anderson wrote, adding, "the concept of class" is "an objective relation to means of production, independent of will or attitude" (Anderson 1980, 40). Erik Olin Wright reaffirmed the objectivist position when he defined class formation as "the formation of collective actors organized around class interests within a class structure" (Wright 1990, 272).

Subjectivists counter that such arguments lead analysts to unfairly chastise workers for not behaving in appropriately "classlike" ways (Somers 1997, 77). Accordingly, subjectivists favor a more relational framework, within which workers construct their own identity in historically and culturally specific contexts that may or may not fit with the revolutionary endgame that objectivists hope for and expect given workers' exploitation under capitalism. The canonical exemplar of this stance is E. P. Thompson, who, in *The Making of the*

English Working Class, insisted, "Class happens when some men, as a result of common experiences (inherited or shared), feel and articulate the identity of their interests as between themselves, and as against other men whose interests are different from (and usually opposed to) theirs." Class is therefore "a relationship . . . defined by men as they live their own history, and, in the end, this is its only definition" (Thompson 1966, 9, 11). Similarly, Katznelson and Zolberg (1986) favor a vision of class formation that is shaped by social relations that include "dispositions," which they define as either shared understandings of the social system or shared values of justice and goodness. Reflecting on Katznelson and Zolberg's framework, Steinmetz (1992) has added that successful cases of working-class formation are those in which workers elaborate coherent narratives about their individual and collective history around the category of social class.

Because the debate hinges on the relative impact of either structural position or identity, scholars of class formation are somewhat at a loss to address the impact of party politics. Przeworski's early research (1977; Przeworski and Sprague 1986), based in part on the work of Antonio Gramsci (see, for example, Gramsci 1971), is perhaps the one exception to this rule.[1] In his now classic critique of objectivism, Przeworski urged an alternative formulation in which "economic, political, and ideological conditions jointly structure the realm of struggles that have as their effect the organization, disorganization, and reorganization of classes" (Przeworski 1977, 343). Here Przeworski attempts to resolve the theoretical antagonism between structure and identity by conceiving of class formation as the effect of both.

This notion of "class effects" finds a strong echo among scholars of democratic party politics. Within political science, Sartori (1969) has argued that parties comprise an "organizational variable" that influences the formation of social cleavages like class and religion. Elsewhere in the social sciences, Ernesto Laclau has criticized as "naïve" the view that "reduces the political forms" to "preconstituted" social groups (Laclau 2005, 7). In the introduction to this volume, de Leon, Desai, and Tuğal use the concept of political articulation to denote the process through which party practices naturalize class, ethnic, and racial formations as a basis of social division by integrating disparate interests and identities into coherent sociopolitical blocs.

Following the political articulation tradition from Przeworski to the present volume, I take a subjectivist stance in regards to class formation, broadly viewing that process as having a relational dynamic instead of a straightforward structural one. However, I suggest that workers may come into their own as a class as they interact, not only with other workers or their employers but also with political parties, whose attempts to naturalize alternate social divisions may occasionally strike workers as disingenuous or worse. Of course, workers may conversely embrace these party alternatives and, in the case of labor parties, may arrive at a class identity precisely *through* political articulation. My own data suggest that Chicago workers (a) accepted the Democratic Party's view that they were members of an aggrieved class of producers together with farmers; then (b) abandoned the Democrats in favor of the Republican Party's view that they were partners in the northern free labor coalition against the slave South; and finally (c) repudiated both major parties as the war came to a close in favor of a view, articulated by socialists and others, that they were a class unto themselves.

METHOD AND DATA

Comparative historical methodology has moved beyond the notion that a single case such as nineteenth-century Chicago is a solitary observation or data point and thus able to generate only tentative theoretical ideas. As Rueschemeyer has argued, single case studies "can test theoretical propositions as well, and they can offer persuasive explanations," in part because they must go through "frequent iterations of confronting" alternative "explanatory propositions with many data points." This iterative process of fitting theoretical ideas to the complexities of a single case "allows for a close matching of conceptual intent and empirical evidence" (Rueschemeyer 2003, 318).

But why choose Chicago to make these particular theoretical propositions? As the queen city in the home state of both Abraham Lincoln and Stephen A. Douglas (the 1860 presidential nominees of the Republican and Democratic parties, respectively), Chicago was a key theater in the transformation of nineteenth-century American politics. Besides the obvious symbolic significance, Chicago manufacturing was then undergoing a dramatic shift from skilled to unskilled production in a variety of trades, a fact that allows us to assess the reactions of workers to industrial wage dependency (Jentz and Schneirov 2012; Schneirov 1998; Schneirov and Suhrbur 1988). Indeed, between 1840 and 1880, manufacturing in Chicago had increased in size from a mere $62,000 in capital investment and 414 total "persons" employed to $72,401,453 in capital investment and 79,414 total "hands" or wage workers employed (U.S. Census Office 1840 [3], 87, 302–309; U.S. Census Office

1883, 960, 1047). Lastly, Chicago workers were at the vanguard of labor unrest that swept across the North in the postbellum era. Not only the Haymarket Affair, but also the nation's first May Day celebration, occurred in Chicago. This suggests that an important rupture occurred after the Civil War in the politics of working people and that Chicago was a critical site of this rupture (Green 2006; Jentz 1991). In all these ways, Chicago was really the crucible for the largest transformations going on in America at the time, prompting one historian to call it "The City of the Century" (Miller 1996).

To document the creation and suppression of competing modes of political articulation, I rely primarily on party newspapers. Nineteenth-century newspapers were the official organs of the political parties and were the principal means through which the far-flung political elites of the early republic tied their leadership and rank and file together in a common public sphere (Cornell 1999; Starr 2004). As Robertson notes, "The principle vehicle for conveying the rhetoric and practice of mass partisanship was a growing network of newspapers" through which "the web of relationships between editors, correspondents, and readers grew and thickened" (Robertson 2004, 67–68).

To document workers' reaction to the parties' attempts at political articulation, I rely on two types of data. First, I analyze letters to the editor and the minutes of labor organizations published in the aforementioned party papers as well as in the *Gem of the Prairie*, the organ of Chicago's antebellum land reform league; the *Workingman's Advocate*, Chicago's English-language trade union weekly; and *The Alarm*, the newspaper of the Haymarket anarchists edited by Albert Parsons. Second, I track presidential electoral returns by ward from 1844 to 1876. The returns are cross-checked against manuscript census reports and other data that describe the wards' ethnic and socioeconomic makeup to discern how majority-worker wards voted from election to election.

FROM PRODUCER TO FREE LABOR, 1844–1860

If Chicago workers' first political organization sought to bar slavery from the western territories, it was because white workers had previously been articulated to the Democratic Party together with white farmers as an aggrieved class of producers, whose economic independence had grown precarious with the advent of the factory and market economy (de Leon 2008).

The rhetorical currency of antebellum Chicago politics was what Fraser and Gordon (1994) have referred to in another context as the "discourse of dependency." Dependency was a state of noncitizenship reserved for sweated wage laborers, slaves, and women, whose current or potential deprivation was said to make them far too desperate and self-interested to reflect on the broad interests of the republic as a whole. Conversely, white male subsistence farmers and artisans were the icons of independence, for it was imagined that they lived comfortably enough off their own labor that they could steer the course of the republic without prejudice to their own enrichment.

The implications of the discourse were threefold. First, it served as the ideological justification for a farmer–worker Democratic coalition. Second, captains of American industry and finance, though economically independent, were not to be counted in the same number as farmers and workers because they were deemed incapable of seeing beyond the horizon of their next speculative scheme. The result is that northern industrialists tended to join southern planters in support of the Whig Party (Ford 1988; Holt 1999; Thornton 1978; Watson 1981; Wilentz 2005). Third, citizenship was confined to self-employed white men and as such was inflected by ethnoracial, gender, and class distinctions (Boydston 1990; Fraser and Gordon 1994; Roediger 1991).

This broad construal of dependency to include and therefore to stigmatize not only women and blacks, but also sweated white men, as unfree, exemplified the dominant brand of Democratic politics in the 1830s and early 1840s. It rendered incipient capitalist institutions such as the Second Bank of the United States the main targets of political attacks (Ashworth 1983; Blau 1954; de Leon 2008; Sellers 1991; Thornton 1978; Watson 1990; Wilentz 2005; Wilson 1974).

When the Democrats changed the terms of debate in 1844 from domestic economic issues to territorial expansion, they justified the policy shift in ways that continued to speak to the economic independence of white workers and farmers. New territory promised additional public domain, and that, in turn, allowed workers and farmers to move on from places where land had largely ended up in private hands to new ones where land was cheap and its use by squatters was essentially free. As one Democrat put it, the effect of cheap land in the West "would be to invite a large number of individuals who had settled in eastern cities, who were half-starved and dependent on those who employed them, to go to the West, where with little funds, they could secure a small farm on which to subsist and . . . get rid of that feeling of dependence which made them slaves" (Morrison 1997, 17; see also Eyal 2007, 148, and Nelson and Sheriff 2008, 12).

The justification of territorial policy as a solution to dependency, however, later divided the Democratic Party as Congress took up debate on the status of slavery in the land settlement to the U.S.–Mexican War (1846–1848). "Free Soil" Democrats sought to prohibit slavery from the territory because a monopoly of the land by wealthy planters would prevent free white men from escaping wage dependency in the nation's cities. Southern Democrats charged that any such prohibition would make southerners second-class citizens, whereas the Democratic leadership sought to quell dissension with a middle-of-the-road policy called "popular sovereignty" that would have allowed settlers to decide by referendum whether their territory should be free or slave.

In Illinois, Congressman John Wentworth led the Chicago Democratic organization in a Free Soil revolt against the state party led by Stephen A. Douglas, which favored popular sovereignty. In a defiant address to the Illinois Democratic Party published in the May 6, 1848, issue of the *Democrat*, the Chicago wing of the party warned that they would not bend to the will of wealthy slave owners as poor white southerners would: "If this issue is forced on them the freemen of the North west will never turn 'dough-faces' at the beck of southern dictation" (see also Pierce [1937] 2007, 389–390fn153, 394). Chicago Democrats made good on their promise in the 1848 presidential election by diverting their votes in Chicago's immigrant majority-worker neighborhoods from the state and national party's nominee, Lewis Cass, to Martin Van Buren, who ran as the presidential nominee of the Free Soil Party. Van Buren carried Chicago with just over 40 percent of the vote, whereas Cass came not in second place but in third, behind the Whig nominee, Zachary Taylor.

The 1844 and 1848 presidential returns in Table 1.1 were not reported by ward but by relatively sprawling precincts and are therefore less precise than the 1852 data, as we shall see, but they nonetheless indicate an emerging shift in the partisan allegiance of majority-worker neighborhoods. The South-East or lakeshore poll and the South-West poll, located just inland from the lakeshore below the mouth of the Chicago River, housed Chicago's most affluent neighborhoods. Table 1.1 shows that in 1844 James K. Polk, the Democratic presidential nominee, carried the city with a comfortable majority and did best in the West and North polling stations, which were in largely immigrant majority-worker communities, breaking the 60 percent barrier in both cases. In contrast, the Democrats were held to well below that mark in wealthier native-born areas. By 1848, the political landscape had changed dramatically.

Table 1.1. Percentage share of Chicago's popular vote for regular Democratic presidential candidates in 1844 and 1848 by precinct.

Precinct	1844 (Polk)	1848 (Cass)
North	62.3	41.7
South-West	56.1	16.6
South-East	52.5	30.4
West	62.7	28.6

SOURCES: For socioeconomic statistics, Einhorn 1991, 261; for 1844 electoral returns, *Chicago Democrat*, November 12, 1844; for 1848 electoral returns, *Chicago Daily Journal*, November 8, 1848.

The Democrats were once again strongest in the North and West, but their support had dropped by double digits throughout the city.

The surviving statements of Chicago workers on the issue of slavery extension explain why the Free Soil message gained traction among less affluent voters. In March 1848, workers organized the Chicago auxiliary of the "National Reform Association" (NRA), which sought to make land an entitlement of free white men (Bronstein 1999, 169; Lause 2005, 99, 100, 102). In the December 8, 1848, issue of their organ, the *Gem of the Prairie*, the Chicago NRA framed their "protest against the further extension of the area of chattel slavery and monopoly of the soil" in this way:

> A denial to the mass of mankind of their equal right to a portion of the earth, must, in the course of events, build up a state of society in which the monopolists of the earth will accumulate all the wealth of the country while the toiling millions, who are the producers of that wealth, must become wage slaves, and sink into hopeless destitution and famine.

The terms of the NRA's opposition to slavery extension are significant in three ways. First, they point to the reasons that workers and farmers had been constituents of the Democratic Party to begin with: Workers assumed a kinship with farmers as fellow "producers" of wealth, and they also hoped to escape wage dependency by one day becoming farmers themselves. Workers thus understood their fate to be bound to that of small farmers. But, second, it is clear from this passage that, whereas in 1844 the Democrats had used territorial policy and the discourse of dependency to articulate a national coalition of farmers and workers, by 1848 Democratic factionalism over the status of slavery in the new territories had disrupted that coalition. Third and relatedly,

Table 1.2. Percentage share of Chicago's popular vote for regular Democratic presidential candidates in 1852, 1856, and 1860 by ward and socioeconomic status (majority-worker wards in boldface type).

Ward	1852 (Pierce)	1856 (Buchanan)	1860 (Douglas)
1	48.7	28.3	36.5
2	In ward 1 count	37.0	42.1
3	65.1	39.1	**46.3**
4	74.9	48.2	**50.05**
5	**56.1**	38.7	"731 short of majority"
6	**73.2**	40.6	34.8
7	**86.8**	55.2	48.2
8	**63.5**	51.1	44.2
9	**In ward 8 count**	51.4	49.1
10	**n/a**	**n/a**	57.8

SOURCES: For socioeconomic statistics, Einhorn 1991, 261, 263; for electoral returns, *Chicago Democrat*, November 9, 1852; *Chicago Tribune*, November 7, 1860; de Leon 2008, 54.

NRA rhetoric was palpably derivative of Free Soil and earlier Jacksonian rhetoric, suggesting that workers came to understand their place in the Republic in part by drawing on partisan discourse.

As the Compromise of 1850 brought the slavery issue to a temporary close and the Free Soil and regular wings of the Democratic Party reunited, the Chicago NRA receded into the background, and the party's traditional strongholds became strongholds once more. Because the proportion of skilled workers throughout the city remained stable at about 25 percent in the 1850s, majority-worker wards (signified in bold in Table 1.2) are those in which unskilled workers comprised at least an additional one-third of the population, giving skilled and unskilled workers together a comfortable voting majority. The resulting ward designations reflect the break between Chicago's affluent lakeshore communities represented by wards 1 and 2 where unskilled workers comprised less than one-quarter of the population, and the interior of the city where the proportion of unskilled workers ranged from more than one-third (wards 5, 6, 8, and 9) to as high as one-half in ward 7 (see Map 1.1; Einhorn 1991, 249, 261).

A majority of voters in the city's affluent wards (1 and 2) cast their ballots for the Whigs. In contrast, the residents of all five of the city's majority-worker wards gave Franklin Pierce convincing majorities ranging from 56 to 95 percent. The Democratic wards consisted mainly of immigrant workers: (a) the North side's seventh through ninth wards were to varying degrees dominated

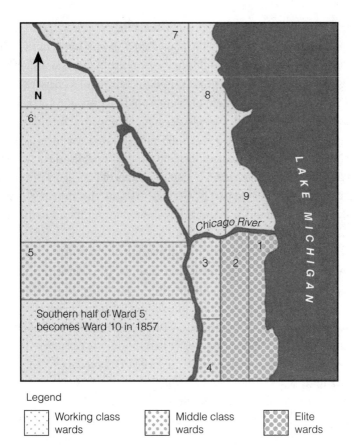

Map 1.1. Chicago ward map.
SOURCES: de Leon 2008, 67; Einhorn 1991, 261, 263.

by German workers; (b) the West side sixth by German and Irish workers; and (c) the southern half of the fifth ward and increasingly the fourth by Irish workers.

It was also in this period of Democratic détente that workers organized the city's first trade unions (*Chicago Tribune*, Oct. 4, 1851; April 23, 1853; May 4, 1853; and Nov. 16, 1853; Pierce 1940, 160, 165, 166; Schneirov 1991, 385), but organizing dropped off as workers renewed their crusade against the expansion of slavery. In 1854 Senator Stephen A. Douglas authored and secured the passage of the Kansas-Nebraska Act to link the lower Midwest to the lands of the Mexican cession (Douglas [1853] 1961, 270). By allowing the residents of Kansas and Nebraska to decide by referendum whether their states should become free or slave (that is, by popular sovereignty), the act abrogated the Missouri Compromise of 1820, which prohibited slavery north of the Mason-Dixon Line. Because slavery could now theoretically be established in the North by a vote of the people, the act raised the specter of a "slave power con-spiracy" through which southern planters would monopolize northern lands and thereby relegate white workers to permanent industrial servitude.

Passage of the law prompted Free Soil Democrats to leave their party again and unite with other antiextension elements in the Republican Party. The new third-party challenge touched off a second exodus of Chicago workers out of the Democratic Party, led in part by German artisans Theodore Hielscher and Eduard Schlaeger, who were esteemed by their community for being "48ers," veterans of the 1848 European revolutions. The minutes of a mass meeting of north-side residents organized by Schlaeger state that the act was roundly condemned for "reducing the free foreigner to the position now occupied by the slave, who is politically without any rights, depriving him of all influence against the phalanx of slaveholders." The residents further resolved, "We have lost our confidence in, and must look with distrust upon, the leaders of the Democratic party, to whom, hitherto, we had confidence enough to think that they paid some regard to our interests" (*Chicago Tribune*, March 20, 1854; see also Jentz 1991, 383; Levine 1992, 204–206).

The 1856 electoral returns listed in the third column of Table 1.2 report that the Democrats retained only three of the seven wards they had carried in 1852 and witnessed an erosion of their base even in the wards they still controlled. Though the Democrats narrowly carried the city, their share of the popular vote dropped steeply. Newspaper and secondary sources confirm that the defection occurred principally in the wards where German workers pre-dominated.[2] According to the *Tribune* of August 26, 1856, north-side residents filled Chicago's imposing German Theatre and then marched in a torchlight procession in support of the 1856 Republican presidential ticket. Significantly, among the chief organizers of the rally were the Turners, a German socialist organization.

Two things happened then that at last secured Chicago and Chicago work-ers for the Republicans. A brief but acute financial panic occurred in 1857, prompting unemployed workers to organize for government relief and rent control. In a city whose total population numbered 93,000, the panic left 20,000 workers unemployed (Huston 1987; Pierce 1940, 156; Skogan 1976). One year later the Democratic Party, led by then President James Buchanan, forced a proslavery constitution on the people of Kansas, the majority of whom were free soilers, effectively reversing their own doctrine of popular sovereignty. The rightmost column of Table 1.2 indicates that the panic and the Democrats' mismanagement of Kansas statehood precipitated the last and decisive defection of worker-dominated wards to the Republican Party. In the presidential election of 1860 between Abraham Lincoln and Stephen A. Douglas, the Republicans captured all but two wards, much as the Democrats had done in 1852.

This outcome is noteworthy for several reasons. First, unlike the Democrats in 1852, Republicans united a majority of voters in the affluent neighborhoods of the lakeshore with majorities in the worker-dominated north and upper west sides. The result is suggestive of an unprecedented cross-class sectional (that is, northern) coalition. Nevertheless, and secondly, the defection to the Republicans in 1860 was much smaller than the 1856 defection. This indicates that the Kansas-Nebraska Act, an artifact of party politics, accounts for more of the shift in workers' political allegiance than the economic downturn (de Leon 2008). Third, while the panic was not strictly a sectional event, the Republicans claimed that it was the direct result of the low tariff, which the Democrats had adopted to the benefit of southern planters and the ruin of northern workers. In effect, the Republican Party was successful in politicizing both the panic and Kansas as two prongs of the same slave power conspiracy. In November 1857, at the nadir of the economic downturn, when the Republicans carried Chicago in the midterm elections of that year, jubilant voters reportedly "drove all through the North side, congratulating their friends on the glorious victory over ruffianism and slaveocracy" (*Chicago Tribune*, Nov. 5, 1857).

This is not to say that workers were somehow oblivious to their plight during the panic. Protests for unemployment relief and rent control suggest otherwise. Yet Republicans successfully discouraged an exclusive working-class–based appeal in favor of a more inclusive appeal to workers as valued members of the "free labor" coalition. This rhetorical strategy allowed the party to condemn socialism even as it hailed workers as independent men and northerners. When the unemployed were laying plans to march on city hall for "bread or work," for instance, the Republican Party deployed a city clerk and 48er named Herman Kriesmann who convinced an audience of some 400 workers that they could not treat the government like a "nursing mother." As a result, the workers canceled their march and established a benevolent society, the *Arbeiterverein*, instead (Schneirov 1991, 384). Newspaper editors and other Republican operatives also stigmatized demands for state relief by comparing them with the paternalistic practices of southern planters. For example, the editors of the *Tribune* wrote,

> When the Slave Power is dominant, then will be the time in which the claims of the poor and unfortunate upon the authorities, for what they eat, drink and wear can be maintained . . . Let us have no European socialism here. (*Chicago Tribune*, Nov. 16, 1857)

Taking advantage of the discourse of dependency, the Republican Party succeeded for a time in branding socialism the political program of slaves who were incapable of standing on their own two feet. Indeed, Chicago did not see a march of the unemployed that month or any month until 1872.

THE CHICAGO WORKING CLASS, 1861–1886

Workers remained articulated to the Republican Party through the opening salvos of the Civil War. South Carolina's attack on Fort Sumter on April 12, 1861, vindicated Republican warnings of a slave power conspiracy and hung the albatross of treachery around the necks of the Democrats, whose Southern Rights faction was the vanguard of the secessionist cause. As soon as the news hit Chicago on April 13, a war fever took hold. The newly elected Republican governor of Illinois, Richard Yates, immediately called for six regiments of volunteers. Among the most enthusiastic were Chicago's immigrant workers. Even the Irish, under the influence of Fenian nationalists, who opposed slavery and condemned the Catholic Church's alliance with the Democratic Party, established the Irish Brigade in the 23rd Illinois under Colonel James A. Mulligan. Organized German workers, however, supplied the most recruits. For example, the German *Turnverein* organized the Turner Union Cadets, who were in the first regiment to muster in southern Illinois on the governor's order. Nationally, the Turners became a giant recruiting agency: Three-quarters of its members enlisted in the army and comprised the core regiments not only in Illinois, but also in Missouri, Indiana, and most famously in Washington, where the *Turnverein* organized the first battalion to respond to the national crisis (*Chicago Tribune*, April 18, 19, 1861; Montgomery [1967] 1981, 94; Pierce 1940, 256, 258, 260).

But no sooner had the war fever begun than dissatisfaction took hold. In Chicago, workers began to reject free labor ideology in favor of a class analysis that recuperated the Jacksonian critique of wage dependency and infused it with immigrant flavors such as European trade unionism and socialism. In this, there can be no doubt that mounting economic deprivation, blamed to a large degree on the conduct of the war, played a part. Labor movement activists grew mutinous, for instance, when they discovered that one could avoid the draft by paying the government $300, an amount well out of reach for most workingmen. The adoption of the greenback as the wartime paper currency resulted in high inflation for necessities from foodstuffs to housing, but the price of labor did not keep step with the price of other commodities. The *Chicago Tribune* estimated, and contemporary scholarship confirms, that whereas the cost of living increased an average of 82 percent between 1861 and 1864, the wages in manufacturing increased only 55 percent. The demand for higher wages was therefore the marquis demand of the labor movement during the war, with calls for pay hikes of as much as 30 percent. The resulting unrest was exacerbated by a series of downturns after the war, culminating in a depression that bottomed out between the fall of 1873 and late 1874 when 20 percent of factory workers became unemployed (Jentz 1991, 245; Jentz and Schneirov 2012, 68; Montgomery [1967] 1981, 45–46, 96–97; Officer 2009, 170; Pierce 1940, 155, 157–158, 500; Schneirov 1991, 385, 396).

Presidential electoral returns confirm that voters in Chicago's majority-worker neighborhoods left the Republican Party toward the end of the war and during Reconstruction. The number of wards grew after the 1860 election, and the ward map was redrawn so that wards 6 through 9 were located in the South Side where Irish workers predominated, whereas wards 15, 16, and 18 were in the Near North Side where German workers remained the majority. Recall that in 1860 the Republicans carried four out of six majority-worker wards. As Table 1.3 reports, with the exception of 1872, when two factions of the Republican Party were on the ballot, the GOP ("Grand Old Party," or Republicans) never carried more than two out of six such wards after 1860 and saw their share of the popular vote drop by at least 10 percentage points in each case. The Republican bloc, in other words, had become a coalition of middle-class and affluent wards.

But wartime economic deprivation and electoral returns tell us only part of the story. A content analysis of period newspapers reveals that Chicago workers came to understand themselves as a class through three interlocking claims. First, the parties' embrace of free market liberalism and the antilabor violence it justified comprised a betrayal of workers' military service to the

Table 1.3. Percentage share of Chicago's popular vote for Republican presidential candidates in majority-worker wards, 1864–1876.

Ward	1864 (Lincoln)	1868 (Grant)	1872 (Grant)	1876 (Hayes)
6	32.3	36.4	54.6	34.0
7	42.5	45.4	58.4	28.8
8	38.0	41.1	47.0	31.9
9	72.6	74.3	41.9	53.8
15	52.7	46.5	68.8	40.2
16	45.9	50.1	68.5	37.4
18	n/a	n/a	46.3	45.7

SOURCES: For socioeconomic statistics, Einhorn 1991, 265; for ethnic settlement patterns, Hirsch 1990, 101; for electoral returns, *Chicago Tribune* November 9, 1864; November 5, 1868; November 16, 1872; and November 9, 1876.

republic and the very promise of the war, which was their emancipation from wage dependency. Second, it was now the duty of workingmen to finish what they started. That is, the new conflict between labor and capital was a logical next step after the war between free labor and slavery. Finally, because they could no longer trust either of the major parties to advocate on their behalf, it was necessary for workers to found their own party.

The response of the political establishment consisted of three interlocking *counter*claims based on a mixture of free market liberalism and antislavery rhetoric. The first claim was that workers' wages and hours were the outcome of a bargain, into which individual employers and employees entered as free and equal partners. In the following passage, for example, the editors of the *Tribune* reject the workers' assertion that wage dependency made them no better than slaves:

> We deny utterly that the "master owns the mechanic" during the hours of labor . . . The mechanic's skill and labor constitute his capital. . . . He says to the capitalist, "I will go into your shop and take charge of your engine, lathe, forge, tools or machinery. I will take the raw material you have provided and shape and fashion it according to your wishes, for a specific cash consideration. I will work by the 'piece' or by the day. You will take all the chances of fire, of loss and depreciation. You shall pay all the public taxes and assessments; and in lieu thereof shall have what the fabric will bring to the market—assuming all the risks yourself." A bargain is struck; the service is performed; the stipulated wages are paid. If the employer finds a favorable market for the product of his shop, he makes a profit. (*Chicago Tribune*, March 26, 1867)

To demonstrate that the mechanic does not sell *himself*, but his own labor or capital, the editors take pains to paint a vivid picture of the wage bargain. It is not enough to assert that neither capital nor labor is enslaved. They show in detail, step-by-step, how the conversation between the worker and his employer takes place in the open marketplace. Significantly, it is the worker who, in this passage, sets the terms of the bargain, while the employer passively consents.

Second, because the wage bargain had become a metaphor for freedom, Democrats and Republicans insisted that it was not the employer who enslaved the worker but rather the trade unionist who enslaved employer and worker alike by attempting to obstruct the wage bargain. For instance, to rationalize the state's repression of Chicago's first general strike for an eight-hour day, the *Tribune* denounced the job action as

> . . . an effort to prevent men from selling their own property (their labor) on such terms as were agreeable to both seller and purchaser. It was the voice of the slave power crying out—You shall work only when, where and on such terms as we dictate. (*Chicago Tribune*, May 3, 1867)

The message of this editorial is quite simply that, whereas the wage bargain is consistent with free market principles, trade unionism represents the second coming of the slavocracy itself, for it binds workers and employers to a *collective* agreement and forbids side bargains on wages and hours between individuals.

Finally, if organized labor now comprised the new slave power, then logically it became incumbent on political leaders to use state violence in defense of free labor. Thus, in an article entitled "Shall Mobs Rule Chicago?" the Democratic *Times* wrote,

> The right of every man in Chicago to work as many or as few hours as he pleases, and to be secure in the enjoyment of that right, must and will be protected. The right of every employer in Chicago to manage and control his own property and to make and carry out such bargains with his employes [sic] as he and they may agree to, must and will also be protected . . . rioters should be swept out of existence by a discharge of artillery. (*Chicago Times*, May 4, 1867)

Here the Democratic editor claims the prerogative to suppress those who would disrupt the wage contract, framed again as the inviolable compact of the postwar Republic. This rationale animated the state's subsequent battles with labor, including the Great Railroad Strike of 1877, in which local police, state and private militia, and the U.S. Ninth Infantry unleashed 20,000 armed personnel to crush labor's uprising in the infamous Battle of Chicago (Foner 1977, 151–156).

As this allusion to antilabor repression suggests, the political establishment's contractual vision of a free society did not ring true to Chicago workers. As early as 1864, when the war was just coming to an end, workers openly declared that political appeals to the slave power conspiracy were irrelevant to them. Thus, Andrew Cameron, editor of the *Workingman's Advocate*, the organ of Chicago's General Trades Assembly, wrote,

> When it can do nothing else it can bleat about "slave-drivers." Alas! gentle-men (?) of the *Tribune*, your old demagoguecial [*sic*] cry is worn out. We are no longer going to permit you to make dupes of us by your false statements and past hypocritical catch-words, nor mislead us from protecting our own interests and rights. You have already made yourselves rich by bleating about the Negro, for whom you cared not a fig . . . This is a white man's question. Our brave soldiers in the field are taking good care of the "slave owners and slave drivers." To them we leave them . . . That game is up . . . We are determined to prevent a wholly unscrupulous set of scoundrelly and hypocritical politicians and purse-proud, moneyed aristocrats from bringing want and slavery to the doors of the FREE LABORING MEN OF THE NORTH [emphasis in origi-nal]. (*Workingman's Advocate*, September 17, 1864)

In this passage, Cameron states in no uncertain terms that the slavery ques-tion is dead. To "bleat about 'slave-drivers'" is described variously as "dema-goguecial," "worn out," and "hypocritical," and it is blamed here for having made "dupes" out of workers, a mistake that Cameron says workers will not soon repeat. To be sure, the editor continues to employ the discursive trope of slavery, but he does so here to fuel an oppositional class politics instead of the preexisting sectional politics. Moreover, to the degree that he referenced the war, he did so to mark the unfinished business of workers' own emancipation. In this sense, the end of the war provided a discursive entry point into an al-ternative political project.

Having risked their lives on behalf of the Republic, Chicago workers, now war veterans, viewed their meager existence and the major parties' high-handedness as a betrayal of their military service and the promise of the war. It was through this fundamentally *political* affront that workers came to see

themselves as a class in opposition to another. At the May Day festivities in-
augurating the 1867 eight-hour strike, one union representative made these
remarks:

> Who conquered the late rebellion? Was it the man who fought against them
> today? [Cries of "No"]. Then that man was a traitor to their cause. It was the
> laborer that had defended the country through war . . . But a few years have
> passed away since the emancipation of our country. Yet look at us now. See
> the factory operatives in Massachusetts, one third of whom die at an early age
> because [of being] overworked . . . Workingmen have their rights, which are
> acknowledged when the capitalist wants their vote, or their services on the
> battle-field, but on the questions of labor they have no rights. Is it the right of
> the workingman to work forever, night and day, to pay a debt contracted while
> he was fighting for sixteen dollars a month? (*Chicago Tribune*, May 2, 1867)

The speaker begins by calling those who attempted to repress the strike "traitors," no more worthy of their respect than the architects of the "late rebel-
lion." Then, in a direct challenge to the parties' free market liberalism, he
scoffs at the notion that Chicago's workers possess any "rights" other than "the
right of the workingman to work forever" to pay off a debt he acquired while
fighting the war for fifty cents a day. It is important to note that the union official identifies the major parties with the "capitalist" who wants their vote and
distinguishes him from "the workingman" and "the laborer." Such rhetoric
clearly bespeaks an analysis of labor and capital as antagonistic classes.

Because they remained unfree, Chicago workers reasoned that the emerging class conflict was simply the next logical step after the Civil War. At a
meeting several days into the eight-hour strike, for example, Eduard Schlaeger, the aforementioned antislavery activist, proclaimed that the workers "had
settled the black labor question, and now . . . would settle the white labor question," adding, "The course of the *Times* and the *Tribune* showed them that they
had nothing to hope from the old parties. They would both join when capital is
endangered. Both were catspaws of the same power—capital" (*Chicago Times*,
May 10, 1867). To "Mr. Taylor," a former rank-and-file Democrat and a striker
at the Illinois Central Railroad, it seemed that "demagogues . . . liked to see
them quarreling about this or that political party. He had himself been once
a democrat, but he was nothing now but a workingman—one of the party of
blistered hands . . . Capital gave them the challenge as the south did at Fort
Sumter, and they had taken it up. Capital considered them as slaves" (*Chicago*

Times, May 12, 1867). Workers' disarticulation from the major parties can be seen in the themes of betrayal, war, and class (as opposed to sectional) identity. Whereas the Democrats were once the champions of producers and Republicans the champions of free labor, now Mr. Schlaeger, once a die-hard Republican himself, called the parties "catspaws" to capital. The phrase, "one of the party of blistered hands," is telling in a similar way. Mr. Taylor has come to understand himself as a worker by being whipsawed by party demagogues, who liked to see him and his fellow workingmen "quarrelling." Finally, both speakers viewed the conflict between labor and capital as the natural successor to the Civil War. For Schlaeger, it was a matter of freeing white labor now that black labor was free, and for Taylor, "the south . . . at Fort Sumter" was equivalent to "capital," which "considered them as slaves" and now confronted them with a new challenge.

It was not long before workers began thinking about a labor party alternative. A railroad striker named W. W. Boyle presaged just such a formation, declaring, "Democrats were 'rottening out,' and republicans would soon 'rotten out.' Then the great laboring man's party would bury both of them and rise sublimely into power" (*Chicago Times*, May 11, 1867). When upwards of 7,000 workingmen gathered at Vorwaert's Turner Hall to discuss solutions to mass unemployment in the city, a spokesperson for the Chicago International during the 1873 Depression was greeted with cheers when he declared that "the two political parties were dead, and the time had come for the workingmen to organize a party of their own and redress their injuries at the ballot-box" (*Chicago Tribune*, Dec. 22, 1873). By 1877, the workingmen had passed a resolution stating, "That we, the working people of the City of Chicago and State of Illinois, do hereby repudiate the Republican and Democratic parties" (*Chicago Tribune*, Aug. 24, 1877). These passages highlight once again the disarticulation of Chicago workers from the mainstream party system. Indeed, they go so far as to declare the parties "dead" and "rottening out." Relatedly, their disarticulation appears to have been an important step in the process by which Chicago workers came to identify and organize as a class. Boyle viewed the process of rottening out as a necessary precondition for "the great laboring man's party" to emerge and bury its predecessors. Likewise, the Chicago International proclaimed that the death of "the two political parties" made it time "for the workingmen to organize a party of their own." And lastly, the aforementioned resolution of 1877 suggests that workers found their voice as "working people" by coming together to "repudiate the Republican and Democratic parties."

It should come as no surprise, then, that the Chicago anarchists who were implicated in the Haymarket Affair would have echoed the immediate postbellum critique of the major political parties on the one hand, yet moved beyond it to explicitly advocate for a new civil war on the other. The once-ardent Republican, Albert Parsons, now editor of the Chicago anarchist organ, *The Alarm*, wrote, "The workers can therefore expect no help from any capitalistic party in their struggle against the existing system. They must achieve their liberation by their own efforts" (*The Alarm*, Oct. 4, 1884). Similarly, in an editorial on the imminent presidential elections of 1884, Parsons held, "The real campaign begins where the political ends . . . One week more and the political phase gives way to the economic, where the daily wants of the working class incessantly clamor for relief" (*The Alarm*, Nov. 1, 1884). In both these passages, Parsons signals the persistent disaffection of the Chicago labor movement with the major political parties. Moreover, as in the early years of Reconstruction, party politics continued to inform the movement's identification as a class. Thus, in the first passage, Parsons sets the "capitalistic party" against the workers, who "must achieve liberation by their own efforts," and in the second passage he distinguishes the "political phase" from the "economic" where the real campaign of labor begins.

But where the earlier Chicago labor movement worked toward organizing a workingman's party and engaged only in crowd violence, for example, in the eight-hour strike of 1867 and the Great Railroad Strike of 1877, the Chicago anarchists called, in programmatic terms, for outright revolution (Foner 1977, 151; Montgomery 1967 [1981], 309, 310; Schneirov 1998, 35; Schneirov 2008, 95). Comparing the revolutionary and civil wars with the impending war against capital, Parsons reasoned that because "two of the systems of slavery have been attacked by bloody war," "bloodshed" would be "necessary" "for the third" (*The Alarm*, Dec. 6, 1884). The problem Parsons identified was the same problem posed by previous working-class leaders in Chicago, that of mounting economic dependency, but the solution had changed. Thus, Parsons noted, "Twenty years ago in the United States every poor man could choose between employing himself and seeking someone to employ him. Today not half of the poor men have got this power." He added, however, that in response to "this terrible fact . . . the laborer must rise and crush it with his heel or he will soon be helpless. Votes and arguments are as nothing in the hands of the poor. Force and force only is his defense" (*The Alarm*, Jan. 12, 1885).

For their part, Chicago political elites continued to see working-class organization (to say nothing of revolutionary anarchism) as a violation of the freedom of contract. On the day after the Haymarket bombing, the Democratic *Times*, for example, sounded a familiar tune: "Those who desire to work" should be "assured of protection in the exercise of their unquestionable right to contract their services upon such terms as they see fit" (*Chicago Times*, May 5, 1886). Further, any contravention of that unquestionable right must be met with state violence. "Mobs that make war against individual rights," the Democratic Party intoned, "must be made objects of war by all men that would maintain their rights" (*Chicago Times*, May 4, 1886).

CONCLUSION

The central empirical claim of this chapter has been that the clash between capital and labor in mid- to late-nineteenth-century Chicago was shaped by the trajectory of political articulation and disarticulation from the Jacksonian era to the Gilded Age. If one of the important legacies of the 1886 Haymarket Affair was the authorization of state violence against critics of capitalism, I have argued that this was prefigured by the North's victory against the South and the party system's embrace of free market liberalism. Having defended industrial capital against the slaveocracy by force, postbellum party elites in Chicago now claimed the prerogative to defend capital against labor. Among the former rank-and-file of the political establishment, the twin processes of articulation and disarticulation fueled the formation of working-class identity. Specifically, the eclipse of the slavery question and the failure of the party system's subsequent strategy to articulate workers with a contractual vision of freedom enabled socialists and others to articulate workers to a different, explicitly class-based political project.

With respect to this edited volume, this chapter illustrates the versatility and explanatory power of the political articulation approach in at least four ways. First, it sheds fresh light on long-standing debates within political sociology. The chapter offers a party-centered alternative to objectivist and subjectivist theories of class formation. Although the data suggest that the subjectivist stance is better able to account for the nineteenth-century Chicago case, I demonstrate that Chicago workers in fact came to their class identity as they interacted with political parties. Second, and as a result, our approach can be brought to bear on key historical conjunctures, in this case, America's transition from slavery to a liberal capitalist democracy. Next, the chapter points to the utility of assuming that little in politics can be taken for granted, least of all the circuit of recognition between party and society. Though the early Democrats and Republicans were successful integral parties, the former was laid low by the intractable debate over the status of slavery in the western territories, while the latter lost its connection with Chicago workers because of the conduct of the war and the turn to free market liberalism. Articulatory dynamics therefore consist not only in the successful naturalization of social cleavages: Formerly dominant articulations may also fail or cease to resonate, thus opening up possibilities for the articulation of new sociopolitical blocs. Fourth, this chapter speaks to the conditions enabling and constraining articulation. Recall that these hinge on the means of articulation: Conditions that enable bloc building are those that facilitate the use of tools uniquely available to political parties, whereas conditions that constrain bloc building are those that impede such use. War is one condition. President James K. Polk's successful prosecution of the U.S.–Mexican War affirmed the Democratic Party's land policy and rhetoric of wage dependency, thereby enhancing the party's ability to articulate workers and farmers as a class of producers, at least until the slavery question became entirely unmanageable. However, war can cut both ways. To be sure, the conflict with the South enabled the Republican Party to forge and maintain a cross-class northern coalition through the use of free labor ideology and official state violence, but the war was fraught with logistical challenges such as its cost and length (which the Republicans addressed by printing greenbacks), inflationary pressures on the home front (due to the greenback itself), and successive military setbacks, which helped to fracture their coalition and make workers susceptible to alternative articulations.

TWO

CONTINUITY OR CHANGE?

Rethinking Left Party Formation in Canada

Barry Eidlin

SCHOLARS OF AMERICAN EXCEPTIONALISM often look north to Canada for comparison (Kaufman 2009; Lipset 1989). The comparison is appealing because the strong similarities between the two countries place the differences that do exist in stark relief. Among those differences, few are as stark as the difference in party systems. Whereas the United States famously lacks a labor party, Canada's New Democratic Party (NDP) is well established. It currently sits as the Official Opposition in the federal Parliament and has governed five of the country's ten provinces. Scholars point to the NDP's presence as a key factor driving U.S.–Canadian differences in health care, labor, and other social welfare policies (Bruce 1989; Card and Freeman 1993; Maioni 1998; Zuberi 2006).

The NDP and its predecessor, the Co-operative Commonwealth Federation (CCF), have attracted much scholarly attention, leading to a rich and varied historiography (Archer 1990; Cross 1974; Johnson and Proctor 2004; Lipset 1950; McHenry 1950; Morton 1986; Young 1969). Although scholars differ on their assessments of the CCF/NDP's success, the character of its membership and political program, its prospects for the future, and more, few have asked why the CCF/NDP has managed to establish itself at all as one of Canada's main political parties. Its existence is taken as a matter of course. After all, in establishing such a party, Canada was following in the footsteps of nearly every other advanced industrialized country, save the United States. To the extent there was anything unusual about the CCF/NDP, it was that it wasn't as large or powerful as its European and Oceanic counterparts, only rarely escaping its "third-party" status.

Existing understandings of the CCF take its establishment as a major party for granted because they are implicitly based on what I call a "reflection" model of politics. By this I mean that they view parties as reflections of underlying social cleavages or institutional arrangements. In the Canadian case, scholars generally point to its parliamentary political system, its "Tory-touched" liberal political culture, or its existing left tradition as reasons for the CCF/NDP's establishment and durability (Duverger 1954; Horowitz 1968; Penner 1977). According to these approaches, the CCF/NDP was able to establish itself and survive because the cultural, institutional, and historical context created favorable terrain for the party to grow.

The problem with such accounts is that, to the extent that these conditions created favorable terrain for the emergence of a major left party, that terrain existed well before the establishment of the CCF/NDP. And, despite that favorable terrain, no Canadian left party was able to maintain a lasting electoral presence prior to the CCF/NDP. Moreover, most advanced industrialized countries, particularly Britain and the other non-U.S. British settler colonies, saw major left parties emerge in the late nineteenth or early twentieth centuries. By contrast, the CCF was founded in 1932,[1] and gained electoral prominence only in the early 1940s. For nearly four decades, Canada more closely resembled its "exceptional" southern neighbor than it did everybody else. Why then did the CCF/NDP succeed where previous left parties failed? And why did Canada take so much longer to establish a major left party?

Answering these questions leads us to focus on the central role of political parties in assembling and disassembling political coalitions, what the editors of this volume have termed the process of "political articulation" (de Leon, Desai, and Tuğal 2009, introduction). For an independent left party to succeed in Canada, two conditions were necessary. First, farmer and labor constituencies that could form the base for such a party had to be detached from their previous allegiances to the two mainstream parties, the Liberals and Conservatives. Second, those constituencies had to be united in a party that was ideologically and organizationally coherent enough to persist over time and resist co-optation while being flexible enough to forge a coalition of disparate groups.

Left party efforts prior to the CCF failed because they did not meet either or both of these conditions. Some, particularly agrarian protest parties, were organized around concrete demands that were easily adopted by mainstream parties and imbued with a vague "antiparty" ideology that impeded their ability to establish durable party organizations even when they achieved electoral success. Other advocates of "laborism" often worked in coalition with the mainstream parties (candidates would run as "Liberal-Labour" or "Conservative-Labour") and based themselves in a labor movement still too small and weak to serve as the foundation of an independent left party. Still others more explicitly influenced by socialist ideology were able to break away from the mainstream parties but were too ideologically rigid to develop a mass base.

I argue that the CCF succeeded where others failed because the mainstream parties' repressive and/or neglectful responses to labor and agrarian protest during the Great Depression created a "common foe" that decisively broke these constituencies away from their traditional party allegiances. This left room for the CCF to articulate the independent farmer–labor alliance that had eluded previous Canadian left parties.[2] Unlike previous left party efforts, the CCF was ideologically and organizationally coherent enough to avoid being co-opted into the mainstream parties while being flexible enough to unite previously fragmented left constituencies.

The case of failed, then successful, Left party formation in Canada highlights the idea advanced in the introduction that parties' "means of articulation" encompass not just what they *say* but what they *do*. Party rhetoric is certainly crucial in assembling, disassembling, and reassembling political coalitions and plays a key role here. But party actions—particularly policy offerings and control of resources—are essential to understanding the success and/or failure of different political articulation projects.

The remainder of the chapter proceeds as follows. First, I discuss existing understandings of the emergence and development of the CCF in greater detail, showing how an implicit reflection model of politics leads to an analysis that takes the CCF's establishment as a major party for granted. After examining in greater detail the evidence that shows the qualitative shift that the CCF represented compared to previous efforts at left party formation in Canada, I then develop an account of left party formation based on an articulation model of politics. I first sketch the history of left party efforts in Canada prior to the CCF, identifying the key factors that impeded left party formation. I then offer an account of the establishment of the CCF, highlighting the key role that the CCF and ruling parties played in disassembling and reassembling political coalitions, leading to a shift from a two-party to a three-party system.

REFLECTION MODELS AND CANADIAN LEFT PARTIES

To the extent that scholars seek to explain the success, albeit limited, of the CCF in Canada, it is usually as compared to the failure of a similar labor or socialist party to take root in the United States. Most accounts highlight the relatively favorable terrain created by Canada's political traditions and institutional arrangements. Although these accounts differ significantly, they share a common "reflection model" of politics, in that they view parties as reflections of preexisting political traditions and party systems as reflections of preexisting institutional arrangements.

Political Traditions

Explanations of the CCF's success that draw on political traditions are most closely identified with the work of Seymour Martin Lipset. From his first book on the rise of the CCF in Saskatchewan (1950) to his last comparing the fates of labor unions in the U.S. and Canada (Lipset and Meltz 2004), Lipset elaborated the idea that the small but significant differences that existed between these two countries that were otherwise so similar derived from differences in political cultures that developed out of the American Revolution (Lipset 1989, 1). According to Lipset, the fact that Canada did not undergo a revolutionary break with the British home country meant that it developed a political culture that retained more of Britain's feudal legacy. While Americans built a "new nation" defined by its "antistatism, laissez-faire, individualism, populism, and egalitarianism" (Lipset and Marks 2000, 30), Canada developed a Tory tradition that led to "a more elitist, communitarian, statist, and particularist (group oriented) society" (Lipset 1986, 442).

Building on Lipset, as well as Louis Hartz's (1964) "fragment theory" of new societies, Gad Horowitz (1968) contrasted the pure "Lockean" liberalism of the United States with the "Tory-touched" liberalism of Canada. As a result, Horowitz contends, "in the United States socialism was alien; in English Canada socialism was 'at home'" (58).

Although they do not necessarily trace Canada's political traditions back to the American Revolution, scholars of the Canadian left commonly refer to the prominent role that British immigrants played in its formation (Naylor 2006, for a critical evaluation; Penner 1992). According to such accounts, those immigrants brought with them traditions of British laborism and Fabian socialism, which in turn influenced the parties they formed and joined in Canada. Additionally, even among those who did not actively join and build nascent Canadian left parties, the large number of British immigrants created an electorate accustomed to supporting such parties.

Institutional Arrangements

According to general theories of party systems, Canada's political institutions occupy a middle ground (Duverger 1954; Lijphart 1999). On the one hand, Canada has single-member plurality voting districts, which tend to favor two-party systems. On the other hand, it has a parliamentary system with strong party discipline, which tends to encourage multiple parties.

In addition to focusing on political traditions, Lipset, Horowitz, and others point to the advantages that Canada's parliamentary system conferred on left parties in general and the early CCF in particular (Horowitz 1968, 48–49; Lipset and Marks 2000, 79–81; Robin 1968, 43). The parliamentary system allowed Canadian left parties to start small, focusing on elections in single districts where they had clusters of support, as opposed to having to contest provincewide or nationwide offices to be taken seriously, as in the United States. And once elected, even a small handful of elected officials could leverage their positions in Parliament to promote their new party.

Unanswered Questions

What these approaches share is a reflection model of politics, the idea that parties *reflect* preexisting social divisions and institutional arrangements. They argue that Canada's historical legacies, national values, demographics, and political institutions created relatively favorable political terrain for the CCF, ensuring its long-term success. Within these variants of a reflection model, the emergence and establishment of the CCF is not particularly problematic, as Canada's political culture and institutions seemed to predict that such a party would take root.

And yet, despite whatever advantages Canada's political culture and institutions offered left parties, it was only with the CCF that anything approaching a lasting, mass left party took hold. Why then did the CCF succeed where other party efforts had failed? And why did the CCF succeed when it did? Explanations based on a reflection model of politics cannot fully answer these questions.

In the following section, I show how an analysis that focuses on the role of parties in assembling, disassembling, and blocking different political coalitions—the process of political articulation—can better account for the CCF's success, as well as the timing of that success. I first outline the history of Canadian left parties prior to the CCF, identifying the key factors that frustrated left party success: intraclass divisions, state repression, and ruling party co-optation. I then provide an account of the emergence and development of the CCF that focuses on how coercive ruling party responses to labor and agrarian protest during the Great Depression created political space for the CCF to articulate a farmer–labor alliance and eventually establish itself as a durable left party in Canada.

THE LIMITATIONS OF PRE-CCF LEFT PARTIES

Two parties established their dominance in Canadian politics relatively soon after Confederation in 1867, with the Conservatives (or "Tories") and Liberals (or "Grits") taking turns in government (Brodie and Jenson 1988, 20–53; Chhibber and Kollman 2004, 180–181). This two-party dominance also prevailed among the nascent Canadian working class and its organizations. Working-class party loyalties were primarily determined by geography, religion, ethnicity, or family ties. For their part, labor organizations played an active role in politics. In fact, early Canadian labor organizations drew a much finer line between workplace and political action than the craft unions that would soon follow. Starting in the 1870s, national organizations[3] such as the Canadian Labour Union, Canadian branches of the Knights of Labor, and even the Canadian Trades and Labour Congress (TLC) were backing union activists for elected office, forming legislative committees to lobby members of Parliament, and putting forth legislative proposals of their own. Also, local groups such as the Workingmen's Progressive Political Party (London), the Canadian Labour Protective and Mutual Improvement Association (Hamilton), and the Workingmen's Election Club (Toronto) represented fledgling attempts at articulating an independent political voice for labor. But, overall, labor's political action at this point confined itself largely to a strategy of identifying with and seeking influence within the established parties. Labor candidates usually ran under "Labour-Liberal" and "Labour-Conservative" banners, although some did run as independents, labor newspapers identified as either Grit or Tory, and political advocacy generally consisted of pleading with legislators or searching for "friends of labour" to advance labor's agenda (Morton 2007, 25–44; Ostry 1960, 1961; Palmer 1983, 119–124; Robin 1968, 1–33).

New strategies began to emerge toward the close of the nineteenth century, as workers began to organize politically more independently of the Grits and Tories. This independent organization took a variety of forms within the heady amalgam of movements that populated the political landscape in 1890s Canada. Spurred on by economic crisis and upheaval, along with social transformations brought about by the growing prevalence of industry and railroad-based westward expansion, numerous strains of ideologies and issues both intermingled and competed for attention. Chief among these were populism, socialism, and laborism.

Although each of these variants enjoyed a certain degree of initial success, that success proved fleeting. In each case, this was due to a combination of their inability to break workers away from their traditional party allegiances and/or their ability to develop a party ideology and organization that was coherent enough to avoid co-optation but flexible enough to unite disparate left party constituencies.

Canadian Populism

An initial attempt at a populist farmer–labor alliance emerged in the early 1890s with the formation of the Grand Association of Patrons of Industry, an organization of reform-minded farmers increasingly disillusioned with the mainstream parties. Initially a U.S. offshoot, the group quickly declared independence and expanded throughout Ontario, Manitoba, and Quebec. It saw itself as a more radical alternative to another U.S.-based agrarian organization, the Patrons of Husbandry, better known in Canada as the Dominion Grange. As part of their efforts to gain a political voice for farmers, they sought to ally themselves with urban workers in a union of "tillers and toilers." In this project they found an initial partner in the Knights of Labor, with whom they shared a "producerist" ideology, which saw a community of interest between those who produced, that is, those involved in manufacturing or extracting goods, as opposed to the idle speculators and rentiers of the financial world. But, by the mid-nineties, the Knights were near collapse, and collaboration shifted toward the TLC, although many Knights continued their involvement in the Patrons. Patrons delegates attended Toronto and other local TLC meetings regularly, and the Patrons as an organization were admitted to the TLC as an affiliate at their 1894 convention. That same year, Patrons candidates won seventeen seats in the Ontario legislature. However, their staunch antipartyism made it difficult for the Patrons to function in Parliament and establish a clear independent political identity. This led to internal divisions and a slide back to established Liberal and Conservative allegiances. Within a few years of their meteoric rise, the Patrons of Industry were wiped out, bringing to a close an initial chapter in the history of farmer–labor alliances in Canada (Conway 1978; Cook 1984; Ferry 2004; Kealey and Palmer 1982).

Canadian Socialism

In the mid-1890s, more explicitly socialist groups began to take root, starting in Ontario. Daniel De Leon's doctrinaire Socialist Labor Party was an early arrival in 1894, but its strident dogmatism, particularly its antiunion stand, ensured that it would attract relatively few followers. More successful was the Canadian Socialist League, established in 1899 (Cook 1984, 5–6; Robin 1968, 34–36). The CSL was much more ideologically ecumenical, and it spread first across Ontario, then Manitoba and British Columbia. It experienced moderate success in the electoral arena, electing a few local officials in Ontario. But it was in British Columbia that it made greater advances. In that province, the various socialist factions—CSL, SLP, and others—were able to unite in a single party, and they managed to elect two socialists to the provincial legislature in 1903. Building off that success, the Socialist Party of British Columbia merged with the CSL to form the Socialist Party of Canada (SPC) that same year. In so doing, the SPC morphed ideologically from its more pluralistic origins in the CSL to a more explicitly Marxist, proletarian form of socialism. The SPC and other more radical forms of socialist organization remained dominant on the independent left in British Columbia for the next several decades and persisted in other provinces through World War I. However, they were never able to establish themselves as a true mass party (Penner 1977, 1992).

Canadian Laborism

Although socialism was a significant pole of attraction for labor politics in turn-of-the-century Canada, many within the labor movement developed a more moderate and eclectic form of working class politics known as "laborism" during this period. As Craig Heron (1984, 50) describes it, laborism "was not an intellectualized doctrine, but more like an inclination and a set of political impulses which proceeded from some common ground. It was the politics not of ideologues but of practical people moving outward from their economic struggles." Drawing on a mixture of Tom Paine–style radical republicanism, agrarian radicalism, and some variants of socialism, laborism was the dominant expression of independent working-class politics in Canada east of the Rockies for the early decades of the twentieth century. Given its practical bent, laborist activity in the electoral arena often involved endorsing candidates from the major parties. This often resulted in the continuation of the "Lib-Labism" of the 1880s, where self-identified labor candidates took their seats as Liberals if and when they won, with all the problems that this posed for independent working-class politics. But at the same time, hundreds of independent working-class candidates ran in municipal, provincial, and national races, resulting in numerous independent mayors, town councillors, and provincial and federal legislators being elected in communities across the country (Morton 2007, 91–95).

Division, Repression, and Left Party Frustration

The political ferment in turn-of-the-century Canada and elsewhere rattled the TLC's traditional commitment to exerting political influence through trying to influence the major parties. In 1906, the British Labour Party experienced its first major electoral breakthrough; that same year, the U.S. AFL issued a call for independent political action. The Canadian TLC followed suit after extensive debate between socialist and laborist delegates, issuing a resolution calling for labor representatives to be sent to Parliament "for the direct purpose of conserving the interests of the working people in this country" (quoted in Robin 1968, 82). The convention further called on provincial affiliates to organize founding conventions for a Canadian Labour Party. However, a combination of internecine squabbling among various stripes of socialists and laborites, along with a continued attachment to old-line partyism among a significant segment of the TLC leadership and membership, hampered initial attempts at labor party formation. Parties managed to get off the ground after a few years in British Columbia, Alberta, and Ontario, while other local parties took shape as well. Together, these Independent Labour Parties (ILPs) marked an initial step toward independent working-class politics in Canada, and in many ways were forerunners of the CCF. Nonetheless, these efforts remained small and limited (Palmer 1983, 158–161; Robin 1968, 62–91).

World War I dealt a major blow to any form of political radicalism, as the Unionist coalition government of Tories and Liberals declared a raft of left-wing and labor organizations to be illegal, banned foreign language publications, and required mandatory registration of "enemy aliens." Even more "respectable" Canadian labor leaders found themselves politically excluded. Unlike in the United States and Britain, the Unionist government enacted key legislation severely restricting wartime labor and civil rights without consulting labor or offering concessions in return. But the end of the war saw an explosion of working-class unrest. Western labor forces in favor of "One Big Union" (OBU), that is, an industrial form of organization, split off from the TLC in May of 1919. Many involved in the OBU split were also involved in the Winnipeg general strike of that year, the high-water mark for syndicalism in Canada. However, brutal government and employer repression crushed the OBU movement, discrediting syndicalism as a strategy and restoring the TLC as the major, albeit diminished, voice of Canadian organized labor. For its part, the TLC renewed its commitment to independent political action at its 1917 convention, even going so far as proposing a united front with the Socialists, but little came of this commitment. State and employer repression of unions of all kinds in the postwar aftermath severely limited labor's ability to organize in any capacity. Although union membership spiked from 205,000 to 378,000 between 1917 and 1919, it plummeted to 277,000 by 1922, and growth remained flat until the late 1930s. Simply put, labor was in no condition to spearhead an independent political movement in the 1920s (Jamieson 1968, 158–213; Kealey 1992; Robin 1968, 119–198).

There was, however, considerable political activity among Canadian farmers, as waves of agrarian protest swept across the country in the postwar period. The main source of discontent was the National Policy (Brodie and Jenson 1988, 21–27, 138–139). Its protective tariffs and railroad subsidies benefited Eastern industrialists, bankers, and railroad magnates, while Western farmers chafed under inflated equipment costs and shipping rates for their crops, leaving them indebted and vulnerable to international price fluctuations (Brodie and Jenson 1988, 159–162; Brym 1978, 340–341). As a result, farmers focused their ire on the "Triple Alliance" of railway, banking, and manufacturing interests. Politically, this protest found its voice in the United Farmers movement, which organized nationally into the Progressive Party of Canada. United Farmers parties were able to form governments for brief periods in Ontario, Manitoba, and Alberta. The Progressive Party of Canada also succeeded in winning fifty-eight seats in the House of Commons in the 1921 election, enough to form the Official Opposition to the governing Liberals, although they declined to do so. But the success of these agrarian parties proved fleeting. Like their populist predecessors, they espoused a vague "anti-party" ideology, which fatally hampered their ability to function as parties when they actually won seats in the legislature. Absent a coherent ideology, their program consisted largely of pragmatic concerns about specific policies, particularly the tariff. This made it possible in some cases for the mainstream parties to bargain with them, co-opting enough supporters to undermine the parties' viability (Thompson and Seager 1986, 29–30). By the mid-1920s most had either ceased to exist or been absorbed into the Liberal Party (Brym 1978; Conway 1978; McMath 1995; Morton 1950; Penner 1977; Robin 1968; Thompson and Seager 1986, 14–37; Whitaker 1977).

However, the experience of the Progressive Party did mark a shift in the structure of Canadian politics. The repressive actions of the Unionist government during the war dealt a serious blow to the legitimacy of the two-party system, as both farmers and workers saw the parties acting more in the interests of the Triple Alliance than their own. As William Irvine, a major figure on the Canadian left at the time, wrote in his book *The Farmers in Politics* (1920):

> On the coming to power of the Union Government, parliament was virtually done away with, its place being taken by orders-in-council [government decrees]. Here was class legislation, the most flagrant and brazen ever perpetrated. Kaiserism made its abode in Ottawa—where it still flourishes. The iron heel of censorship was placed on the neck of every protestor. Literature in opposition to plutocratic class rule was banned, and the worst features of the inquisition were not to be too bad to be resurrected and brought to Canada to do service in the interest of a class tyranny of the most shameful kind. (quoted in Penner 1977, 191)

This repression at the joint hand of the Grits and Tories created an opening for independent left politics, driving important segments of farmer and labor groups away from the mainstream parties. The Progressives mounted a serious challenge to the two-party system, but with a labor movement divided and crushed by state repression, the farmers on their own could not sustain their movement. Nonetheless, a rump group of Progressive Members of Parliament (MPs) who did not return to the Liberal fold did manage to unite with two Independent Labour MPs to form a "Ginger Group" in Parliament that held aloft the banner of independent politics through the 1920s (Brodie and Jenson 1988; Penner 1977; Pentland 1968, 161–162; Robin 1968).

In sum, while Canada had a vibrant history of independent agrarian and working-class political action, the track record up until the early 1930s was disappointing. Electoral efforts had either foundered after initial success due to infighting and/or state repression or had been absorbed into one of the ruling parties. Similarly, efforts at forging farmer–labor alliances had proved fleeting. As a result, Canada distinguished itself at the outset of the 1930s as one of only two industrialized countries lacking established labor or socialist parties, the other being the United States.

POLITICAL ARTICULATION AND THE CCF

Given its historical development, traditions, and institutional structures, many would have predicted that a party like the CCF would take root in Canada. But despite the relatively favorable political terrain, efforts at left party formation had largely foundered prior to that point. There was no inherent reason to believe that the few dozen people who gathered in Calgary in 1932 to create the CCF would be any more successful than any number of parties that had gone before them. What made the difference in the case of the CCF?

To understand what happened, we must examine the role of parties in shaping political alliances. In this case, the analysis centers on how ruling party responses to labor and agrarian protest sparked by the Great Depression decisively detached key farmer and labor groups from their traditional allegiances to the mainstream parties, and how the CCF articulated those fragmented groups into a new political alliance. The Grits and Tories had defeated such challenges in the past, using a mix of coercion and co-optation. This had played a key role in frustrating left party formation up until that point.

With the onset of the Great Depression, farmer and labor insurgency flared once again, to which the ruling parties responded with a policy of repression and neglect. This raised once again the question of independent political action for workers and farmers alike. But whereas ruling party coercion and co-optation had worked in the past, this time was different. By the end of the 1940s, the CCF had established itself as a significant presence on the Canadian political scene, holding one-eighth of the seats in the House of Commons, receiving the support of approximately one-fifth of the Canadian electorate in public opinion polls, forming the government of one province (Saskatchewan), and forming the Official Opposition in five others (McHenry 1949, 366).

Unlike in previous episodes, the ruling party response was largely coercive, not co-optive. This created a "common foe" that decisively severed past party loyalties and gave the CCF an opportunity to articulate the farmer–labor alliance that had eluded past left party efforts. But why was ruling party co-optation no longer an option? And how was the CCF able to create a unified alliance including farmers and workers? Here we must consider the characteristics and actions of the CCF itself. Organizationally, it did not suffer from the antipartyism that undermined many agrarian political efforts. Ideologically, its distinctive brand of socialism, mixing elements of British Fabianism, European socialism, social gospel, and agrarian radicalism, was coherent enough to pose a more primordial threat to the Liberals than past left challenges. This predisposed them to try and defeat the CCF, not co-opt it. At the same time, CCF ideology was flexible enough to appeal to disparate groups. Ruling party hostility pushed them away, and CCF organization and ideology pulled them together (Horn 1980; McHenry 1950; Naylor 1993; Smith 1975, 231).

Depression and Unrest

The economic and political situation for Canadian workers and farmers was bleak at the outset of the 1930s (Horn 1984). With its National Policy predicated on tariff-protected industry in its central region and export of primary sector goods from its western and eastern peripheries, the Canadian economy was particularly vulnerable to fluctuations in international markets. The collapse of world agricultural and manufacturing markets in the early 1930s sent the Canadian economy reeling. Regions dependent on export of primary staples had no markets in which to sell, which meant in turn that domestic, tariff-protected industry was deprived of its home market. Wheat prices, which accounted for nearly one-third of exports, fell by two-thirds between 1929 and 1932 (Leacy, Urquhart, and Buckley 1983, Series M228). Mean income for wheat-dependent prairie farmers fell by an astonishing 94 percent between 1929 and 1934 and by 64 percent for farmers in other provinces. Wages in export industries fell by half, and even wages in domestic, tariff-protected industries fell by 37 percent (Lipset 1950, 123). Retail trade fell by a third between 1930 and 1933 across the country (Lipset 1950, 126).

Worker and farmer organizations were ill equipped to address the crisis. Union membership stood at 13.1 percent of the nonagricultural workforce in 1930 and was fragmented among U.S.-affiliated TLC unions, national unions affiliated with the All-Canadian Congress of Labour (ACCL), confessional Québécois unions affiliated with the Canadian Catholic Confederation of Labour (CCCL), the Communist-led Workers Unity League (WUL), and numerous independent unions (Labour Canada 1980; Leacy et al. 1983, Series E175–177). Farmer organizations were internally divided on the question of political action (Anderson 1949; McMath 1995).

As for the government, not only were its leaders generally oblivious to the depths of the crisis the country faced, but there was little impetus to try and solve anything (Brodie and Jenson 1988, 148; Owram 1986, 161; Whitaker 1977, 9–10). So deluded was Prime Minister William Lyon Mackenzie King that, even two months after being voted out of office due to the crisis, he could still write in his diary that "the country was happy and contented, [manufacturers] & labour alike but for the election propaganda" (King 1930). Part of the problem lay in the structure of Canadian federalism, which delegated responsibility for relief programs to the provinces and municipalities, which were singularly unequipped to handle an economic disaster of this magnitude. However, there were also ideological barriers to government intervention in the economy and provision of relief benefits (Brodie and Jenson 1988, 162; Horn 1980, 6–9).

Mackenzie King's Liberal government was replaced in 1930 by R. B. Bennett's Conservatives, but he proved equally unable to address the crisis, doing little beyond increasing tariffs and proposing piecemeal and ineffectual proposals to shore up collapsing farm prices (Brodie and Jenson 1988, 162; Horn 1984, 7–9). Mainly he sought to scapegoat and target those who were organizing the poor and unemployed to demand relief. He revived Section 98 of the Criminal Code, which prohibited a broad array of "seditious" and "subversive" activities, and declared that Communism was to be stamped out by "the iron heel of ruthlessness" (Jamieson 1968, 217). Under the Code's provisions, prominent Communists were jailed, and the Party was banned, activists were deported, radical literature was censored, and meetings were routinely disrupted (Imai 1981; Petryshyn 1982; Roberts 1986). Bennett had groups of idled young male workers rounded up and shipped off to remote work camps. Under Communist/Workers Unity League leadership, some of these unemployed workers organized the "On to Ottawa Trek" in 1935, which sought to journey by train from Vancouver in the west to the Canadian capital in search of economic relief. Their trek ended in Regina, Saskatchewan, where the Royal Canadian Mounted Police forcibly dispersed the riders under government orders (Hewitt 1995). Still, the Depression continued.

Mackenzie King's Liberals were returned to office in 1935, but as party supporter and McGill professor Brooke Claxton put it, the Liberals seemed "devoid of imagination, ideas, organizing ability and drive" (quoted in Owram 1986, 135). The Liberals' (as well as the Tories') perceived lack of imagination was symptomatic of a general crisis of faith not only in the mainstream political parties but also in the ability of capitalist ideas to solve the crisis. There was intellectual and political space for new ideas and new political formations to take hold (Brodie and Jenson 1988, 164; Horn 1980, 11–13; Owram 1986, 161).

It was in this uncertain environment that the CCF took shape. The initial 1932 meeting in Calgary consisted of four groups: (1) agrarian populists from the United Farmers movements of Alberta, Manitoba, and Saskatchewan; (2) labor unions, represented by Aaron Mosher, head of the ACCL-affiliated Canadian Brotherhood of Railway Employees (CBRE); (3) representatives of local and provincial labor party organizations, along with a rump "Ginger Group" of Progressive and Independent Labour MPs; and (4) a group of Fabian academics from McGill and the University of Toronto, organized as the League for Social Reconstruction (LSR) (Lipset 1950, 114; McHenry 1950, 23–25). Although each group had disparate interests and divergent analyses of the crisis and how to solve it, the specific conditions of the Great Depression, and the Canadian state's response to it, created the "common foe" necessary to bring them together (Penner 1977, 194; Thompson and Seager 1986, 230–235).

Farmers: The Need for a Coalition

Canadian farmers were no strangers to the politics of protest by the early 1930s. In successive waves dating back to Confederation, generations of farmers had organized to protect themselves from the vagaries of the market. In every instance, though, farmer protest had ended in either dissolution or defeat.

The rise and fall of the Progressive Party in the early 1920s, although a failure, nevertheless marked a shift in Canadian farmer organizing. Taking advantage of the mainstream parties' disarray following World War I, it broke a layer of farmers away from the two-party system and left them open to other political alternatives (Archer 1990, 9–11; McMath 1995, 541). The experience of the Progressives showed that a solely farmer-based party could not succeed. What was needed was a reform coalition with urban workers (Brodie and Jenson 1988, 111–112). However, Canadian workers' organization remained in tatters following the violent state and employer counteroffensives of the post–World War I period, making such a coalition impossible in the early 1920s (Kealey 1992; Penner 1977, 174–175).

Farmer organizing continued throughout the 1920s, particularly through the formation of cooperative wheat pools in the prairie provinces. This process both revitalized and radicalized the farmers' movement in many areas. In Saskatchewan, the dynamic Farmers' Union merged with its more sedate rival, the Saskatchewan Grain Growers' Association (SGGA), to form the United Farmers of Canada (Saskatchewan Section) (UFC [SS]) (Lipset 1950, 99–117; Solberg 1987, 198–202). Together with more moderate United Farmers organizations from Alberta, Manitoba, and Ontario, they would form the base of the agrarian constituency at the founding meeting of the CCF in Calgary.

The collapse of the global wheat market in 1929 and the onset of the Great Depression accelerated the process of agrarian radicalization, as did the federal and provincial governments' inability to cope with the crisis. This led farmers to turn once again to independent politics and to search for political allies outside the major parties (Anderson 1949, 146–167). The agrarian groups remained acutely aware of the need for labor allies but also of labor's weakened state. G. H. Williams, president of the UFC(SS), wrote to a colleague in 1930:

> In the political field the farmers have lacked the leadership to a very marked degree and there is no one who has appealed to the people's imagination as the leaders of the people's party in Canada . . . Labor in Canada is very poorly organized . . . Labor organizations in the industrial East . . . is [sic] a local matter rather than a national one. *Were the workers really organized, I believe agriculture is sufficiently organized to carry her end of a political movement, but an agricultural group which ends at Winnipeg* [i.e. does not include the industrial East] *and has no means of communication with the industrial workers eastward is like an army with its left flank up in the air* . . . The situation will not continue forever, and the time will come, having accomplished our economic development, we will carry them into the field of political legislation, but that time is not yet. (Anderson 1949, 150; italics added)

One set of allies that was already available was the members of the Parliamentary "Ginger Group," led by former Methodist minister J. S. Woodsworth. This group consisted of left-wing Progressive Party MPs who had refused to be absorbed into the Liberals, as well as a handful of Independent Labour MPs. These legislators in turn had connections with a loose network of provincially based labor parties, some of which had begun meeting starting in 1929 as the Western Conference of Labour Political Parties. In 1932, this group invited farmers' organizations to attend their meeting in Calgary, which is when the CCF was formed.

Another group in attendance at the Calgary meeting, the intellectuals of the League for Social Reconstruction (LSR), brought into the emerging coalition a new and critical element: a program and unifying vision for the party.

CCF "Brains Trust": The League for Social Reconstruction

The Canadian left prior to the 1930s was conspicuous for its paucity of intellectuals (Horn 1980, 11–12, 204–205; Penner 1977, 40–45). As the Great Depression challenged the legitimacy of capitalism as an economic system, and the mainstream social, political, and economic institutions proved unable to cope with the crisis, that changed. Small groups of academics at the elite University of Toronto and McGill University in Montreal, joined by other intellectuals and professionals, began to gather in 1930 to survey the situation and discuss proposals for change. In February 1932 the group drafted a manifesto and christened itself the League for Social Reconstruction (Horn 1980). The manifesto denounced capitalism as "unjust and inhuman, economically wasteful, and a standing threat to peace and democratic government." It called for the establishment of "a new social order which will substitute a planned and socialized economy for the existing chaotic individualism," that will end "the present glaring inequalities" and "eliminate the domination of one class by another" (28). The organization set up a branch structure, and members began to join from across the country, far afield from the main Toronto–Montreal axis.

Although initially constituted as a nonpartisan organization, LSR members observed the emergence of the CCF with great enthusiasm. Several members attended the 1932 Calgary meeting as observers, although they did not officially affiliate at the time. Soon there was discussion about affiliation, though, and when Woodsworth approached LSR leaders Frank Underhill and Francis Scott about drafting the CCF's manifesto, they readily agreed. The product, unveiled and endorsed at the official founding convention of the CCF in Regina in 1933, became known as the Regina Manifesto. It echoed in many ways the same analysis and proposals contained in the LSR's manifesto. LSR members went on to amplify the themes of the Regina Manifesto in two subsequent books that proved quite influential: *Social Planning for Canada* (1935) and *Democracy Needs Socialism* (1938). LSR members like David Lewis also took on important leadership roles in the new party.

The intellectuals of the LSR were crucial in the formation and development of the CCF, both in providing ideological cohesion to the group itself and in moving the CCF into a position of moral and intellectual authority on the national political scene. In contrast to the United States, where Franklin Delano Roosevelt's New Deal offered, if not a coherent program, at least "a feeling of high adventure, a sense of iconoclasm, genuine 'radicalism'" (Horowitz 1968, 32–33), the Canadian ruling parties offered little aside from unimaginative and timid conservatism. The LSR and CCF were able to fill the political and intellectual vacuum and became a pole of attraction. As the cadre of intellectuals who entered the Roosevelt administration were dubbed FDR's "Brain Trust," so too were the LSR-affiliated intellectuals of the CCF (Horn 1980, 46–47; Horowitz 1968, 33).

The CCF in the 1930s: Promise and Uncertainty

By the mid-1930s, the CCF held a great deal of promise as the organizational expression of a new politics in Canada based on a class alliance of labor and farmers. This was signaled by early electoral strength in British Columbia, where the party polled 31.5 percent of the vote in 1934, and in Saskatchewan, where the CCF was able to form the Official Opposition by 1938 (Lipset 1950, 146; Young 1976, 152). However, serious problems remained. First, there was the issue of agrarian support. Although United Farmers groups from four provinces attended the 1932 Calgary meeting, three—those from Alberta, Manitoba, and Ontario—had all disaffiliated from the CCF by the end of the decade. They were uncomfortable with the overly socialist rhetoric of the Regina Manifesto, as well as the generally radical orientation of the group in practice. Only the Saskatchewan farmers remained (Brodie and Jenson 1988, 170–172). Second, there was the problem of regionalism. Aside from a few LSR intellectuals in central Canada, the CCF was overwhelmingly Western in composition. It would be difficult to contend on the national political stage without spreading their organization eastward, particularly into Ontario, as Williams had predicted, and even optimistic assessments by party leaders admitted this (Lewis 1943, 471–472). Additionally, the party's support for a strong federal government did not play well in Quebec, and their lack of outreach to the francophone population ensured that they would remain a marginal political presence in that province, which would have serious consequences for the party's future development (Naylor 2006, 291; Penner 1977, 57–59).

Third, and perhaps most important, there was the problem of labor representation. Although the party conceived of itself as a farmer–labor alliance—

its full official name was "Cooperative Commonwealth Federation (Farmer-Labour-Socialist)"—in reality the "labor" component such as it existed in the 1930s consisted almost exclusively of regional labor party organizations, not actual trade unions. In fact, organized labor as a whole kept an arm's-length relationship with the CCF for much of the party's first decade (Abella 1973, 73–74; Logan 1948, 433). CBRE and ACCL head Aaron Mosher attended the 1932 Calgary meeting and the 1933 Regina convention but did not formally affiliate the CBRE or ACCL with the CCF (Barnes 1960, 254–256; McHenry 1950, 163–166). Indeed, given the federalized structure of the CCF, there was no formalized way for national-level organizations such as trade union confederations to affiliate. The CCF did allow union locals to affiliate, but very few had done so by the end of the 1930s (Barnes 1960, 252–253; Palmer 1983, 215). The farmer–labor alliance within the CCF remained more rhetorical than real.

Labor and the CCF: The Missing Link

As with their agrarian counterparts, the economic desperation of the Great Depression had a radicalizing effect on Canadian workers and led to an increase in labor militancy. But this increased militancy did not win concessions from the state (Heron 1996, 65–67). On the contrary, it often provoked further hostility from both federal and provincial governments, as police and troops were sent in to break up strikes in logging, mining, paper, auto, textile, and other industries (Fudge and Tucker 2001, 153–227). In Ontario, as workers in several cities engaged in sit-down strikes, Premier Mitchell Hepburn vowed that "invading unions," meaning Congress of Industrial Organizations (CIO) organizers coming up from the United States, would be turned away at the border (Abella 1973, 7; Palmer 1983, 219). In Quebec, Premier Maurice Duplessis enacted the infamous "Padlock Law" in 1937, which allowed the state to seize the property—literally padlock the doors—of any group suspected of promoting Communist ideas, which often included unions. And, at the federal level, Prime Minister Bennett used Section 98 of the Criminal Code to prevent "seditious conspiracy" and "unlawful association" among workers and applied a broad interpretation of immigration law to deport so-called undesirables, who often included union activists (Fudge and Tucker 2001, 212–213; Petryshyn 1982; Whitaker 1986). Although Mackenzie King reversed some of the most egregious Bennett antilabor policies on his return to office in 1935, including Section 98 and the relief camps, he rebuffed calls for labor policy reform (Fudge and Tucker 2001, 193). Provincial and federal governments did respond to some of the more egregious employer abuses of the day by enacting regulatory laws regarding minimum wages and hours of work, and some proposed rudimentary frameworks for establishing collective bargaining rights. However, these were largely piecemeal reforms, and none sought in any way to deepen state involvement in collective bargaining. Labor in the 1930s remained politically excluded and largely deprived of basic organizing and collective bargaining rights (Fudge and Tucker 2001, 153–227; McConnell 1971).

Meanwhile, as their agrarian counterparts were exploring independent politics, Canadian labor leaders were largely hewing to their old voluntarist model, summarized in the maxim of "reward your friends and punish your enemies." The TLC's resolution on political action at its 1935 convention persisted in recommending "that the Congress continue to act as the legislative mouthpiece for organized labor in Canada independent of any political organization engaged in the effort to send representatives of the people to parliament, the provincial legislatures, or other elective bodies of the country" (Fudge and Tucker 2001, 196; Logan 1948, 433).

The upsurge in class conflict in the mid-1930s galvanized Canadian labor. Inspired by the CIO upsurge in the United States, Canadian workers organized under the CIO banner, even though U.S. CIO officials were largely unaware of Canadian efforts, let alone supporting them (Abella 1973, 4–5). Despite lacking any equivalent to the U.S. Wagner Act, Canadian union membership spiked by 36 percent between 1935 and 1937 (Leacy et al. 1983, Series E175–177).

Canadian labor's struggle against the state for recognition had a unifying effect. While many of their parent unions in the United States split into rival AFL (American Federation of Labor) and CIO federations that engaged in bitter internecine conflicts, Canadian unionists joined together to protest the lack of basic labor rights. The TLC expelled its CIO unions only in 1939, two years after the U.S. split, and then only under direct pressure from the AFL. It is important that the TLC did not purge local labor councils when it expelled its CIO affiliates, leaving local councils available to affiliate with the CCF (Forsey 1958, 82). Also, unlike in the United States, Canadian CIO unions sought reunification with the TLC from the start. Although the TLC rebuffed these overtures, the Canadian CIO did increase labor's organizational unity by merging with Mosher's ACCL to form the Canadian Congress of Labour (CCL) in 1940 (Abella 1973, 33–53; Galenson 1960, 49–72). The Canadian state's refusal to recognize labor rights did not dissolve interfederation rivalries, but it did mute their political significance.

War, Repression, and the Labor–CCF Alliance

Although state intransigence to Canadian labor's demands fostered greater organizational unity, it also blocked the possibility of labor's co-optation into the ruling party coalition. It did so by pushing supporters of political voluntarism within labor toward official support for the CCF (Forsey 1958; Horowitz 1968, 166–185).

As the question of labor's role in politics became more urgent, some CCL officials, like Mosher and Steel Workers Organizing Committee (SWOC) head Charles Millard, advocated closer ties with the CCF. Others, such as United Electrical Workers (UE) Canadian President C. S. Jackson, were more influenced by the politics of the Communist Party of Canada (CPC). And still others, most notably CCL Secretary-Treasurer Pat Conroy, continued to insist on labor's traditional nonpartisan role in politics (Abella 1973, 73–77, 139–140). These three positions coexisted uneasily for several years, until the strains of class conflict and state repression during World War II brought them to a head.

With the onset of Canada's involvement in the war, the ruling Liberals recognized the importance of securing labor's cooperation to mobilize for wartime production speedup. To that end, Mackenzie King met with labor leaders in June 1940. The labor leaders insisted on a statement of labor principles, to which Mackenzie King agreed. As a result, his war cabinet (Fudge and Tucker 2001, 229–230) issued an order, PC 2685, stating that workers in war industries should have collective bargaining rights. However, the order was merely advisory, provided no enforcement mechanism, and was universally ignored by employers. Additionally, as with the previous Great War, labor was systematically excluded from any wartime planning agencies, despite repeated entreaties to be included. This politicized wartime labor conflict, as state repression of strikes exposed the gap between the promises of stated government policy and the reality of steadfast government intransigence. As such, at their 1941 convention, the same year that the U.S. AFL and CIO agreed to no-strike pledges for the duration of the war, the CCL affirmed a resolution on strike policy stating:

> The [CCL] believes in the observance of contracts, and is therefore opposed to any strike where it is clearly and definitely established that such a strike

is unjustified. The Congress desires to point out, however, that the refusal of employers to accept the Labour policy of the Government with regard to the right to bargain collectively often creates situations beyond the control of the Congress, but for which the Government has the remedy through the enforcement of its stated policy. (Canadian Congress of Labour 1941, 23)

Escalating industrial conflict across Canada in 1942 and 1943 created many situations beyond the control of the CCL leadership. The number of strikes nearly doubled between 1941 and 1943, from 231 to 402, with the number of workers involved spiking from 87,091 to 218,404 (Labour Canada 1977). As pressure mounted on the King government to address the labor problem, the response was a series of ever more repressive Orders in Council further restricting picketing and strikers' civil liberties (Camfield 2002; Fudge and Tucker 2001; Jamieson 1968; MacDowell 1978; McInnis 2002). At the same time, the spiraling conflict led to a breakthrough in political support for the CCF in Ontario, where the Hepburn government was attempting to smash the CCL. The harbinger of change was a February 1942 by-election in the deep Tory blue riding of York South, where CCF candidate Joseph W. Noseworthy defeated former Prime Minister and Conservative Party leader Arthur Meighen (Granatstein 1967). But the real CCF success in Ontario came in the provincial election of August 1943, when the party took thirty-four seats in Parliament with 33 percent of the popular vote, enough to form the Official Opposition (Caplan 1963, 102–104). Reflecting on the results, King wrote in his diary:

> The CCF have made a telling run in all industrial constituencies, particularly where there has been political unrest, making clear the combination of the industrial CIO with the political CCF. . . . The collapse of the Liberal Party in Ontario . . . may be the beginning of the end of the power of the Liberal Party federally. . . . [Results may] show some members of the government the necessity of being less extreme in their attitude toward labour. (King 1943)

Having branched out beyond their Western agrarian base and allied with the industrial working class in Ontario, the CCF no longer had "its left flank up in the air." It was now a much more serious electoral threat for the Liberals. The party's success also showed voluntarist labor leaders that a class-based political party could be viable.

Declaring that he was "sick and tired of going cap in hand to Mackenzie King to get Labour policies adopted," Conroy backed a resolution at the 1943

CCL convention recognizing the CCF as the "political arm of labour" (Canadian Congress of Labour 1943, 53–56). Conroy was a reluctant CCF supporter and came down decisively in favor of independent political organization only at the 1946 convention, after a series of factional disputes with Communist Party supporters. But the combination of the Liberals' intransigence toward labor's demands and the CCF's demonstration that it could be viable pushed Conroy and his supporters away from voluntarism and toward CCF affiliation (Abella 1973, 73–80; Canadian Congress of Labour 1946, 79–81). The ruling party's policy of repression and neglect prevented labor from being absorbed into the Liberal coalition. Instead, it allowed the CCF to articulate an independent farmer–labor alliance, paving the way for the CCF to take root in Canada.

CONCLUSION

Although many aspects of the Canadian NDP/CCF have been the subject of intense scholarly research and debate, few have questioned why the party was able to establish itself as one of Canada's main political parties at all. Rather, the idea that the NDP/CCF or a similar party would take root in Canada is taken for granted. More specifically, the argument is that Canada's parliamentary system, its political culture suffused with a "Tory-touched" liberalism, and a small but significant preexisting left tradition created a political terrain that was relatively favorable to independent left parties.

Yet, despite these potential advantages, what is surprising is that no left party was able to establish a major and durable electoral presence prior to the CCF. Until that point, Canada was joined with the United States as the two "exceptional" countries without a major labor or socialist party. Why then did the CCF succeed where previous left party efforts had failed, and why did it succeed when it did?

Existing explanations for the CCF's establishment are insufficient because they are based on a reflection model of politics, whereby parties reflect preexisting social cleavages and institutional arrangements. These approaches can correctly identify the factors that create terrain favorable for the emergence of independent left parties, but they cannot specify why they were less favorable prior to the emergence of the CCF and more so afterwards.

To construct a more adequate explanation, I proposed an account based on an articulation model of politics. Such accounts emphasize the role that parties play in assembling, disassembling, and blocking different political coalitions. In the case of the emergence of the CCF, the ruling Liberal and Conservative parties' coercive response to labor and agrarian upsurge sparked by the Great Depression decisively detached key farmer and labor groups from their traditional party loyalties, leaving them available for a new independent political alliance. Meanwhile, CCF organization and ideology was coherent enough to prevent it from following previous left party efforts down the path toward co-optation or dissolution. At the same time, it remained flexible enough to incorporate disparate and previously fragmented constituencies, allowing the CCF to articulate a previously elusive farmer–labor alliance. Although the actual content and stability of that alliance remained in doubt well into the 1940s, the decisive moment occurred in the midst of World War II. At that point, the glaring discrepancy between the ruling Liberals' stated commitment to labor rights and the reality of state repression of labor drove previously noncommittal labor leaders to back the CCF. This made the envisioned coalition of labor and farmer groups more real, allowing the CCF to take root as a major left party in Canada.

Empirically, these findings refine our understanding of left party development in Canada. Although recognizing that the CCF drew on and was part of a broader left tradition, the analysis highlights the qualitative shift that the establishment of the CCF represented. Prior to the CCF, no left party had managed to maintain a strong electoral presence for more than three election cycles. And, after the CCF was established, the previously varied left ecosystem became bifurcated between the dominant CCF/NDP and everything else. Additionally, the account illustrates how political and class struggle, mediated by parties, reshaped the Canadian political landscape, allowing the CCF to take root.

However, the articulation framework proposed here does not dismiss the importance of culture, ideologies, and institutions, that is, the existing political terrain. Rather, it highlights the ways in which they predisposed, but did not predetermine, certain outcomes. For example, the Canadian political landscape certainly had features that encouraged left party formation. But, given the country's political economy, such a party required a farmer–labor alliance to be viable on a national scale, a coalition that remained elusive for several decades. It was the interaction of Canada's political structures with the political-economic struggles of the Great Depression that led to the political landscape we observe today, where the NDP serves as the federal official opposition.

Theoretically, this chapter's findings highlight the importance of seeing parties not as mere interest aggregators or class or group representatives but rather as active organizers—and disorganizers—of interests and class coalitions. In so doing, this study offers a way of reintegrating the study of parties into political sociology. As the editors note, that field has largely been left to political scientists since the defining interventions of Lipset and Rokkan (1967) and Sartori (1976). Sociologists studying state–society relations have tended to focus either on nonstate actors such as social movements (McAdam, Tarrow, and Tilly 2001) or on the state itself, primarily its administrative bureaucracies (Evans, Rueschemeyer, and Skocpol 1985). Although parties are commonly used as a regression variable (usually termed "left party strength") used to explain variation in state structures (Huber, Ragin, and Stephens 1993), this chapter seeks to develop a more active conception of parties as shapers of state–society relations. In so doing, it offers a means of integrating these two perspectives and developing a more robust understanding of the interaction between state and society.

More broadly, political articulation provides conceptual tools for developing a more dynamic understanding of cross-national policy variation within the context of "sticky" cultural practices and institutional arrangements. Current research has moved well beyond the structural determinism of midcentury modernization theory (Wilensky 1974). Instead, scholars have focused on identifying variations in institutional arrangements. The resulting schemas have helped to understand how institutional differences have driven cross-national variation (Esping-Andersen 1990; Hall and Soskice 2001). But although these approaches explain persistent differences, they are less suited for explaining change processes. Political articulation injects an element of instability and contingency into our understanding of cross-national differences, allowing a deeper understanding of how those differences evolve over time.

THREE RELIGIOUS POLITICS, HEGEMONY, AND THE MARKET ECONOMY
Parties in the Making of Turkey's Liberal-Conservative
Bloc and Egypt's Diffuse Islamization

Cihan Tuğal

THIS CHAPTER SEEKS TO DEMONSTRATE the autonomous role of politics in crystalizing and prioritizing certain cleavages and rebuilding society around them. It first focuses on the Republic of Turkey, with its complex political scene and multiple cleavages, to demonstrate this claim. Divisions between Kurds and Turks, secularized and pious sectors, upper and lower classes, and ultimately the ruling elite and the people have influenced the political scene for decades. Even though these divisions seemed to naturally find their expression in the division between the center left and the center right until the late 1980s, Islamist leaders embarked on revising these divisions after that point. By redefining the normal citizen as a *mağdur* (wronged, mistreated) yet hard-working and entrepreneurial Muslim, they attacked the secular ruling elite. They thereby rendered free market identity "popular" and built consent around it. Islamists mobilized Kurds and Turks for this new project, while at the same time increasing piety among all sectors, including some parts of the (hitherto) secular elite. They built an "equivalential chain" (Laclau and Mouffe 1985): They structured politics around a set of oppositions between entrepreneurial Muslims and bureaucratic elites, the pious and the secular, the oppressed people and the oligarchy, and the free market and state regulation. Standing on one side of the divide on any of these issues came to necessarily mean taking a predetermined stance regarding all of these binaries.

Although similar trends can be observed elsewhere in the Middle East, Turkey remains an exception, as this social transformation was led by a political party. To support this claim, this chapter discusses how the lack of a legal, professionalized, unified, mobilizing Islamic party has restricted (though not completely undermined) the process of Islamic neoliberalization in Egypt. Contradictions in this country have revolved around axes such as Arabs versus Israel and the United States, labor versus capital, integral religion versus official and Sufi religion, and the ruling elite and police state versus the people (as well as the less frequently politicized and nationalized issues such as lower Egypt versus upper Egypt, the state versus the nomads, and so on). The Muslim Brotherhood has not been able to establish chains of equivalence among these contradictions, in contradistinction to the Justice and Development Party in Turkey.

This difference of outcome is all the more striking in the light of certain similarities between Turkey and Egypt. The governing Islamic party in Turkey has roots in an Islamist movement that took the Egyptian Muslim Brotherhood as one of its models. Historically, therefore, the two movements resembled each other, especially in their intent to shape society, the state, and the economy along a solidaristic interpretation of scripture. Adding to the similarities between the cases, the dominant secularist regimes tried to absorb Islamism after the 1970s, but, due to Islamic actors' divergent responses, the attempted absorption produced contrasting results.

In the language of the political articulation research program, both movements had integral orientations; however, the Turkish movement also had the organizational capacity to realize its integral aims. The Turkish Islamist movement established an integral party as early as the 1970s. The Brotherhood, by contrast, remained an integral organization with low levels of professionalization and also failed to unify the Islamic field once it ultimately established its party. The outcome was that the Turkish Islamists were able to articulate blocs (woven around the equivalences mentioned in the previous paragraphs), whereas their Egyptian counterparts weren't.

The chapter ends by pointing out that, after the events of 2011, Egyptian Islamic actors were handed the chance to move in the Turkish direction but have been unable to use the opportunity. However, the post-2011 world political and economic climate has also highlighted serious limits to Turkish Islamism's hegemonic capabilities. The analysis of recent developments further highlights the differences of the articulation approach from state-centered approaches.

ISLAMIC OPPOSITION: STATE, CIVIL SOCIETY, OR POLITICS?

In studies of religious mobilization in the Middle East, sociology and political science have either naturalized the secular–religious divide or put emphasis on state traditions. It is true that, both in Turkey and Egypt, civil society on the one hand and state on the other have had a great impact on shaping cleavages. However, we cannot understand their impacts fully without bringing in the political party and other political activities that have rechanneled their influence on the making of cleavages.

The literature on civil society in the Muslim world draws our attention to the creativity of the actors on the ground (Norton 1995–1996; Özdalga and Persson 1997; Singerman 1995). This literature emphasizes that popular sectors build their own networks, which might even have an impact on formal institutions (White 2002). In this account, Islam or Islamism enters after the fact of civic creativity, as a political or religious channel that gives a voice to the already formed communities and identities. Spontaneous associational activities are at the root of the Islamization. This literature takes the transition to a market economy as a broad background and argues that economic liberalization has strengthened the hand of society against the state, making the flourishing of civil society possible. Political interventions in social processes are usually absent from these accounts.

Even scholars who have revised and developed the civil society paradigm by recognizing the intersections between politics and civil society hold that networks exist before politics and that "institutions are products of the underlying society" (White 2002, 21, 26). By contrast, I take civil society as an effect of hegemonic projects. Citizens indeed associate together to take control over their lives, but this gathering is deeply influenced by political organizations.

Although networks, communities and divisions within society *precede* politics and ideology in the civil society literature, my account shows that politics is partially *formative* of society, communities, and the cleavages that pit communities against each other.[1] Islamist politics and community are mutually constitutive.

Civil society is not so much a countervailing force against the state, but both civil society and the state are battlegrounds for competing hegemonic projects. Because civil society, as the realm of civic activity and network building, is by definition more intertwined with the creativity of actors on the ground, hegemonic projects need to be open to this bottom-up creativity to secure a foot in civil society. I hold that Islamism's novelty and difference from other hegemonic (and less hegemonic) projects in Turkey come from being more open to this creativity when establishing its hegemony. In other words, Islamism appeals to the people not because it simply liberates them as against an oppressive state (as in the civil society perspective) but because it successfully intervenes in the constitution of their communities and absorbs their creativity when implementing its own project.

State-centered accounts of Islamic mobilization in Turkey and Egypt emphasize the incomplete secularization of state policies. Either the state's top-down Islamization to fight the left or the breakdown of secular state capacity lies at the root of Islamization. This literature, which draws on the state-centered turn in political sociology (Evans 1979; Evans et al. 1985; Skocpol 1979), takes two shapes: (1) looking at repression and divisions within the secular state, which Islamists make use of; and (2) looking at how the state becomes an active agent of Islamization. Echoing Jeff Goodwin's (2001) argument that repressive and exclusive states with low capacity encourage revolutionary movements, scholars posit that indiscriminate and reactive repression leads to radicalization (Hafez 2003). Some scholars likewise suggest that inclusion of activists and a decrease in repression would increase the likelihood of deradicalization (Baylouny 2004).

Scholars focusing on institutional openings (Arjomand 1988, 114–128; Hafez and Wiktorowicz 2004; Tepe 2006; Zubaida 1989) account for the rise of Islamism by referring to divides among secular elites, emergence of sympathetic elites, the availability of religious institutions in the absence of secular institutions of opposition, declining capacity or willingness of secular states to repress dissent, the fragmentation of the political system, and the collapse of the center parties. Such factors can indeed partially explain the political and institutional context of Islamic mobilization. But they cannot fully explain the divergent paths of Turkey and Egypt.

Turkey and Egypt have both witnessed divisions among secular elites and the emergence of pro-Islamic factions among the elite. Nevertheless, Islamic actors have made quite different uses of similar openings. Scholars have also shown that in Egypt (Starrett 1998; Zubaida 1989) and Turkey (Cizre-Sakallıoğlu 1996) officially secular states have furthered Islamizing policies to undercut the influence of bottom-up Islamic mobilization and create obedient citizens. However, this has culminated in a fluctuating exclusion of Islamists in the former country (under the Sadat and Mubarak regimes) and their gradual absorption in the latter, signaling that we have to bring in other factors for a full explanation.

Moreover, the secular state's willingness to repress Islamism (consistent in Egypt between the mid-1990s and 2011 and declining in Turkey after 2001) cannot be simply handled as an independent variable that induces Islamic liberalization, as this willingness (as well as the capacity) partially depends on Islamist strategies. For example, the reduced willingness of the Turkish state to repress dissent can be traced back to emerging divisions within the Islamist camp (that is, the emergence of a promarket Islamic party in 2001). Another example of the political structuration of repression is the crackdown on the Brotherhood in 2010, which will be further explored in the sections on Egypt.

In sum, repression, institutional openings, and the state's role as an active Islamizer are the most important factors that come out of this literature as possible explanations of diverging paths of Islamization. I posit that any sound analysis of this divergence should integrate the mentioned factors but also thoroughly take into account political society's responses to them.

Although civil society and state-centered accounts provide important insights, they do not really account for the variation between the results of secular and Islamic struggles in Turkey and Egypt. Even though rigid secularism has been undermined in both countries, why has one ended up with a state and society largely built along neoliberal Islamic lines (and in opposition to secular workers and bureaucrats)? In Egypt, Islamic mobilization has mostly focused on the issue of Islamic law (it has been "legalistic"),[2] and the popular experience on the ground is focused on the classical texts of Islam (which are also the basis of Islamic law itself). Why has Egypt ended up with a state and society where Islamic law is central and neoliberalism lacks legitimacy? Why aren't the lines of battle as clearly drawn in Egypt? Why were Islamic forces unable to establish control after the ouster of Mubarak, even though they were by far the most organized?

This chapter's central claim is that neither civil society, nor political society, nor the state in isolation can explain the divergence of these otherwise similar cases. Only by investigating how political society refashioned these other two can we accomplish this. Political society is the domain of political parties, sociopolitical organizations, municipalities, and charismatic leaders. Civil society is the domain of associations.

The word *sociopolitical* is used to designate a comprehensive project that touches on a broad set of issues regarding politics and society. Such comprehensive vision is what differentiates sociopolitical organizations from social movement organizations. Even though this is a working distinction that will have to be further refined elsewhere, what differentiates actors in civil society and political society is specifically this urge to be comprehensive.

I take the primary activities of state actors as administration and coercion. State actors devise and implement programs, and the same actors or others discipline those who do not abide by them. Political actors, by contrast, are defined here by leading people—in other words, mobilizing them for social reproduction or transformation. Although state actors might also act as political actors (that is, also invest in and work on mobilizing citizen participation in favor of their policies), this combination of the two roles is not necessary, and it is not a social given. Municipalities sit on the boundary between the state and political society. They devise and implement programs. However, as was the case in Turkey in the 1990s, they can become the institutional vanguards of a sociopolitical project that attacks the established order, and one of the chief mobilizers of people on the ground against this order.

The following sections will point out that the characteristics that differentiated Turkish (Islamic) political society from its Egyptian counterpart were unification and professionalization. These characteristics also intensified the capacity of political articulation in Turkey.

CONSTRUCTION OF THE CONSERVATIVE BLOC IN TURKEY

The solidification of an Islamic "ethical party" in Turkey accounts for much of the difference between the two cases.[3]

In the initial decades of the republic's history, the Turkish state had the strongest influence on sociopolitical organization but (starting in the 1950s) was also aided by political parties. All these actors aimed to create secular citizens who downplayed their differences through their common allegiance to Atatürk (the founder of the republic) and his legacy. The secular system they established was replaced by a more Islamic polity starting in the 1980s.

During the process of Islamization, changes in political society became the key to social transformations. The rapid fragmentation of the party system in the 1980s and the inability of the major parties to organize the population intensified an emerging crisis. The failures of center-leftist and center-rightist parties engendered a shift to the extremes and opened the door to a new political society.

Concomitantly, Turkish civil society (rich with divisions along multiple lines but mostly divided along a right versus left axis from the 1960s to the mid-1990s) came to be divided mostly along the secular–Islamic axis starting with the 1990s. Also, secular civil society became less influential[4] as Islamic associations grew at an unprecedented pace. The weakening secularist associations' cooperation with the military and paramilitary organizations (for example, during the 1997 coup and then again during alleged coup attempts around 2007) further fueled Islamic mobilization, this time in the name of democratization.

Islamization from above, implemented by a military regime in 1980 to fight leftist as well as Iran-inspired radical Islamic movements, also paved the way for an Islamization from below. In this process, some of the major institutions (such as the police forces) were staffed with religious conservatives, long before the empowerment of the (Islamic) Justice and Development Party in 2002. Although secularist forces within the state, political society, and civil society were incapable of providing alternatives to Islamism, they had a significant (if sometimes unintended) impact on how Islamic political society and civil society were structured, through repression, partial incorporation, selective alliances (Turam 2007), and countermobilization. It should be emphasized once again that the political articulation approach does not deny the influence of such state-level factors but seeks to integrate them into the study of the making and unmaking of integral and institutional parties.

Ever since the 1970s, a diverse Islamic political society in Turkey revolved around a successive chain of legal Islamist parties (National Salvation Party–Welfare Party–Virtue Party). Nevertheless, political society was not always central to Islamization in Turkey. As Islamic organizations were banned, only underground Sufi communities could carry out any meaningful Islamization during the republic's initial three decades. They then passed the torch to (mostly anticommunist rather than primarily Islamic) youth associations in the 1960s, the minor players in a civil society field dominated by leftists and right-wing nationalist forces.

Islamist politicians first became nationally influential with the foundation of the National Salvation Party (MNP) in the early 1970s (Sarıbay 1985). At first, they were able to subordinate Sufi communities and youth associations (which gradually became more interested in Islamization than fighting against communism, attesting to the influence of the party on civil society). However, as the Islamic youth radicalized under influence from Egypt, Pakistan, and Iran, they split from the party at the end of the 1970s. The military intervention in 1980 closed down the National Salvation Party, along with all other parties. When the Islamist party reemerged under the name the Welfare Party, it had a more radical, social justice–oriented platform. In the early 1990s, it attracted the formerly disillusioned radicals thanks to its electoral victories. In other words, the party effectively deployed the means of articulation (policy, rhetoric, and cadre change) and thereby laid the basis of unification in the Islamic field.

The MNP combined the forces of disparate sectors under an antielitist, vaguely social justice–oriented program. These sectors did not come together as a natural result of preexisting Muslim–secular divide in society, as the civil society approach would assume, but were severed from the center right and articulated to a new project by the MNP. Formerly conservative subjects were reinterpellated as Islamic subjects. Had the center-right parties kept these sectors in their orbit through the necessary concessions and maneuvers (through the right kind of "institutional politics" in Laclau's sense), the Islamist challenge in Turkey would never have been as serious.

The 1980 junta both expanded official Islam's sphere to fight the Left and suppressed autonomous expressions of Islam so as to prevent the emergence of a religious opposition. On the military's closure of all existing parties and civil organizations in 1980, a new center-right party (ANAP) led neoliberalization, supported by secular businesspeople, pious tradespeople, and a secular professional class. (Society was still divided mostly along class lines.) The Islamists were again going to win some of these sectors to their side in a decade, attesting to parties' incessant disarticulation and rearticulation of social sectors, which civil society and state-centered explanations are not well equipped to explain.

After the failures of the center right and then the center left, the Welfare Party came out of the 1995 national elections as the leading party. It managed to form a coalition government with the center right, with the Welfare Party leader Erbakan as prime minister. In the 1980s and 1990s (the heyday of a rigid, comprehensive, textualistic interpretation of religion), Islamists attacked secularism in Turkey and transformed everyday behavior and uses of the body. The Islamic political party, municipalities, and radical organizations (in one phrase, political society) led this attack, thoroughly shaping the activities of civil society (pious associations, foundations, communities, and networks). These activities included teaching people how to pray or the proper way of praying, arranging Islamic wedding ceremonies, encouraging or imposing Islamic ways of clothing and Islamic facial hair, and imposing alcohol bans or making people quit alcohol. They introduced Islamic practices (most of all the prayer and the separation of the sexes) to central locations as well as offices and workplaces.

The median, "normal" Islamic subject, as interpellated through these interactive political practices, came to be a politicized, pious, and cautious activist. This combination demonstrates that the political party does not simply express grievances from the electorate but molds popular concerns. This process suggests that, in the absence of the party, the civil society actors would probably have followed different paths: The sufi orders would remain more moderate, and the youth would radicalize further. Focusing on the state and civil society, therefore, would not be sufficient for a full account of how certain political identities and dispositions become more central than others.

Together with still supporting provincial businesspeople and artisans, the Welfare Party's program placed a strong emphasis on redistributive social justice. On one hand, the party furthered the interests of an expanding pious business class. With the changing needs of this class, heavy industrialization was dropped from the program to emphasize flexible production. The party's proposed socioeconomic program, on the other hand, envisioned a world where morality dominated the market (Erbakan 1991). Such a market bound by morality would enable small business owners to operate without exploiting the poor, who would also be protected by the state. These promises, which articulated an acceptance of open markets with communitarian socialism,[5] brought with them immense urban poor support.

The Welfare Party came out of the 1994 municipal elections as the leading party (Çınar 2005), following which Islamist municipalities carried out a redistribution of urban resources. Also, the ideological impetus of the party had enabled it to stay relatively clean in the post-1980 environment, where secular actors pursued the corrupt wealth generated by irregular privatization. These moves of the Welfare Party increased its popularity, and it came out of the 1995 national elections too as the leading party. The Welfare Party's policies led to protests by secularist, middle-class civil organizations that implicitly called for a military intervention. The military, responding to these demands, gradually pushed the Welfare Party out of government and then out of legal existence (February 28, 1997–1998).

The actions of the state (here, the military, the courts) once again set certain limits on action. Yet, as will be seen in the following discussion, these were translated into solid sociological results only through mediation and internalization based on parties.

The 1997 intervention culminated in the founding of the Virtue Party. The Virtue Party got rid of the rhetorical anticapitalism in the Welfare Party's program. Rather than reacting against global competition from the West, the Virtue Party sought to negotiate the terms of this competition. It declared itself a prohuman rights party. It expected help from Europe against secularist authoritarianism, which never came. Yet, in line with the MSP–Welfare Party tradition, it was an Islamist party and desired the replacement of the secular elite—which again exemplifies how political parties are crucial in articulating hitherto unrelated demands (here, populist Islamization and democratization). The secularist courts closed down the Virtue Party, too (Koğacıoğlu 2004), after which the Islamists formed a new party, the Felicity Party. The moves of the military against Islamic education and clothing met wide street protests. However, Islamists could not (or did not) make use of street action properly in the 1990s and later, mostly due to top Welfare and Virtue Party leaders' reluctance, their authority over and incorporation of some radicals and party youth, and their marginalization of the others (which are among their chief means of articulation). The many abortive attempts to establish radical organizations and failed street protests reinforced existing tendencies of deradicalization, as the disappointed and disillusioned radicals repented and started to seek Islamic change within the system. This resulted in the absorption of once antisecular leaders, activists, networks, and lifestyles into secular democracy.

The preceding should not be read as a one-sided political explanation of deradicalization, as other trends also affected this process. For instance, former radicals' engagement in trade and hence operation in a market economy made them question the viability of a completely distinct "Islamic economy." However, this questioning was restricted until a new Islamic political party normalized the market economy and the secular state. The former radical activists and networks joined the party and started to work for its empowerment. For instance, Ömer Çelik, one of Turkey's prominent Islamic intellectuals, still attacked global capitalism and sided with the anti–World Trade Organization (WTO) protests in Seattle at the end of the millennium; he was to become one of the primary advisors of the Turkish prime minister in a few years and cease his criticism of the WTO and similar neoliberal bodies. Hence, it is not the direction taken by civil society but its interaction with political society that determines the ramifications of mobilization. If trends in civil society single-handedly dictated the path of social change, the strengthening of civil society against the military could perhaps radicalize activists (especially the students and intellectuals). Yet, an entrenched political Islamic tradition tempered even the existing radicalism.

The (neoliberal, relatively prodemocratic, and pro-U.S.) younger generation of the Virtue Party first tried to take over the existing party structure. Because its leaders had lost at the ballot during a major party congress (in May 2000), they established a new organization in 2001—the Justice and Development Party (AKP or Ak Party). The leaders of the Justice and Development Party promised the secularist media and the military that they would not use religion for political purposes. They reframed their appeal in center-conservative terms, emphasizing their allegiance to the free market (in line with the interests of their own bourgeoisifying base), parliamentary democracy, and the EU process. They also incorporated politicians from the now failed center-right parties. The "liberal" (less rigidly secularist, more pro-American, and less authoritarian) wing of the military, as well as center-rightists in the secular media, gave signals that they would be willing to work with such a reformed Islamic party.

As this book's Introduction points out, preexisting intellectual formations also influence the process of articulation. One crucial factor in Turkey was the consolidation of the intelligentsia around liberal themes in the 1980s and 1990s (although liberalism in pure form never became a mass ideology, even in a restricted way). What marked the new intellectuals most distinctively from the intelligentsia of the former decades was their disappointment with secular, nationalist authoritarianism; they were willing to support any force that promised to undermine the (old regime's) official ideology. Liberalized intellectuals of all backgrounds (ex-Islamists, ex-nationalists, ex-Marxists) looked for a political home throughout these decades, without any stable success. They first invested hopes in secular business parties. The failure of such parties in the 1990s was crucial in the displacement of their hopes and their investment in Islamic politics. Small "libertarian-left" political groups, who were under the influence of the ex-Marxists among these liberals, also became keys to the establishment of Islamic market hegemony.

Certainly, the Islamic political forces could have ignored this complex scene. Yet, as different from its predecessors, the AKP did not seek to dethrone *all* the ruling secularist elites (up until 2011, at least). Responding to its conciliatory tone, a vast number of non-Islamist politicians, intellectuals, and voters soon joined its ranks. This granted the AKP a resounding election victory in

November 2002—34 percent of the vote in a highly fractured multiparty system where the second party (the Kemalist,[6] or the Republican People's Party, henceforth CHP) got only 19 percent and the other parties all below 10 percent. Despite mounting secularist opposition, the party increased its vote to 46 percent in the 2007 elections. The AKP thus (re-) constituted the social by disarticulating several sectors from the center-right, liberalism, and nationalism and rearticulating them to an Islamic project. Without the AKP's move to expand its hegemonic bloc, it is unlikely that these widely divided forces would have reorganized out of the familiar opposition of Islamism and the center-right. The cold-blooded professionalism with which the AKP engaged in the necessary policy and rhetorical shifts to draw people from many different camps (while remaining within an Islamic idiom) was what differentiated this party from the Egyptian Brotherhood.

By the mid-2000s, a molecular absorption of pious life patterns characterized Turkey. The result was what we can call (with some caveats)[7] liberalized Islamization. Liberalized Islamization can be defined as a flexible implementation of gender segregation and female covering; flexibility and (business and political) utility orientation regarding the daily and Friday prayers; flexibility and attention to economic implications in the restriction of un-Islamic practices. So, the question is, how did Turkish Islamists shift from propagating a somewhat legalistic understanding of religion to this new interpretation?

The integral orientations of the AKP (in its interaction with civil society and the state) were the key driving mechanism. The AKP appropriated countersystem mobilization to reinforce existing systemic patterns. For example, whereas prayer lost its centrality to everyday life, Islamic leaders and activists made a point of praying before and after public political meetings (Tuğal 2009). Such public shows have been central to the careers of center-rightist politicians throughout republican Turkish history. These politicians lead Westernized lives but mobilize Islamic symbols for mass appeal. As center-right parties weakened in Turkey, Islamic parties moved in to fill the gap but internalized some center-right strategies while doing so. In other words, the changes in the place of prayer in social and political life resulted from changes in the structure of political society rather than solely the secularist impositions of the state.

The interlocking activities of political society and civil society put an end to the separation of sexes in workplaces, while however reproducing a tamed variety of gender segregation in less visible neighborhoods. Segregation was unofficially practiced, but in official venues like the municipality or party meetings it lost its prominence. Professional and business-oriented women gained more visibility in this new context of flexibility. Instead of attempting to ban alcohol everywhere (the Islamist utopia), the AKP imposed restrictions on alcohol sale and use, after the American conservative model.

We can take the Justice and Development Party's supple attempts to apply Islamic law and force as further demonstrations of liberalized Islam. A case in point is pious cadres' gradual infiltration of state institutions such as the police, the judiciary, ministries, and public education. Combined with a major court case against (alleged) civil and bureaucratic coup attempts (the "Ergenekon" case), which resulted in an uneven, but effective, purge of secular cadres from the state, this amounted to an Islamization of official cadres. Moreover, many government critics were weeded out from the media throughout the same legal process. This can be taken as an instance of Islamic coercion. However, note that, in contradistinction to Iran (and Egypt between 2011 and July 2013), the government and institutions allied with it (for example, the police) carried this process out with every attempt to remain within (national and international) secular legitimacy and legality (until mid-2013). Moreover, many intellectuals (including secular liberals and ex-Marxists) propounded the Ergenekon case as the Turkish state's ultimate democratization. In short, an integral party could sell even its authoritarian moves as exemplars of liberty and transform a court case into a means of articulation.

A bourgeois-Islamic civil society slowly blossomed in the liberalized atmosphere the AKP created, and the existing Islamic civil society molecularly changed in a modern direction, giving rise to new understandings of religiosity. Cultural centers and networks of friends, mosques, and Islamic schools manufactured a pragmatic and business-oriented spirituality. For example, whereas the Welfare Party and Virtue Party leaders encouraged their members and contacts to pray whenever the call to prayer was cited, the AKP leaders and members chose to emphasize how hard work itself is a part of religion and did not publicly incite people to pray (Tuğal 2009). Religion, still practiced though less vigorously, was more individualized (for example, former activists no longer put pressure on people around them to perform the daily prayers communally). Furthermore, some neo-Sufi communities further professionalized and individualized (Turam 2007)—and these more professionalized became more prominent when compared to the other neo-Sufi communities.

Finally, some sectors of the elite appropriated this emergent religiosity and became more observant themselves.

These behavioral changes were paralleled by changes in the goals of Islamists. Goals and motivations may be more difficult to measure, as we cannot neglect the possibility that actors are hiding their true motivations from public scrutiny. With this qualification in mind, the available information indicates that support for an Islamic state declined throughout the nation during the 2000s (Çarkoğlu and Toprak 2006). This was a significant development, given that Islamists across Egypt and Turkey used to share a comprehensive vision of Islam (including the goal of an Islamic state), but political and civic dynamics (at least apparently) led most Islamists in Turkey to drop this objective.

These developments show how institutional opportunities and threats do not impose a direction on mobilization; political organization mediates their influence. If we were to follow the (state-centered) political opportunities logic, Islamism would radicalize or liberalize only in response to the various moves of official institutions. However, even though these moves did have an impact, the party's relations with youth mobilization and other forms of activism (that is, the interaction of political society and civil society) also had an impact on the tone of the movement in Turkey.

In sum: The AKP was successful in merging ex-Islamists, the urban poor, intellectuals, business families, and professionals around a neoliberal "democratic" program. These groups were integrated into a new, more conservative, stronger regime (as the AKP transformed the Turkish state in such a direction after 2002).

Failed Articulation

Although secularist social movement organizations in Turkey were determined to fight the Islamists through street action, the military, and the courts, the Kemalists lacked an effective party that could articulate all these forces and deal a decisive blow to the AKP. The failures of the main anti-Islamist party (the Republican People's Party, or CHP) in this regard once again demonstrate the importance of parties in sociopolitical battles.

The CHP became a popular party in the mid-1960s, after it moved away from secular authoritarianism and adapted a populist platform. This expanded the party from an exclusive coalition of bureaucrats, notables, and professionals to include working classes, peasants, and Kurds. After the CHP was closed down by the 1980 military intervention, it reopened under the name SHP (Social Democratic Populist Party) and attempted to shift from populism to European-style social democracy. However, once in power in the early 1990s, the SHP failed to make any progress on the Kurdish question, ultimately costing it the Kurdish vote. The Kurdish vote was ultimately divided between Islamists and Kurdish nationalists. Moreover, the SHP's corruption at the municipal level destroyed its credibility.

Another reason for the SHP's marginalization was its shift to the rigid secularist position of the pre-1960s CHP. As a result, the center left's base shifted from a working- and middle-class coalition to one of (secular) professionals, (secular) bureaucrats, and the worker aristocracy. During the 1990s, pious Kurds and informal workers (two partially overlapping populations) began to desert the center left and join the Islamists. This disarticulation spelled the end of the party as a governmental alternative.

Once the CHP reopened in the mid-1990s, it relied mostly on its pre-1960s mission of authoritarian secular nationalism, further weakening the leftist elements within the now-defunct SHP. The CHP thus became the political leader against Islamism. However, due to the liquidations of its prominent social democratic leaders, it alienated even (some) secularized sectors.[8] While the party abandoned its mission of social protectionism, it did not replace that with a new social vision, which could allow it to articulate new sectors.

If the CHP had reinterpreted its leftist turn of the 1960s under the new conditions, rather than purging social democracy from its ranks, the social scene in Turkey would probably look different today. The left could possibly produce (with its own original interpretation) either the class-based, populist articulation seen in Venezuela and Bolivia or the social-liberalism witnessed in Chile and Brazil.

The recent unsuccessful attempts of a CHP leader (Kemal Kılıçdaroğlu) to shift the party in a left-wing direction demonstrate that the AKP's articulations were so naturalized in the 2000s that no major actor could take a step without falling back on the chains of equivalence the governing party had set up. The pro-AKP media (ranging from conservatives and ex-Islamists to secular liberals and liberalized Marxists) repeatedly accused the new CHP leadership of having a hidden agenda to resurrect the authoritarian military state; according to them, the new leader was just a naïve prop of a deep coup plan. (Liberal and conservative journalists and politicians also told the public that student protests against privatization of education and massive strikes were parts of the same coup plot.) Subsequently, all public attempts to support a leftward move in the CHP were (counterintuitively) interpreted to be authoritarian conspiracies. Under different conditions, left-wing critiques of secularist authoritarianism in the CHP would appear to be democratic, but, in the 2000s, the obviousness of the identification between the AKP and democracy was so entrenched that anything that would hurt the interests of the governing party was seen to be undemocratic. The old guard authoritarian secularist forces in the party used this suspicion-ridden environment to render the leftist attempts of the new leader ineffective. Although they were able to prevent a left-wing swing within the party, this did not necessarily help either them or the party on the national scene: Locking the party in the very positions liberals and conservatives attributed to it (secular, elitist, nationalist authoritarianism devoid of any economic promises, save a nostalgia for national developmentalism), they marginalized the party even further.

The fluctuating trajectory of Kemalism has important lessons for the sociological study of parties. First, Kemalist parties' popularity from the mid-1960s to the mid-1990s (when some pious workers and Kurds used to vote for them) demonstrates that the weight of the secular-religious (or the center-periphery) cleavage in Turkey is dependent on parties' articulating practices rather than being the governing logic of society and politics. Second, although social movements and civil society organization are indispensable weapons for any social project, they cannot by themselves compete against rival projects that have strong party leadership. In the absence of articulation, they lose orientation and make recourse to extreme measures (as in the case of pro-CHP civilians investing hope in military and paramilitary resolutions). The CHP's insistence to stick to a shallow institutional party model hurt both the party and the sectors that still supported it.

The Kurdish Peace Process: Contingent Articulation
The soft underbelly of Turkish liberal-conservative hegemony was the Kurdish issue (Tuğal 2009). The victories, fluctuations, and restrictions of the governing Islamic party in Turkey demonstrate that, even in quite hegemonic cases, articulation is an open process, which remains challenged, at least from some directions.

After it came to power in 2002, the governing AKP made some inroads into Kurdistan by granting new rights (for example, more linguistic and educational freedom and an official television station in Kurdish). However, because the guerrilla itself had become partially hegemonic in Kurdish areas over the course of a three-decades civil war, these means of articulation proved feeble. The Kurdish insurgency persisted, due to the multiple levels of political work the guerrilla had engaged: The Kurdistan Worker's Party, known by its acronym, the PKK, had built formidable links with the Kurdish agrarian and urban populations through municipal, legal party-focused, civic, and armed struggle, blending violence, threat, redistribution, and consent (a mixture the composition of which fluctuated based on the responses of the Turkish state, other opposition forces, and the balances among the guerrillas). Further AKP attempts to pacify the guerrillas failed under Turkish nationalist pressure, both from within and from outside the governing party. These restrictions in the party's democratization program raised questions among Turkish and European liberal supporters of the party.

In early 2013, however, the new regime wisely mobilized the secular and Islamic liberals by constituting a commission of "Wise Men" who would build public support for the peace negotiations between the Turkish Prime Minister Erdoğan and the Kurdish guerrilla leader Öcalan. The aura of apathy among the liberal intellectuals dissipated almost overnight thanks to this creative means of articulation. There was an explosion of enthusiasm again in favor of the new regime. Liberal, conservative, and even some leftist intellectuals, artists, and politicians were raised to the status of officially recognized rational actors ("Wise Men"), which boosted their credibility among the pro-AKP masses and the new regime's credibility on the intellectual and international scene.

The unity of Turkey hence preserved its delicacy. The AKP's hegemonic project certainly addressed some of the wounds but was far from being a final seal, an ultimate suturing. Nevertheless, the Turkish Islamists' headaches paled in comparison to the Egyptian Islamists', not least when it came to sustaining national unity, an issue that hardly troubled Egypt's old regime.

EGYPT: RESTRICTED NEOLIBERAL ISLAMIZATION, FRACTURED AND DIFFUSE RELIGIOUS COMMUNITY

Egypt also experienced the spread of liberalized Islamic practices, but these did not become predominant as in Turkey. After the overthrow of the colonially backed monarchy in 1952, the new Egyptian republic started out as a secular-nationalist project. Islam was marginalized, especially after 1954 under President Gamal Nasser, as in the first three decades of the Turkish regime. The Free Officers coup disbanded all political parties in its first months

(Moustafa 2003, 888). Even though Nasser initially became a charismatic hero, the defeat of his pan-Arabist strategy (Shorbagy 2007, 179), as well as the slowing down of development toward the end of his term (Waterbury 1983), discredited both him and his one-party regime. However, ongoing repression ensured that all competing parties (the liberal Wafd, the conservative Ahrar, and so on) remained marginal and uninfluential until 2011. This repressive structure was one of the factors that allowed illegal Islamic political organizations (including the Brotherhood) to become the major players in political society and civil society (exceptions include the non-Islamic Labor Party, which became Islamic at the end of the 1980s).

As was the case in Turkey after the military intervention of 1980, the rulers after Nasser (Sadat and Mubarak) coupled neoliberalization with a fluctuating absorption of Islamic activism to cope with the emergent crisis. Even during the relatively more liberal 1980s, Egypt was much more authoritarian than Turkey, but, still, certain periods of the Sadat and Mubarak regimes provided much greater opportunities to Islamic activists and politicians than to the rest of society. Despite these comparable opportunities, Egypt and Turkey diverged, suggesting that we need to take into account political moves in understanding how similar political opportunities might sometimes give rise to contrasting results.

Most important, what we have to account for is the sustained rise of a text- and law-focused Islam in Egypt. Although it is true that state and Islamic forces have been able to further naturalize Islamic identities in both countries, the meaning of this identity has come to be different in the two contexts. Although many Turkish conservatives freely mix secular and Islamic ways of life, this mixture is more cautious in Egypt (despite a bourgeoning literature on Islamic fashion shows and the like). A very simple example of this is the behavior of cab drivers. Many in Egypt listen to the Qur'an while working and repeat the verses along with the preacher on the radio (to memorize as much of the holy book as possible). One would hardly encounter such persistent behavior in Turkey, where even conservative cab drivers usually tune into popular music channels (of *arabesque* and *taverna* music, which feature some Islamic themes but are usually abhorred by Islamists and Islamic scholars; see Stokes 1992). In short, everyday practices in Turkey are predominantly market oriented (even when they articulate Islamic elements), whereas they are textuality oriented ("legalistic") in Egypt.

As different from Turkey, courts and al-Azhar scholars (as experts of Islamic law) also propel Islamization in Egypt, in order to claim radical Islam's
ground and limit its effectiveness (for example, see Mehrez 2001, 11–12), demonstrating that the state–society interaction can produce legalistic rather than
liberalized Islamic results. Given that there are liberal Islamic trends also in
Egypt, how can we account for the persistent predominance of legalistic Islam
(despite similar turning points in the state's relation to Islam and Islamists
around 1980 and the mid-1990s)? Why has the state–society interaction
turned liberalized in one country and remained legalistic in the other?

We have to turn to political dynamics to find an answer. The Muslim
Brotherhood is the central node in Egyptian Islamic political society. It was
founded in 1928 by Hasan al-Banna and, in its first decades, developed as
a sociopolitical movement organizing itself around athletic clubs, evening
schools, welfare provision, and anticolonial activism (Lia 1998; Mitchell 1969).
The founding leaders of the Muslim Brotherhood had an anti-institutionalist
bias: They did not want to be established as an association, club, or anything
"official" but rather presented their group primarily as "an Idea." To clarify
this further, the Brotherhood was never against expansive *organization*, but it
remained suspicious of legal and formal institutionalization (and hence, of a
formal political party). An analysis of this initial anti-institutionalism and its
consequences can shed a light on the differences of process and outcome from
Turkish Islamism.

The 1960s were the most radical years, when the Muslim Brotherhood propounded a violent overthrow of the regime by a revolutionary vanguard. Both
the increasing authoritarianism of the regime and the group's radicalism isolated the Muslim Brotherhood, preventing it from operating in conjunction
with associations during this decade. Privatization and deregulation from
the 1970s to the 1990s moderated the Muslim Brotherhood's position.[9] These
reforms brought with them sustained growth in the first half of the 1980s
along with declining real wages and increasing unemployment and poverty
(Kienle 1998).

This resulted in bread riots in the late 1970s and in more and more strikes
and violence in the beginning of the 1990s. In the 1970s and 1980s, the regime's
overall strategy was the inclusion of Islamic radicals and partial democratization to deal with increasing unrest. The Brotherhood tried to help the regime
prevent Islamist students from demonstrations, strikes, and sabotage, but

because it was not organized as a political party, it could not control the students completely (Baker 1991, 55–56). This provides an important contrast to Turkish Islamic political society, which had considerable control over Islamist students in the 1980s: The political societies in these two countries had quite different relations to the means of articulation.

In the 1970s, Islamists strengthened within the student body, and the public influence of al-Azhar was bolstered. Sadat wanted to use both against the left (Zeghal 1999), boosting the importance of Islamic legal scholarship in Egypt. However, Sadat's monopolization of power at the end of the 1970s interrupted the cooperation with Islamists. After Sadat's assassination in 1981 and the regime's relative liberalization, the Brotherhood started to participate in municipal, associational, and parliamentary elections. This taught the Brotherhood to play by the rules of the game, just like the Turkish Islamists.

In this decade, as before, the Muslim Brotherhood defined its own goal and the goal of the state as enhancing individual piety—including intensified worship, good manners, and overall abidance by Islam (Zahid and Medley 2006). As in the Turkey of the 1970s through the 1990s, Egyptian Islamic parties of different stripes enforced cleanliness, correct worship, and Islamic morality through their newspapers, magazines, books, conferences (Ismail 1998, 211–212), and the monitoring of neighborhoods and streets (Ismail 2006), as well as providing cheap urban services and low-cost Islamic clothing (Kepel 1995, 113). Ever since the 1970s, Islamic groups in universities have been instituting gender segregation (Ismail 1999; Rahman 2002).

Despite this similarity in the everyday implications of Islamization in the 1980s and 1990s, Egyptian Islamism has focused more on implementing Islamic law when compared to Turkish Islamism. What seems on the surface to be only a result of contextual difference (the Egyptian state recognizes a restricted version of Islamic law, whereas the Turkish state does not) turns out on closer scrutiny to be also a contrast in religious strategy.

The Islamist movement in Egypt was always concerned with Islamic law. What changed starting with the 1980s is that this point of concern moved further toward the center of the Muslim Brotherhood's agenda. More particularly, the Brotherhood rendered its tone conciliatory especially after the government declared Islamic law as the only source of legislation in May 1980.[10] After this move, confrontation was mostly removed from the Brotherhood's vocabulary (Sullivan and Abed-Kotob 1999, 57). Although some techniques of Islamization resembled the Turkish case even after this turning point, holding the government accountable to Islamic law gradually became the Muslim Brotherhood's main public activity under the old regime. So, available opportunities did have an impact on the type of Islamization, as the state-centered approach would predict, but their ultimate influence was molded by the way political society responded.

In the process of this absorption into existing power structures, the Muslim Brotherhood gave up its remaining radical ideas. During the 1980s and 1990s, some of the cornerstones of its agenda (such as a transnational Khilafa state) were dropped (Tamam 2010, 8–10). By 1994–1995, the Muslim Brotherhood declared its support for (a restricted version of) democracy, women's rights, and minority rights—though some scholars and activist women remained suspicious of the sincerity of these declarations (Harnisch and Mecham 2009, 199–200). After this point, the Muslim Brotherhood even started to use old Islamic modernist arguments (for example, *shura* as an Islamic equivalent of democracy) in favor of a plural party system (going against al-Banna's condemnation of parties; see el-Ghobashy 2005). Do these trends indicate a consistent shift in a more liberalized direction?

These moves away from a comprehensive understanding of Islamization were indeed paralleled by liberalization of religion on the ground. For instance, veiling became less conservative, more revealing, and a component of new urban chic (Herrera 2001), paralleling the transformation of Islamic clothing in Turkey. Among the poor, although religiosity still maintained its salience by integrating them to the city, everyday life became less puritan through an acceptance of fashionable dancers, singers, and expensive vacations (Ghannam 2002, chapter 5). However, because (unlike the Justice and Development Party) the Brotherhood's leadership was still not in sync with this liberalized form of religiosity, there was no force in Egyptian political society that would normalize this new face of Islam. In sum, though the transition to a market society and the strengthening of civil society prepared the conditions for the predominance of liberalized Islam (just as in Turkey, as the civil society approach would predict), liberalized Islam did not flourish due to differences in political society between Turkey and Egypt. So, why was the leadership not accommodating of these practices?

Urban middle-class and peasant elements were poorly integrated within the Egyptian Islamist movement, which inhibited a monopoly of the Brotherhood over Islamic political society and reproduced influential violent Islamist organizations. This lack of monopolization of political capital was a core dynamic differentiating Egypt and Turkey. Although intermittently using the Brotherhood against Islamic radicals, the old regime feared the influence of these radicals over the Muslim Brotherhood. In the 1980s and 1990s, radical armed organizations (Jamaa and Jihad) appealed to the urban and rural poor,[11] whereas segments of the Muslim Brotherhood appealed to rentier capitalists, the labor aristocracy, petty merchants, and professionals (Ismail 1998, 200–201). Jamaa (led by university graduates of middle-class and working-class origin; southern; social justice-focused) situated itself in opposition to the Brotherhood, which supported some free market policies and backed landowners against small farmers (Fandy 1994). At least until the mid-1990s, the countryside was open to agitation by radicals. Southern Egypt became associated with "terrorism." This provides a contrast to Turkey, where conservatives in the east and the west of the country are relatively more integrated through Islamic civil society and political society. Even though the countryside and the fringes of the cities are homes to poverty also in Turkey, the poor are connected to official institutions through patronage networks of political parties. The AKP's further organization and institutionalization of these patronage networks (an institutional tool turned into a means of articulation) can be taken as one reason why economic exclusion (which results from the transition to a free market) does not automatically lead to radicalization. Hence, comparable economic divides[12]—in these two cases did not dictate outcomes—they were mediated by politics.

Hence, there was no unification in Islamic political society (no monopolization of political capital) as in Turkey. The Egyptian state's sustained crackdown in the second half of the 1990s (which was in part a reaction to the Algerian civil war (Ghadbian 1997, 101) interrupted further strengthening of independent radical Islamic organizations. The crackdown was not followed, however, by the Muslim Brotherhood's absorption of radical Islamists, due to the Muslim Brotherhood's organizational semiprofessionalism: the Muslim Brotherhood did not have a spelled-out, coherent program (Tamam 2009) and the structure of a political party, which in combination could provide an alternative route to these radicals, incorporate them, and deradicalize them (as happened in Turkey). That the Muslim Brotherhood leaders remained suspicious of the idea of turning into a political party well into the 1990s is indicative of the legacy of semiprofessionalism.

In short, official repression does not dictate social outcomes; political organization shapes its influence. Throughout this historical process, regime type prevented the emergence of "ethical politics," but the structure of the Islamist field, as well as the structure of the Brotherhood's internal organization, further prevented the Brotherhood from becoming an effective integral party.

Between 1995 and 2000, the Muslim Brotherhood was afflicted with stalemate, as innovators were imprisoned (as was Erdoğan for a while after the 1997 coup in Turkey), and conservatives used repression as an excuse to have their candidate appointed as the top leader of the movement. Only in the beginning of the new millennium did the liberalizing youth have influence again. This influence became more decisive after 2004, with the death of a conservative top leader (el-Ghobashy 2005; Stark 2005). However, even following this partial liberalization, the Egyptian regime was distrustful of Islamism and continued mildly and selectively repressing the Muslim Brotherhood. Consequently, the organization fluctuated between a revival of conservative tendencies and small gains by reformists, with conservatives gaining more ground during 2009 and 2010. The Brotherhood's conservatives ousted many of the liberals in the last years of the old regime, and the regime used this as an excuse to crack down on the organization, saying that the organization was now controlled by fundamentalists. The structure of political society and the state led to a very different interaction than that in Turkey. Both old regimes had in the past looked for excuses to repress Islamists, but the Muslim Brotherhood provided more excuses than Turkish Islamic political parties. This prevented a possible transition to liberalized Islam and strengthened the hand of legalistic Islam.

These several shifts of balance within the Brotherhood suggest that some Islamists perceived the possibility of a more liberalized path. However, their attempts were thwarted not only by crackdowns but also by the conservatives' use of these crackdowns. In sum, whereas the Turkish Islamists recoiled to a liberalized form of Islam when their totalizing version of Islam was defeated, Egyptian Islamists recoiled to a legalistic position (once again demonstrating the political nature of responses to military defeat and hence the limits of an exclusively state-centered approach).

There was, in short, a convergence in the mid-1990s in Turkey and Egypt in terms of state response (the turn away from the inclusive policies of the 1980s as a reaction to Islamists gaining ground at home and Islamists fermenting civil war in Algeria), but, partially due to differences in the structure of political society, the results were different. In contrast with the Turkish case, state repression did not culminate in the emergence of a separate, liberalized

Islamic organization. To understand why, we need to focus on how the internal organization of political society differs in the two cases. Looking at repression and available opportunities is necessary but would not be enough.

The linchpin of the Egyptian Islamic movement's absorption to the system was also its changing relations to the economy, but these relations were mediated by politics. Developing a counterhegemonic position, figures within the early Brotherhood propagated Islamic socialism (Ismail 1998, 207). After prosecution by Nasser, Brotherhood members escaped abroad and engaged in economic activity, which they continued in Egypt starting with Sadat's opening to markets. In the 1970s and afterwards, the creation of jobs in the private sector and explosion of foreign trade benefited these Brotherhood members; many became rich (Ates 2005). The emigrant money coming from the Gulf escaped state control and was invested in Islamic banks. The financialization of the economy and the turn away from industrial investment were thereby legitimized Islamically in the 1970s and 1980s. Trading with the West or on the black market was also deemed Islamic through religious verdicts (Ismail 1998, 213–214).

As a result of these changes, the Brotherhood emerged as a proponent of a loose and community-based welfare system contradictorily married to an Islamic integration to neoliberalism. In the 1980s and 1990s, its overall economic program supported the state's and community's taking care of the poor, the narrowing of class gaps, and social security for all citizens. The program of the 1987 election alliance with other Islamic parties supported the shrinking of the government bureaucracy, promotion of the private sector as the backbone of the economy, promotion of alms giving, a noninterest banking system, and comprehensive government regulation and strategic planning of the economy (Abed-Kotob 1995, 326–327; el-Ghobashy 2005). The apparent contradictions here are reminiscent of the Turkish Islamists' Just Order program in the 1980s and 1990s (that is, before their full neoliberalization).

Yet, at the same time, economic liberalization drove a wedge between radicals (the losers of neoliberalism) and the MB (the partial winners). There was no hegemonic combination of the two as in Turkey, signaling the limits of Islamic hegemony in Egypt. Radicalism came as a handy excuse for the regime to block a full absorption into the system. Starting in the 1970s, the Egyptian regime gave many concessions to Islamism, which amounted to "Islamization without an Islamic state," in Asef Bayat's (2007) terms.

After the 1990s, too, the Brotherhood's position with respect to market reform was quite uneven. There were increasingly more neoliberal economists associated with the Brotherhood. The organization also supported liberalization in the countryside. However, even in the 2000s, the newspapers, election platforms, and other publications of the Brotherhood still combined elements of protectionism and free-market dynamism. In the 2005–2010 parliament, Brotherhood-connected MPs fought for higher wages, supported strikes, and made some moves against privatization. In short, no consistent Islamic path, whether pro- or antimarket, has emerged out of these decades of inconsistencies, demonstrating once again the limits of Islamic mobilization when compared to that in Turkey.

In sum, while the Islamists in Egypt were able to thoroughly Islamize society, this happened in such a diffuse manner that no coherent blocs, no coherent programme, no coherent identities have emerged. (Speaking in poststructuralist terms, we could say that there is no chain of equivalence in Egypt that has become hegemonic, though this chapter's analysis points out that there are organizational and structural reasons behind this.) An inchoate sense of a good Egyptian as a Muslim person distinct from Copts, the seculars, and especially defined in contradistinction to Israel became common sense—but this identity did not really shape the political arena, as perhaps 90 percent of the population fit it anyway. It is no surprise, then, that once a revolutionary situation erupted, the Brotherhood could not forge a contentious bloc.

THE JANUARY UPRISING: ARTICULATION RESHUFFLED OR FURTHER DISARTICULATION?

In this section, the period between 2011 and 2013 will be taken as a primary example of a point when a liberalized Islamic path was possible but was not taken.

Before the 2011 protests, the Brotherhood was shifting in a more and more conservative-protectionist direction. During 2009 and 2010, the regime ratcheted up the pressure against the Brotherhood. As a response, some members of the Brotherhood decided to boycott the parliamentary elections of 2010. However, the conservative-dominated Guidance Bureau (in alliance with the elected assembly of the organization) opposed this idea; the organization participated in the elections. What was remarkable in this debate about participation was not only the content of the arguments. The Guidance Bureau used a heavily moralistic language in condemning the people who suggested that the organization should boycott the elections. Questioning the decision of the leaders, the Bureau held, was "immoral" and against Brotherhood etiquette. This was emblematic of the organization's traditionalistic and unprofessional orientation to politics.

The Brotherhood could win only one seat in the heavily rigged elections. The governing National Democratic Party secured about 80 percent of the seats. After this, the opposition within the Brotherhood was further emboldened. They started a campaign against the Guidance Bureau, which in turn threatened to expel them.

After the 2011 protests, a deeper rift emerged. The Guidance Bureau remained silent during the protests of January 25, which started the revolutionary uprising in Egypt. Despite that, many Brotherhood members went to Tahrir Square. After it became obvious that this was turning into a popular uprising, the Bureau switched its position and declared that it was a part of the uprising! In order not to attract too much Western attention, the organization downplayed Islamic slogans, even when it turned out in large numbers onto the streets. Along with smaller leftist groups and soccer fans, the organization was the leader of the effort to defend Tahrir Square against thugs and undercover police. The military discipline that the organization had instilled in its members (not for the sake of revolution but mostly to get ready for a possible war with Israel) was put to extensive use.

Once Mubarak stepped down and the military, now taking charge, invited the protesters to go back home, the Guidance Bureau again called on the Egyptians to end the protests. Even more provocatively, their leaders called the strikes spreading all over Egypt "factional" (*fi'awiyya*), and one of them went one step further by raising doubts that it was actually counterrevolutionaries who were inciting the strikes.[13] At this juncture, Brotherhood members in Tahrir Square held meetings with leftist and nationalist groups, at the end of which they declared that they supported the strikes. They also said they were going to remain in the Square until the demands of the revolution were met. This new coalition of forces also asked the government to raise wages, build a wider social safety net for all Egyptians, and expand syndical freedoms.

Many analysts have pointed out that the protests did not feature Islamic slogans. Based on this information, they concluded that Egypt was now in a post-Islamist phase, where even pious people were more concerned with liberal democracy than in spreading piety and Islamic law. This, however, was too simplistic a generalization. Although the protests were not Islamic, it was

also significant that no slogans or mass protests in any city called the centrality of Islamic law in the Constitution (and in society at large) into question.
Public debate, as well as the protests, focused on other nondemocratic aspects
of the Constitution. Only a handful of Coptic intellectuals, along with a few
secular intellectuals, raised the question, but they did not find mass backing.
This situation shows that orthodox Islamic law has become unassailable as a
result of the efforts of the Brotherhood and its interactions with the old regime
over the decades (hinting that there are elements of a solid, but nonliberal,
interpellation in the Egyptian Islamic project).

The ruling military council appointed a committee of judges to make revisions in the Constitution (instead of drafting a new constitution, as the revolutionary uprising demanded). One member of this committee was reputed to
be a Brotherhood member. The head of the committee was a former critic of
the Mubarak regime and known to be an Islamic conservative. The committee showed no signs that it would discuss the second item of the Constitution
(which states that Islamic law is the primary source of legislation in Egypt).
The following amendments to the Constitution reproduced the authoritarian state structure. The amendments were approved by a crushing majority of
Egyptians, despite resistance by the revolutionaries and the liberals.

We again see here how preexisting intellectual formations influence the
process of articulation. In Egypt, just like in Turkey, there was a growing intellectual trend of questioning secular authoritarianism. This had even led, in
the mid-2000s, to anti-Mubarak coalitions across the secular–Islamic divide.
However, unlike in Turkey, the liberals and the nonauthoritarian left never
uncritically invested all of their hopes in the major Islamic political forces.
Moreover, the military's and the Brotherhood's capacity to mobilize the vote
against the revolutionaries and the liberals (partially a result of the lack of ties
between the masses and the oppositional intellectuals) also raised questions
about whether the revolutionary uprising would produce any solid transformation. As an organization with low integral capacity, the Brotherhood
(unlike the AKP) counted more on the military and less on the liberal intellectuals, a strategy that turned out to be fatal for the organization.

The questions that faced a political articulation analysis in 2011 were: How
would the Brotherhood manage these uncertain times? Would it be possible
for the organization to share power with the military to keep Egyptian Islam
on a law-focused path (as the constitutional committee signaled) but also engage in a compromise with militaristic neoliberalism? Could the deployment

of such means of articulation lead to a bloc as hegemonic as that in Turkey, or were these weak when compared to their counterparts in Turkey?

The Perpetuation of the Terminal Crisis

Since then, the Brotherhood not only has failed to constitute a liberal-conservative bloc, it was also unable to prevent the further proliferation of differences. Its incapacity became dramatically visible after it was enthroned as the governing party in 2012. New cleavages emerged, rendering the Egyptian sociopolitical scene much more complex. Speaking in Laclauian language, there was an accumulation of unfulfilled demands. Even though the mainstream Western press wanted to reduce this complex map to a simple binary (secular versus Islamic, which allegedly overlapped with the opposition between the urban elite and the people), the Brotherhood actually failed in articulating such blocs. But other, competing attempts of articulation (by leftists, left-wing nationalists, and secular liberals) failed as well.

The list of unresolved oppositions is long and expanding: central versus provincial, democracy versus authoritarianism, neoliberal policies and the business class versus the striking workers of the industrial towns Mahalla and Tanta, the Brotherhood versus other Islamists (primarily, the Nour Party), and so on.

Let's first look at the central versus provincial tension. Whereas the most troublesome provincial issue before 2011 was the integration of the Sinai tribes into a nation-state structure (certainly compounded by Egypt's lack of full sovereignty over the area due to international agreements), the post-2011 scene witnessed the eruption of other anticentralization tensions. The Suez Canal cities forged a new, libertarian identity against Cairo. Some prominent voices even demanded independence from Egypt. The Muslim Brotherhood government sought to calm down the Suez Canal rebellions in 2013 by promising free trade zones, but this fell too short of meeting the broad economic and political demands of the protesters (an end to the police state foremost among them).

Second, the Brotherhood was also far from satisfying the foremost demand of the revolutionary uprising: freedom. In early 2013, this resulted in the entrenchment of political violence in Egypt. Not only was the Brotherhood unable (and partially unwilling) to dismantle the old regime's police state mechanisms,[14] it unleashed its own militias against protestors. There were even claims that the Brotherhood was moving in a more violently authoritarian direction compared to Mubarak. The contradiction between the police state and the people (and the politicization of this contradiction), then, persisted after 2011.

Third, labor protest had been simmering for a decade (Beinin 2012). The revolution further added national political demands to labor's agenda, which had been mostly focused on class-related (even if not narrowly "economic") issues until 2011. Although the mobilized workers still demanded higher wages, better working conditions, and freedom to organize, they now also demanded democracy for all Egyptians and occasionally a minimum wage throughout the country and an end to privatizations. The Brotherhood government, however, did not take any steps to answer the demands of strikers and other militant workers, who were mostly concentrated in the industrial towns Mahalla and Tanta. The only consolation the Brotherhood could have was that these workers did not form solid links with Cairo's youth and were less likely to form such links with the more locally focused protesters along the Suez Canal. To put it differently, the Brotherhood was fortunate not to have an integral party as its competitor.

Another result of the revolutionary process was the consolidation of challenges against the Brotherhood's monopoly over the Islamic field. The Salafi organizations, which most commentators did not take seriously before 2011, became major players in Egyptian politics. However, these strengthening radical right political forces did not have the chance to ultimately marginalize the Brotherhood and constitute a new Islamic hegemony. It is likely that the more the radical right politicizes, the more divided the religious field will be. The Salafis used to be meticulous in their efforts to separate religion from politics: They had mostly stayed away from (publicly open) politics in the old regime. The revolution opened the gates to politicization. As a first response, the Salafis separated their religious and political institutions. However, the divisions within their political institutions spilled into their religious institutions (divisions in Hizb al-Nour led to divisions in Da'wa Salafiyya).[15] Therefore, the real significance of the hard right in Egypt lay not in that it presented a hegemonic alternative to the Brotherhood regime but in that it destabilized the Brotherhood by (1) inhibiting its monopolization of religious and political capital; (2) pulling it to the right politically and religiously; and (3) criticizing its economic policies based on an Islamic sense of social justice.[16] In short, the fragmentation of the Islamic field further curtailed the Brotherhood's integral capacity.

The failure to forge blocs out of these contradictions also transformed the local crises into national and diplomatic crises, that is, an inability to define working relations with international institutions. Against all expectations, the Brotherhood was not able to quickly and effectively negotiate with the International Monetary Fund (IMF) for a loan. In early 2013, IMF managing director Christine Lagarde said, "The IMF needs to have the commitment of the political authorities that can actually endorse the programme, own it, and propose it to the population as theirs." But there was no *organized, professional, integral* political actor to do this, unlike in Turkey. It is not enough just to "want," and an emphasis on this point further highlights how the political articulation approach differs from voluntarism: The Brotherhood's inability to enforce IMF policies was not due to its own unwillingness but rather due to the failure of the overall process (instability was not introduced only by the forces previously listed, but also by al-Azhar and the Salafis who opposed the Brotherhood on many occasions, such as details regarding legislation on Islamic bonds, which caused further uncertainty in financial markets in early 2013). As a result of all of these dynamics, the Brotherhood never felt comfortable enough to "own [the IMF plan], and propose it to the population as theirs," as the international community desired.

The IMF process further demonstrates the crucial differences between the two countries. In Turkey, a professionalized Islamic party that held monopolistic control over the religious field was able to normalize Islamic neoliberalism ("propose [the IMF program] to the population" as its own). The fragmented and semiprofessionalized Islamic political society in Egypt, by contrast, could not even start to implement the IMF reforms. There were many actors within and outside the Brotherhood who tried to push it in a neoliberal direction, but the organization never took that path in a consistent fashion due to its low integral capacity.

In other words, against the possible argument that "the AKP just came to power fortuitously and then implemented successful infrastructural reforms (in education, transportation, and health care) within the boundaries of neoliberalism," the question becomes: Why couldn't the Brotherhood do the same when it also happened to come to power? If one obvious reason for this is the revolutionary process, other reasons are the Brotherhood's low capacity of articulation, the fragmentation of the political field, and low levels of professionalism among Islamists, all of which reinforced each other and disabled the

Brotherhood from mobilizing intellectuals and masses on behalf of its neo-liberal reforms while simultaneously quieting all opposition, as the AKP did.

The July 2013 coup and its aftermath further reinforce these points. Neither the coup mongers nor the Brotherhood were able to form a persistent bloc against their enemies that could mobilize the majority and express the voice of the "normalized" Egyptian. Force rather than consent now holds together the increasingly fragile Egyptian society. The country is on the brink of a civil war.[17]

In short, there has been an accumulation of contradictions in the Egypt of the recent years, but there has been no equivalential chain. In line with our argument in the Introduction, this chapter theoretically analyzes this contrast between the two cases (rather than providing a solely historical narrative). It is logically possible to build equivalent chains out of the multiplying contradictions in Egypt (certainly, the right-wing Brotherhood, the liberals, and the leftists would do this in quite different ways). Yet, without any entrenched organizations in place, the leftists and the liberals cannot generalize their way of thinking throughout the country. Even though the Brotherhood does have some organization that could communicate its hypothetical equivalential articulation, its orientation to politics has not shaped along *professional* hegemonic lines that could enable the formation of such an articulation (an orientation, as the section on Turkey has shown, develops in decades rather than overnight).

A Sociological Alternative to the
State-Centered Study of Crisis

A discussion of the state-centered analysis of revolutionary failure, which is based on institutions and legitimacy, further highlights the distinctiveness of our approach, which is based on ethical politics and consent. In a brilliant analysis of the two years that followed the toppling of Mubarak, Ellis Goldberg emphasized institutional legitimacy (and mass protests that undermined it) as the driving factors in Egypt. The Army and the courts seemed to be the only legitimate institutions (even though there were a lot of grievances against them too), whereas the parliament and the presidency could not acquire enough legitimacy.[18] Although this argument captured some important elements of the Egyptian postrevolutionary situation, it left unanswered the central question: Why were the parliament and the presidency not legitimate even before July 2013? Why weren't they able to rule, even though they were backed by the most organized religious and political force in Egypt (the Muslim Brotherhood), which was perceived (and therefore supported, grudgingly and with reservation and caution) by the Western and pan-Arab mainstream as the only force that could bring stability to post-Mubarak Egypt?

What Goldberg's analysis lacked was the concept of the integral party. If the Brotherhood had been hegemonic enough, it could have articulated all of these institutions into a legitimate bloc and then have weeded out what was unnecessary or whatever threatened its interests.

Goldberg's comparison of Egypt with the classical revolutionary cases (French, Russia, and China) resonated with Skocpol's (1979) understanding of the central factors in these cases (state collapse and initially uncontainable mass mobilization). Egypt presented a revolutionary situation (the old elites could no longer rule, and the masses were persistently mobilized), but one in which two institutions of the old regime, the Army and courts, had not collapsed. The contrast I want to point out with these classical cases is the lack of a professionalized integral party in Egypt, rather than limited state collapse (which I recognize is a central factor).

In France, the Jacobins played this role (though, as Gramsci emphasizes, politics did not become thoroughly hegemonic before the late nineteenth century, even in Western Europe; in that sense, the integralism and the party-ness of the Jacobins do not match the political orientations of the actors analyzed in this book, though they were the harbingers of what was to come). The Bolsheviks initially acted as an integral party and were therefore able to carry out a social revolution, though in time the Russian Communist Party descended into an institutional party. The Chinese Communist Party was forged through the Long March and (despite destructive experiences such as the Cultural Revolution and the Gang of Four's policies) remained an integral party, with sustained links to the masses and ongoing cultural and political work that articulated their demands with a "sinified Marxism" (Anderson 2010; Hung 2011).

In other words, it might be true, as Ellis Goldberg pointed out, that one factor that differentiated Egypt from the classical revolutionary cases was the survival of two old regime institutions, but what he neglected was that an integral political force could further undermine the surviving institutions of the old regime through successful manipulation of mass mobilization. The Islamists were very much aware of this and did their best to deploy the streets in their endeavors to infiltrate and subordinate the judiciary. Yet, their *capacity* in this regard paled in comparison to the Turkish AKP's mixture of mass mobilization (not only of hard-core Islamists, as in the Brotherhood's attempts, but of liberals and even some leftists) and international public relations (where even the liberal Anglophone press was summoned), which ultimately subordinated and contained the Turkish military (through the Ergenekon court case). The AKP, I argue, is the true heir to the Jacobins (and Machiavelli) in the Islamic context, despite the Kemalists' and other secularists' deep-rooted (and misleading) self-designation as Jacobins. The contrast with the Egyptian case suggests that integral parties are central to the realization and consolidation of revolutions (and passive revolutions), though this insight will be further elaborated elsewhere in the light of a discussion of other cases.

POST-ARAB UPRISING TURKISH DISARTICULATION?

The resurgence of Islamist hopes throughout the region after the Arab revolt has thrown Turkey, too, into disarray. Due to space considerations, the details will not be explored here, but some implications for the theory of articulation, blocs, and the integral party will be shortly noted.

Already before the Arab revolt, the Turkish AKP had started to give greater weight to Islamist themes due to the post-2008 global recession, which had set structural limits on its ability to apportion neoliberal spoils. The AKP leaders saw an imperial possibility after 2011 and further intensified their resort to Islamist themes. While appealing to the pious sectors in the broader region, this dynamited both the AKP's Western alliances and its coalitions at home.

Threatened by these newly rediscovered Islamist themes were not only secular business and new middle-class allies but anti-Islamist, conservative Islamic groups as well. One key conservative constituent of the conservative bloc, the Gülen Community, first stealthily, then publicly, attacked the AKP's Islamist tendencies (in issues ranging from the Kurdish question to relations with Israel). The Gezi Revolt of 2013 erupted in this context and further exacerbated the rift between Gülen and the AKP.[19]

The Gezi Revolt had many reasons and temporarily united all sectors that had a problem with at least some AKP policies (including many groups and individuals who had not only voted for, but fought side by side with the AKP). Yet the timing of this fleeting coalescence was indicative: It followed a chain of regional and global revolt, which not only inspired citizens of Turkey but also signaled the unraveling of global diplomatic and military balances. This unraveling created an exaggerated sense of imperial possibility and overblown confidence in the AKP. The result was the move away from consent at home to prepare for major imperial undertakings.

The party thus evolved toward a more militantly Islamic and less articulative position as a response to global recession, the Arab Spring, frictions with Gülen, and the Gezi Revolt. There is now a possibility that some conservative groups might part ways with the AKP and return to their old regime alliances (and hence refragment the currently united Islamic field), effectively undermining not only the integral-ness of the AKP but also the hegemonic-ness of the Turkish regime.

Though the Turkish experiment of liberal–conservative articulation has not come to an end yet, these moves demonstrate the fragility and constant remaking of articulation. Unlike in state formation and civil society accounts, the political articulation approach does not assume that social cleavages have deep, almost unshakable roots. Though some articulations might be more resilient than others, disarticulation is always a possibility. Due to its solid basis in a more professionalized and united political society, Turkish Islamism has been more capable of forming blocs when compared to Egyptian Islamism. The stability of the resulting regime (which becomes an outcome rather than the primary cause as in state-centered account) allowed the Turkish Islamists to rule at least for eleven years, whereas the Egyptian Islamists could not properly rule even for a year. Yet this certainly does not mean that the lines between these blocs (or, for that matter, the liberal–conservative new regime) have become "fate" for the citizens of Turkey.

CONCLUDING NOTES

As a result of all these differences, the hard-working, market-oriented Muslim identity has not become "common sense" in Egypt. In Brotherhood and other Islamist circles, a good Muslim is still evaluated in terms of dedication to the faith, intensity of religious practice, and fighting for Islam. Only some Islamic nongovernmental organizations (NGOs) (for example, those associated with a previous Brotherhood preacher, Amer Khaled) emphasize efficient market activity as a central part of being a good Muslim. In contrast, a huge chunk of practicing Muslims in Turkey shifted to a market-oriented religious identity.[20]

More important, "hardworking Muslims" form no separate community from the overall population or the secular elite, in contrast to Turkey. The pious Muslims are too divided to form a single bloc against secularized Muslims, and piety is quite diffuse. Moreover, the Brotherhood is not an uncontested leader of practicing Muslims, unlike the (pre-2013) Turkish AKP. The religious divisions in Egypt crystallize around the Coptic–Muslim difference, rather than the secular–Muslim divide. In this sense, the Brotherhood's project of articulating differences around a good Muslim (in distinction from infidels and nominal Muslims) is not hegemonic.

Up until 2013, business families, the (privately employed) new middle-class, and urban poor coalesced in Turkey against bureaucrats, public employees, and the formal working class (overlapping with the religious democracy versus secularist dictatorship divide). Neoliberal subjects were defined as religious-democratic too. This coalescence erected "chains of equivalence" between certain classes and classifications. No such clear neoliberal class (and classification) alliance was formed in Egypt. There was no naturalized identification of religion and/or democracy with neoliberalism either. As of early 2014, there were no "new balances" (Arrighi 1994) of classes and classifications. Instead, religiosity was diffused across the Muslim population, setting it apart from the Christian population (a division feebly contested by the liberals and the left). In this sense, the Brotherhood's success has also been its failure (Islamic religiosity became so much identified with being Egyptian that it lost its bite).

In short, although the transition to a market economy has set the context for a vibrant civil society in both cases, it has not dictated the form and content of the new politics. Political parties and their relations with allied associations, together with their links to the state, have deeply influenced the formation of cleavages in this process of transition. Where there were expansively organized political parties with strong links to civil society and the state, new actors were able to redefine cleavages and reshape society. In the absence of such parties, political projects were either defeated or diffused, or they shaped cleavages only to a limited extent.

None of this implies that articulation is a win-win game without costs. As we pointed out in our Introduction to this volume, both the articulating actor and the articulated sectors and identities risk thorough mutation or even dissolution throughout this process. As this chapter has shown, Turkish Islamism has been successful in constituting an integral party with a high capacity of articulation, yet the cost for the movement has been a devolution from Islamism (as a distinct civilizational project) to Western-style conservative liberalism. The articulated sectors have also paid a price, as most clearly seen in the case of the liberals and some leftists, who have become the advocates of conservative causes and interests. Perhaps we can even say that, not having endured a complex game of articulation over the decades, Egyptian leftists, liberals, and Islamists have remained true to their causes, though the price has been powerlessness for all of them (and the failure to unseat the military elite)—leading to the catastrophic events of summer 2013.

The contrast between Egypt and Turkey also informs us on how the activities of integral parties are conditioned, limited, and facilitated by existing political balances. Most important among these are the activities of other institutional and integral parties. The Kemalist left's move away from articulation has reduced the largest Turkish opposition bloc to an institutional party (and an increasingly awkward one at that, sheepishly falling into the binary oppositions set up by Islamic forces), further facilitating the rise of the Islamic integral party. Nevertheless, Turkish Islamism's potential of articulation has been seriously restricted not only by its less articulating orientations towards the Kurds but also by the entrenched presence of a rival integral actor in Kurdistan (the Kurdistan Worker's Party). In Egypt, the major institutional party, the old regime party, has failed, without being challenged by an integral party. The result is not simply a lack of democratization, but the threat of breakup of the whole social fabric in Egypt.

FOUR

**DEMOCRATIC DISARTICULATION
AND ITS DANGERS**

Cleavage Formation and Promiscuous
Power-Sharing in Indonesian Party Politics

Dan Slater

INTRODUCTION AND ARGUMENT

Even the most strongly felt cultural and ideological identifications do not necessarily find enduring expression in national politics. Whenever politics proximately appears to be shaped by such identities, it is only because political organizations, particularly party organizations, somehow channeled them historically. Social forces cannot be articulated into the political blocs that actually have access to and can exercise state power except through the active efforts of political parties. It should be a core task for historically oriented social scientists to uncover how such attempts at *political articulation*—the building of blocs—have unfolded over time and across the world.

To speak of attempts at articulation, however, is to foreshadow their possible failure, weakness, or even absence. If political parties are decisive agents in shaping social and political order, it naturally follows that their inactions and missteps can lead to unforeseen fragmentation and fraying of a polity. When political parties cease articulating cleavages and building blocs, society's constitutive elements have little if anything to hold them together in the political arena. Politics can thus become largely divorced from any deeper social purpose and sadly reduced to elitist struggles among opportunistic factions and individuals to win power and to draw benefit from it.

Political disarticulation—the deterioration of parties' ideologically defined linkages with their core constituents and the disintegration of political blocs—may occur through parties' inactions as surely as political articulation arises through parties' actions. This chapter explores the phenomenon of democratic disarticulation in a case where the process is still very much unfolding and where its outcome is still very much uncertain (because disarticulation is never either total or irreversible). The case is Indonesia, the world's largest Muslim country and largest new democracy.

To understand how Indonesia's democracy has become increasingly disarticulated, it is critical at the outset to recognize that political parties are not only power-*seekers*: They are also power-*sharers*. The role of parties in shaping social and political order thus depends not only on how they *act* but on how they *interact*. To be more concrete: Party competition along clear lines of ideology or identification *during* elections can at times be followed by opportunistic elite collusion across those lines of cleavage *after* elections. In extreme cases, such "promiscuous power-sharing" can make a mockery of the ideological cleavages that have shaped voter choice and loosen parties' primary source of connection to society in the process (Slater and Simmons 2013).

My argument in this chapter is that Indonesia is indeed an extreme case of democratic disarticulation through promiscuous power-sharing—though by no means a hopeless case. When Indonesia democratized in the late 1990s, it appeared that party competition would be characterized by two primary cleavages that had been incubated under Suharto's authoritarian "New Order" (1966–1998), a *regime cleavage* pitting reformist opponents of the recently fallen dictatorship against its holdovers and a *religious cleavage* distinguishing parties by their views on the proper political role for Islam, as well as the centrality of religious pluralism in the definition of Indonesian national identity.

Yet, some fifteen years later, neither a reformist nor a religious bloc exists in Indonesian politics. This chapter seeks to explain how this surprising outcome came to pass. In so doing, it aims to highlight the dangers that democratic disarticulation poses not only in Indonesia but in young democracies around the world.

BUILDING AND UNBUILDING BLOCS:
THE CASE OF INDONESIA

No country is more culturally and ideologically diverse than Indonesia or has seen its cultural and ideological divisions find greater political and organizational expression throughout the twentieth century. By the 1920s, the Dutch colony that would become the world's largest Muslim country had spawned the two largest Islamic mass organizations in the world, the Nahdlatul Ulama (NU) and Muhammadiyah. It had also seen the emergence (and Dutch repression) of two mass parties with leftist and nationalist ideologies, the Indonesian

Nationalist Party (PNI) and the Indonesian Communist Party (PKI). By the mid-1940s, the PNI and PKI would resurface and be joined by a new Islamic party (Masyumi) to mobilize mass resistance among their respective constituencies to Dutch reoccupation after World War II. Quite unlike India— southern Asia's other great multicultural demographic behemoth—Indonesia gained its independence through the mass mobilization of a panoply of diverse political organizations, rather than a single vanguard nationalist party.

Party pluralism would continue to channel cultural and ideological pluralism after independence. Indonesia's decade of parliamentary democracy (1949–1958) witnessed party mobilization along what Clifford Geertz (1976) famously described as "*aliran*" lines. Even under the authoritarian and militarized regime of Suharto (1966–1998), which sought to demobilize party politics and destroy party–society linkages with its "floating mass" policy, there remained two officially sanctioned parties in place to reflect (if definitely not proactively channel) Indonesia's broadly Islamic and nationalist "streams." The persistent relevance of Islamic and nationalist organizations and identifications was witnessed in 1998, in the leading role played by figures from NU, Muhammadiyah, and the PNI's descendant party, the Indonesian Democracy Party (PDI) in inspiring—and by nationalist and Islamist student groups in accomplishing—the contentious overthrow of the Suharto regime. Unsurprisingly for those with a keen sense of Indonesian political history, the party system that emerged from democratic parliamentary elections in June 1999 exhibited considerable continuities with the *aliran*-based party system produced by the country's previous free and fair national elections in 1955 (King 2003; Ufen 2008).

As of 1999, there was no reason to doubt that Indonesian political cleavages would map onto cultural and ideological cleavages in the twenty-first century in much the same way as they had throughout the twentieth. The reintroduction of democratic politics had removed all authoritarian obstacles to parties' mobilization of support along the lines of familiar and, by century's end, largely naturalized political identities. Democratization also offered the prospect that the political parties and organizations that had collectively played the leading roles in toppling Suharto might forge an enduring reformist bloc in Indonesian politics, working to weed out the worst practices and most controversial figures associated with Suharto's "New Order" regime. The emotive intensity of the anti-Suharto struggle seemed to demand and promise nothing less (Aspinall 2005; Hefner 2000; Slater 2010).

Some fifteen years later, these expectations have not been borne out. Rather than continued and strengthened processes of articulation, Indonesia has witnessed a novel and marked disarticulation between political parties and their presumptive social constituencies. *If the twentieth century was an era of building blocs, the twenty-first has thus far been one of unbuilding blocs.* The primary reason for this disarticulation process is not that Indonesia has undergone considerable socioeconomic change in recent decades. If anything, the two main social changes roiling Indonesia since the 1970s—strengthened societal Islamization and increased economic inequality—would point to the sharpening of religious and class cleavages, not their dulling. Nor has disarticulation occurred because neoliberalism has superseded old categories of identification (Aspinall 2013) or because Indonesian voters care more about personalities than parties when casting their ballots (Mujani and Liddle 2010). Nor has it happened because reformist and religious themes have somehow lost their resonance among Indonesia's voters.

Democratic disarticulation has emerged because Indonesia's political parties have largely abandoned their cleavage-based commitments: not so much during elections as after them, when power-seeking makes way for power-sharing. If "neoliberal fragmentation" prevails in Indonesian politics today (as Aspinall compellingly argues), and if Indonesian voters choose their candidates on personal more than partisan grounds (as Liddle and Mujani have persuasively shown), this is primarily because Indonesian parties have manifestly failed to suture together ideological blocs that could serve as viable coalitional alternatives to these neoliberal and personalized modes of political interaction. They have failed, I attempt to demonstrate through my following historical discussion, despite the considerable raw material for bloc building with which they were initially endowed. They have focused their energies more on colluding to share the perquisites of state power than on consistently competing to serve and represent distinctive social constituencies—much less transcending their core constituencies to build broader, majoritarian political blocs. The disarticulation of parties and their presumptive support blocs has left reformist and religious social forces without the party champions necessary to secure collective expression in national politics.

This chapter locates the origins of this disarticulation process in the elite deal making that accompanied the formation of the first democratic government under Abdurrahman Wahid in 1999 and the subsequent parliamentary impeachment of Wahid in 2001. Both of these critical episodes were characterized by what I call *promiscuous power-sharing*: an especially flexible coalition-building practice in which parties express or reveal a willingness to share executive power with any and all other significant parties after an election takes place, even across a country's most important political cleavages (Slater and Simmons 2013).

By promiscuously sharing power across cleavage lines, party leaders fostered voter dealignment in the 2004, 2009, and 2014 elections. This has undermined Indonesia's initially workable party system in turn. As of 1999, a manageably small number of parties enjoyed wide enough support to have "coalition potential," in which a group of parties "finds itself in a position to determine over time, and at some point in time at least one of the possible governmental majorities" (Sartori 1976, 8). These processes of disarticulation and dealignment have loosened Indonesia's leading parties' ideological links to their core constituencies. This has ominously left Indonesian democracy vulnerable to the unpredictable politics of individuals rather than institutions and opened the door to populist and antisystem challengers.

THE CHAPTER TO COME

The first empirical section in the following pages provides a necessarily cursory overview of historical cleavage development in Indonesia from the inception of its revolutionary struggle for independence to the waning days of Suharto's New Order. We will see that political struggles have not simply taken place among preexisting cleavage groups; they have taken place in large measure to determine which cleavages would find expression in national politics at all. Struggles have been *over* cleavages, not simply *between* them. The second section explores the role of political organizations in reshaping sociopolitical cleavages during Indonesia's contentious transition to democracy. I will argue and attempt to demonstrate that two meaningful cleavages existed as of the 1999 elections, as a joint product of both long-term and shorter-term political developments, a *regime* cleavage pitting reformist opponents of the fallen dictatorship against its holdovers and a *religious* cleavage distinguishing parties by their varying views on religious pluralism and political Islam.

These two cleavages helped define the June 1999 parliamentary elections, in which the five major parties secured an impressive 86 percent of the vote. But, ironically, *the regime and religious cleavages would shape the process but not the outcome or the aftermath of the initial democratic struggle for power*. As I show in the subsequent empirical section, neither the regime cleavage nor the religious cleavage would define the political blocs that emerged from the MPR session. Instead, the political settlement involved *all* political parties securing a share of executive power and setting aside ideological differences over regime and religion in the process. In short, Indonesian party politicians formed a "party cartel" (Ambardi 2008; Katz and Mair 1995, 2009; Slater 2004), grounded in collective control of the cabinet.[1] This cartel arrangement was reasserted in 2001 when compromise president Abdurrahman Wahid, the long-time leader of NU, was impeached and removed from office with the support of all major parliamentary parties after reneging on his promise to share the cabinet with them.

By 2001, then, a pronounced political disarticulation of Indonesia's party system was already in evidence, as Indonesia's major parties had compromised and at times contradicted their expressed positions on questions of religion and regime in the process of collectively seizing and sharing state power. The chapter's final empirical section traces the downstream effects of this disarticulation process on Indonesia's subsequent democratic elections in 2004 and 2009. *In both elections, all five parties saw their vote share decline*—a rather astonishing result, considering that their cartelized ruling arrangement should have made it exceedingly difficult for voters to locate and choose viable party alternatives. After winning more than 86 percent of the vote in 1999, the five main parties won barely 65 percent in 2004 and less than 45 percent in 2009.

Indonesia's originally workable democratic party system has thus suffered not just disarticulation but dealignment. Reformist and religious credentials now primarily reside in particular individuals rather than well-organized and socially embedded political parties. Even the two parties that most effectively channeled reformist and religious energies to generate electoral support in 2004 and 2009—the Democratic Party (PD) of President Susilo Bambang Yudhoyono and the Islam-oriented Prosperous Justice Party (PKS)—have failed to rearticulate the reformist and regime cleavages and start rebuilding the blocs that Indonesia's initial "big five" parties have unbuilt.

The chapter's conclusion also serves as a coda, preliminarily assessing the possible effects of the ongoing 2014 national elections on Indonesia's democratic disarticulation—and perhaps even its very democratic fate. On the one hand, the reform-oriented and religiously pluralist candidacy of Jakarta Governor Joko Widodo (also known as Jokowi) offers the tantalizing prospect that ideological cleavages might once again gain clear expression through discernible interparty blocs. Yet the parallel candidacy of a self-styled populist and once-disgraced army general from the Suharto era, Prabowo Subianto, who has opportunistically coalesced with Indonesia's most conservative Islamic parties in support of his bid for power, offers a far more frightening prospect: that Indonesia's fledgling democracy might soon experience "democratic careening" via demagogic attacks on democratic institutions (Slater 2013) or even suffer outright democratic reversal through the imposition of "electoral authoritarianism" (Schedler 2013). Such is the vulnerability and unpredictability of any democratic party system that fails to build blocs.

AN AGE OF ARTICULATION: POLITICAL ORGANIZATIONS AND CLEAVAGE FORMATION IN THE TWENTIETH CENTURY

> *Indonesia's postcolonial experience has tended to reinforce the original identification of political and cultural cleavages in such a way as to make the separation of party and aliran difficult. . . .*
>
> *On the other hand . . . though the identification of a particular community with a political party has tended to be stable in the postcolonial period, the present pattern did not always exist, and there is no reason to be sure it is now immutable.*
>
> **Ruth McVey (1970, 21)**

Indonesia had relatively sharply defined social cleavages before it developed formal political parties—but not before it developed mass political organizations. The first major cleavage to gain organizational expression was not between Islamic and non-Islamic groups but within the Netherlands East Indies' majority Muslim population itself. Specifically, the founding of Muhammadiyah in 1912 gave institutional birth to Indonesia's urban, "modernist" Islamic wing, whereas the countervailing rise of NU in 1926 did likewise for its more rural, "traditionalist" Muslim community. The modernist-traditionalist subcleavage has repeatedly hindered attempts to construct a majoritarian Islamic political bloc in Indonesia (Bush 2009), as we shall soon see. Religious cleavages in Indonesian politics and society have divided not only non-Muslims and Muslims but different types of Muslims.

This social and organizational bifurcation meant little in political terms so long as the Dutch maintained colonial control and disallowed party mobilization among the colonized. Dutch repression not only prevented any possibility for the emergence of a mass-based Islamic party but kept the nationalist PNI (founded in 1928, disbanded in 1931) and the communist PKI (founded in 1924, outlawed in 1927) from mobilizing constituencies and articulating cleavages as well.

The Japanese occupation from 1942 to 1945 blew the lid off the Dutch colonial state and ignited a new era of mobilization and politicization. The Japanese founded a new organization to mobilize Muslim political support, called Masyumi, and symbolically shared political authority with leading non-Islamist figures in Indonesia's long-suppressed nationalist movement, the most important being the youthful, charismatic PNI founder, Sukarno. When Japan surrendered in 1945, the organizational ground was thus laid for Islamic social forces to overcome their historic modernist-traditionalist division and for the nationalist movement to undertake the radical mass mobilization for independence that had been politically impossible before the Japanese occupation.

The two rapidly emerging organizational manifestations of these Islamic and nationalist political wings were Masyumi (officially reborn in November 1945) and the new PNI (formally refounded in January 1946). Despite their shared interest in preventing the Dutch from returning to power, the two wings needed to overcome friction over the proper place for Islam in the emerging political dispensation. Even before Japan had surrendered, a controversy had erupted over whether Indonesia's Muslims should be obliged to follow the syariah, or Islamic law. Words to that effect were proposed as an addition to the constitution being drafted by Indonesian nationalist and Islamic leaders, in what became known as the "Jakarta Charter." Thankfully for the cohesion and ultimate fate of the nationalist movement, Sukarno deftly deflected the controversy—although by no means resolving it—by grounding the 1945 constitution in a pluralist national ideology, the Pancasila, whose first principle was a belief in a single God rather than a specific God. This masterfully codified the mandatory monotheism demanded by Muslim leaders, yet without forcing all Muslims to follow strictures perceived by many as more Arab than indigenous. Islam-oriented and Pancasila-oriented figures remained equally central to an independence struggle that explicitly embraced both ideological wings.

After four years of bloody revolution, Indonesia gained its independence in late 1949. Because the communist PKI had generally played a background role in the revolution and had been violently crushed in 1948 when PKI forces attempted to seize control over the anti-Dutch struggle, Masyumi and PNI

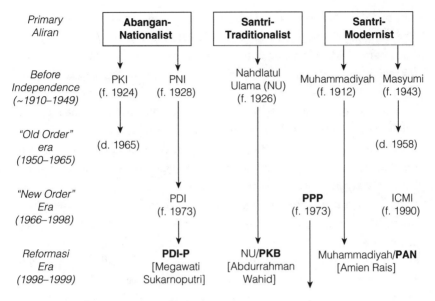

Primary Aliran	Abangan-Nationalist		Santri-Traditionalist	Santri-Modernist	
Before Independence (~1910–1949)	PKI (f. 1924)	PNI (f. 1928)	Nahdlatul Ulama (NU) (f. 1926)	Muhammadiyah (f. 1912)	Masyumi (f. 1943)
"Old Order" era (1950–1965)	(d. 1965)				(d. 1958)
"New Order" Era (1966–1998)		PDI (f. 1973)	**PPP** (f. 1973)		ICMI (f. 1990)
Reformasi Era (1998–1999)		**PDI-P** [Megawati Sukarnoputri]	NU/**PKB** [Abdurrahman Wahid]	Muhammadiyah/**PAN** [Amien Rais]	

Figure 4.1. Indonesia's age of articulation.
SOURCE: Slater 2014, 297.

were the most important and deeply rooted political parties as the Dutch departed. In Geertz's classic terms, Masyumi aimed to mobilize Indonesia's "*santri*" (or pious Muslim, hereafter "Islamic") community, whereas the PNI targeted "*abangan*" (nominally Muslim) and non-Muslim voters (hereafter lumped together as "nationalist").[2] (See Figure 4.1 for a visual overview of party and cleavage development in Indonesia, to clarify the discussion thus far and guide the discussion to follow.)

By the time Indonesia's first (and final) national elections of its initial period of parliamentary democracy approached in 1955, both Masyumi and PNI faced concerted opposition from within their own *aliran*. On the Islamic side, Masyumi split in 1952, and NU formed its own party, restoring the modernist-traditionalist split that the umbrella Masyumi group had papered over for nearly a decade. Within the broadly nationalist (or non-Islamic and nominally Islamic) *aliran*,[3] divisions were becoming more effectively articulated as well. The PKI initially remained hesitant and hobbled in the aftermath of its massive revolution-era repression by the newly formed Indonesian military, or ABRI, but, as elections approached, the party gained mobilizational momentum as a clear leftist alternative to the PNI. In sum, the 1955 election would see four major parties competing along three major lines of cleavage: (1) religion (the Islamic NU and Masyumi versus the nationalist PNI and PKI); (2) class (the communist PKI versus noncommunist Masyumi, NU, and PNI);[4] and (3) region (the Java-centered PNI PKI, and NU versus Masyumi). Religion, class, and regionalism were the cleavages in play as voters went to the polls.

The election would settle nothing. All four major parties gained a nearly equal share of the national vote,[5] and a series of unstable multiparty coalitions shuffled into and out of government power. After regional rebellions erupted on the islands of Sumatra and Sulawesi in the late 1950s, President Sukarno banned Masyumi, which he perceived as complicit in the revolts against Jakarta's writ, and asserted stronger executive control under his "Guided Democracy" system. Indonesia's regional cleavage was thus settled through force rather than votes. The same would occur with Indonesia's emergent class cleavage in the mid-1960s, as an apparent failed coup by military forces loyal to the rising PKI culminated in the genocidal army-led annihilation of the party and its perceived sympathizers in 1965–1966. *Despite the obvious persistence of extreme regional diversity and class stratification in Indonesian society, neither region nor class would become salient political cleavages in Indonesia's party system again.*

Yet the Islamic-nationalist divide—the core religious cleavage—would remain articulated in Indonesia's party system. Although he rose to power in 1966 with the clear intention of decimating and demobilizing party politics, General Suharto eventually calculated that his regime would be best served by allowing and guiding the emergence of tightly controlled elections and parties. Rather than working through an existing party such as the PNI, which could prove unhelpfully independent (or even worse, openly Sukarnoist), Suharto backed the transformation of an existing organization of progovernment "functional groups" into a new quasi-party, Golkar, which all civil servants were required to join.

After Golkar romped to a stage-managed and strong-armed victory over cleavage parties such as the PNI and NU in the 1971 elections,[6] the Suharto regime forced all parties besides Golkar to consolidate into just two parties, the Islamic PPP (United Development Party), and the nationalist PDI. That these new authoritarian fabrications were intended to house the followers of the old and now abolished Masyumi and NU parties (in the case of the PPP) and PNI (in the case of PDI) was unmistakable. (The PDI was not intended to house former followers of the PKI, which had been targeted not merely for abolition but annihilation.) That the New Order's plan was to bridle rather than mobilize these broad Islamic and nationalist cleavage groups—even while continuing to articulate and even essentialize them—was unmistakable as well. This was seen most clearly in the regime's "floating mass" policy forbidding the existence of PDI and PPP branches at the local level. Authoritarian party politics under Suharto thus exhibited the skeleton, but not the flesh and blood, of nationalist and Islamic articulation.

Yet the bloodstreams of nationalist and Islamic political attachment would continue to flow, whether the New Order's leaders liked it or not. On the Islamic side, it was almost inconceivable that the regime would disband NU or Muhammadiyah as mass organizations, particularly because Suharto and the military initially gained much of their most active support from these stridently anticommunist Islamic quarters. On the nationalist side, mass attachment had long been directed toward the charismatic anticolonial personage of Sukarno more than the party he had helped to found. Hence banning the PNI served more to break the nationalist bloc's bones than its spirit.

Suharto's divide-and-conquer strategems would ironically both restrain and reinforce political identifications along the nationalist–Islamic religious cleavage. In 1984, growing Muslim protests over their own political exclusion and the perceived dominance of Indonesia's small Christian minority culminated in the massacre of Islamic activists in the Jakarta neighborhood of Tanjong Priok. Soon thereafter, Suharto demanded that all political organizations embrace the vague humanist philosophy of Pancasila as their sole ideological foundation, making a mockery of the "Islamic" PPP when it could no longer claim Islam as its basis.

The New Order would also fail to keep Islam's modernist and traditionalist wings encaged in the same party prison. NU leader Abdurrahman Wahid pulled the mass organization out of the PPP in 1984. By ostensibly moving the NU out of politics entirely, Wahid's clever gambit allowed his mass organization to practice politics on its own terms rather than the regime's. Wahid's NU, the unrivaled champion of Indonesia's traditionalist-Islamic *aliran*, quickly became the sharpest social thorn in the New Order's side. Suharto responded in 1990 by forming ICMI, a proregime institution of primarily modernist Islamic intellectuals, to ensure that the awakening of Islamic politics did not occur on terms he could not control. Intense rivalry between

Wahid's traditionalist NU and the modernist-dominated ICMI would shape Islamic politics and complicate the unification of Islamic opposition to Suharto throughout the 1990s.

Indonesia's nationalist cleavage would be reactivated later than its Islamic subcleavage, but more explosively. This would importantly coincide with the emergence of a *regime* cleavage in Indonesian politics, as political organizations began for the first time in decades to express opposition—if often obliquely more than openly—to the authoritarian status quo. In response to the unwelcome demands for regime liberalization emanating from PDI leader Soerjadi in the 1992 elections, Suharto engineered his downfall and replacement with the late Sukarno's seemingly demure daughter, Megawati Sukarnoputri.

This proved a colossal error. Megawati quickly used her inherited charismatic status to stake out an even more critical position for the PDI, prompting the Suharto regime to reverse course and engineer Megawati's downfall at a rump party congress in 1996. Violence erupted at the PDI's Jakarta headquarters between Megawati loyalists refusing to exit the premises and military forces attempting to force them out. The ensuing bloodshed would mark a dramatic end to the New Order's cherished (if always coerced) stability and the beginning of the opposition's cross-class struggle for democratic reform. Even as the regime cleavage gained novel expression in the increasingly contentious anti-Suharto struggle, historically familiar Islamic and nationalist forces were the decisive articulators of Indonesia's dramatic antiauthoritarian turn (Aspinall 2005; Hefner 2000; Slater 2010).

RELIGION AND *REFORMASI*: SUHARTO'S FALL AND DEMOCRATIC ELECTIONS, 1998–1999

Once Indonesia's traditionalist Islamic stream (via Wahid's NU) and Sukarnoist nationalist stream (via Megawati's rump PDI) had slipped out of the iron grip of the New Order's formal authoritarian institutions, the Suharto regime found itself in a far more difficult and tenuous political position. A third *aliran*-based challenge emerged in the rise of Amien Rais as leader of Muhammadiyah, the organized champion of modernist Islam. Even while continuing to serve with fellow modernist elites in Suharto's ICMI group of Islamic intellectuals, Amien became "the most outspoken critic of the government and had been calling for the replacement of Suharto since 1992" (Madrid 1999, 20, 24).

By the time Indonesia was devastated by the Asian financial crisis in 1997–1998, therefore, Suharto confronted an increasingly strident triangle of political oppositionists, calling for political reform and regime change from their powerful institutional positions atop Indonesia's *santri*-modernist, *santri*-traditionalist, and *abangan*-nationalist blocs. Amien, Megawati, and Wahid would all play broadly supportive and inspirational roles in the massive student-led protests that erupted and toppled Suharto in May 1998.

Although they uniformly called for the resignation of Suharto, the end of massive government corruption, and meaningful democratic change, the *reformasi* protests initially only secured the first of their goals. Suharto had fallen after more than thirty years in power, but, in resigning, he had handed power to his perceived stooge of a deputy, Vice President B. J. Habibie. Protests thus continued as a wide array of civil-society groups demanded immediate democratic elections to replace Habibie as president and to crack the effective duopoly of Suharto-era Golkar apparatchiks and military appointees in the national parliament.

Although student-led protests could express their democratic ideals toward the halls of power, it was political elites who had the power to articulate what *reformasi* would mean in a more definitive sense. The key moment came in the so-called Ciganjur meeting of November 1998, when Amien, Megawati, and Wahid joined the widely respected Sultan of Yogyakarta . . .

> to formulate a common platform for reform. The "Ciganjur Four" were essentially moderate in their positions. The eight-point declaration said they did not favor establishing a transitional government, preferring instead to work toward a fair election as a way out of the nation's political and economic crises. Also, they preferred to phase out the military's political role and presence in Parliament over six years rather than immediately. . . . Condemning corruption, the statement included a commitment to investigate Soeharto's wealth, though his fate was otherwise left unsettled. However disappointing to students who had hoped for a more radical statement, the Ciganjur declaration was significant as a point of reference for the movement and helped establish a common agenda. (Weiss 2006, 203).

Suharto's most powerful opponents thus expressed their commitment to pursuing the democratization path after Suharto's resignation. Even before the Ciganjur gathering, Habibie had been pressed by a combination of civil-society protest and his own desperation to cement his badly wobbling legitimacy (both at home and abroad) to accelerate the timetable for national elections to June 1999 from 2002, as constitutionally scheduled. Concerted pressure from the Ciganjur reformists and their civil-society allies helped keep Habibie's feet to the democratic fire. Besides maintaining his pledge to hold early elections, Habibie pushed through laws reforming the electoral system and restoring freedom of the press, thus making free and fair elections a genuine possibility. Such democratic concessions make sense only against the backdrop of a highly salient regime cleavage, as Habibie's leading opponents prioritized the ending of authoritarianism as much as the advancement of their own nationalist and Islamic communities.

As the June 1999 elections approached, therefore, the spirit of democratic reform was palpable, not just among ordinary voters but among leading party elites. The older bloodlines of Geertz's *aliran* were palpable in party politics as well. As Figure 4.1 indicates, four of the five major parties (acronyms in bold) arising to contest the parliamentary vote could evidently be positioned in traditional *aliran* terms and represented clear inheritors of long-term patterns of political development.

The elections duly delivered on their democratic promise. Turnout was massive, and voter enthusiasm for continuing political reform ran high. Of particular interest for the question of political articulation, voters rallied in hordes behind parties mobilizing social blocs along familiar *aliran* lines. As seen in Table 4.1, the top five parties received nearly 87 percent of all votes cast. Furthermore, in preelection surveys, 86 percent of Indonesian voters expressed a party preference and 52.5 percent declared some level of attachment to their parties of choice, figures far surpassing most longer-standing democracies in regions such as Latin America and Eastern Europe (Liddle and Mujani 2000, 32; Mainwaring 1998).

Table 4.1. Vote totals from Indonesia's June 1999 national election.

Party	Percentage
PDI-P	33.8
Golkar	22.5
PKB	12.6
PPP	10.7
PAN	7.1
	86.7%

SOURCE:, Slater 2014, 301.

In what ways and to what extent did the 1999 election reflect the salience of cleavages in Indonesian party politics? As depicted in Figure 4.1, the top vote-getter, Megawati's PDI-P, was an obvious reflection of Indonesia's nationalist political stream. Because Megawati's popularity also clearly rested in her image as the "primary victim" of New Order repression, her massive victory signified the continuing salience of Indonesia's regime cleavage as well.

Much the same could be said of the third-place finisher, the Wahid-led and NU-based PKB, and the fifth-place finisher, the Amien-led and Muhammadiyah-based PAN. Although all three parties strove to recruit support beyond their core *aliran*—mostly by burnishing and highlighting their hard-earned democratic credentials—their grounding in those familiar social blocs was unmistakable. Meanwhile, the fourth-place finisher, the New Order–created PPP, was an explicit manifestation of Islamic politics. Only Golkar, which finished in second place, could be said to be a true "catch-all" party transcending any single *aliran*, rather than a cleavage party.[7] Yet, as the party founded and long led by Suharto himself, Golkar clearly played the "ancien regime" role against which other parties proclaimed their democratic agendas—making the party's showing relevant for the regime cleavage if not the religious cleavage.

It is critical to stress the point that religious cleavages were not the only cleavages at play. Of equal significance was the recent emergence of a *regime* cleavage distinguishing parties whose leaders had explicitly opposed the authoritarian New Order (Megawati's PDI-P, Wahid's PKB, and Amien's PAN) from those who had served as civilian ballast in Suharto's military-dominant regime (Habibie's Golkar and, to a lesser extent, the PPP). To be sure, all major parties vocally backed the new democratic order; yet only a year removed from Suharto's dramatic fall, voters had been strongly primed to perceive a distinction between democrats by conviction and democrats by convenience. The desire for meaningful regime change was most pronounced on Indonesia's most populous island, as "Golkar . . . was scorched and being discredited across Java" (Ambardi 2008, 105). Because Golkar had no clear positioning on the Islamic-nationalist divide, this discrediting only makes sense as a manifestation of Indonesia's meaningful regime cleavage as of 1999.

It had been more than forty years since Indonesian citizens had been afforded the opportunity to use the ballot to force a housecleaning in the halls of power. Considering that more than 53 percent of voters sided with the PDI-P, PKB, and PAN, despite these parties' massive infrastructural disadvantage vis-à-vis Golkar, it seemed that a major blow for deepened democratization and a thoroughgoing changing of the political guard had been struck. The New Order's ruling party was on the verge of being replaced by a coalition of the New Order's most vocal and powerful opponents, grounded in the same overarching Islamic and nationalist *aliran* that had characterized Indonesian party politics for most of the past century.

How, then, was this widely anticipated outcome derailed?

FROM IDEOLOGICAL CLEAVAGES TO PROMISCUOUS POWER-SHARING, 1999–2001

Parties are no longer expected to hold on dearly to their ideologies, values and platforms, which are now all expendable at the right price. To some extent, this new development has also had a positive effect: the withering away of aliran politics (a term popularized by anthropologist Clifford Geertz), or political currents that are very much shaped, influenced, and directed by socio-religious and traditional values, which once polarized the country politically. But, basing the politics of coalition solely on the principles of pragmatism only demonstrates the nakedness of power politics at the expense of public interest and meaningful politics.

—**Bahtiar Effendy (2009a)**

As noted in the introduction to this chapter, political parties are not only power-seekers, but power-sharers; they not only act, but interact. And these critical party interactions are shaped, at least in part, by electoral rules. In the case of Indonesia in 1999, the most important electoral rule in question was the indirect selection of the president by parliament. The vote totals from June 1999 had determined what percentage of the 500-seat parliament, or DPR, would go to each party (not counting the thirty-eight seats still set aside for the military, now renamed TNI). Those 500 members would convene with 200 additional appointed members at a special parliamentary session, or MPR, in October 1999, to determine whether Habibie would remain president, and, if not, to choose his successor. *Voters had proposed in June, but elites would dispose come October.*

Because no single party had won an electoral majority, it was up to multiple parties in parliament to suture together a winning coalition to constitute the new democratic executive. For all of Indonesia's social and political complexity, *building a majority coalition in a cleavage-consistent manner was*

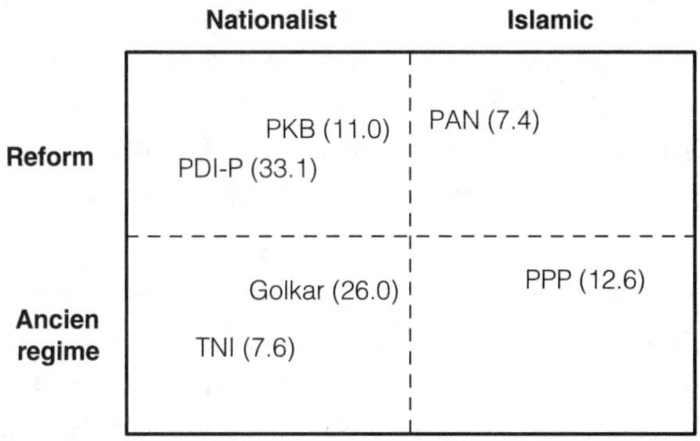

Figure 4.2. Cleavages and approximate party positioning (with 1999 seat shares).
SOURCE: Slater 2014, 303.

far from politically impossible. Parliamentarians in fact had several options
for how to translate political cleavages, as they had long been articulated by
political parties and more recently been expressed by voters, into a winning
majority. Figure 4.2 arrays the major forces at the MPR session along the two
major cleavages noted earlier, the regime cleavage and the religious cleavage.
As indicated by the bolded headings, the further to the left a party is situated,
the more it favors a nationalist or "Pancasilaist" as opposed to an Islamic view
of the state. The higher a party lies on the chart, the stronger its reformist and
democratic credentials as of the 1999 election and MPR session.[8]

How might the MPR have assembled a cleavage-consistent majority from
this distribution of party power? Figure 4.2 helps us see that at least two, and
perhaps three, distinct cleavage-consistent options were available. One was a
reformist coalition, encompassing the three parties in the top half of the chart:
PDI-P, PKB, and PAN, which combined for 51.5 percent of the parliamentary seats. Such a grouping could have coalesced around these three parties'
minimal mutual desire to ensure the consolidation of civilian supremacy over
the military, the furtherance of deepened democratic reforms, and the exclusion of notorious New Order "corrupters" from executive positions. A second
option was a *nationalist* coalition, encompassing the groups on the left side
of the graph. If all four nationalist players were to coalesce, a grand coalition including over 75 percent of all parliamentary seats could be assembled
around a shared commitment to preserving the religiously pluralist policies
of the so-called Pancasila state. A third possibility was for Golkar, still led by
ICMI founder Habibie, to fracture the potential reformist alliance by working

to suture together an *Islamic* ruling coalition with stoutly Islamic parties as well as PKB and PAN: the avowedly pluralist parties grounded in Indonesia's two gigantic Islamic mass organizations, NU and Muhammadiyah. All three of these interparty constellations exhibited "coalition potential" in Sartori's terms; in short, there were multiple options for building a new majoritarian ruling coalition.

The MPR session kicked off with a sweeping parliamentary rejection of Habibie's mandatory "accountability speech," effectively dethroning him as president and seemingly displacing Golkar as Indonesia's long-ruling party. Some sort of reformist bloc thus appeared poised to prevail, as Megawati and Wahid became the two frontrunners for the presidency. Yet appearances were deceiving. *Even as the advent of a reformist presidency was becoming inevitable, the triumph of a reformist bloc was becoming nearly impossible.* To understand why, consider again the regime and religious cleavages and the parties that institutionally manifested them, as depicted in Figure 4.2. For Wahid to defeat Megawati, he would need to enlist the support of Islamic or ancien regime types such as the PPP and, in all likelihood, the greatest ancien regime party of all: Golkar. For Megawati to defeat Wahid, she would require the support of political forces that were more Pancasilaist than the "Central Axis," but by no means more reformist; that is, Golkar and the TNI, or military. *Once Megawati and Wahid had become pitted against each other, the only alliances with majoritarian "coalition potential" would have to draw support across the reform–ancien regime divide.*

Ancien regime forces did not simply bide their time until the coalitional math worked in their favor, however. Recognizing that both Megawati and Wahid needed additional support to reach the 50 percent threshold, Golkar's newly anointed leader, Akbar Tandjung, managed to elbow his way into the political action. Instead of standing aside while Megawati and Wahid engaged in a face-to-face contest for the presidency, Akbar announced his intention to contest the presidency as well. He then rescinded his candidacy at the last second and endorsed Wahid, in a transparent bid to extract a quid pro quo from the presumptive winner. Wahid indeed prevailed over Megawati, by a 373 to 313 margin. After outraged PDI-P supporters demonstrated and rioted in Jakarta and Bali over the MPR's denial of the presidency to Megawati, the special session elected the PDI-P leader to the vice presidency in a landslide, thanks to yet another last-second tactical withdrawal—and presumably the extraction of an additional quid pro quo in terms of power-sharing—by Golkar leader Akbar.

This coalitional maneuvering by political elites at the 1999 MPR session has not been detailed here simply to provide descriptive context. Appreciating the process of elite self-dealing is essential to understanding why, *even after Indonesia's two leading nationalist/reformist figures became ensconced in the presidency and vice presidency, the ascendance of a ruling nationalist/reformist bloc had ironically become foreclosed.* The difficulty was that, in winning the top two posts, Wahid and Megawati had accumulated political debts to Islamic and ancien regime political forces. Once the MPR session was complete, it was time for political payback.

Instead of an ideologically compatible coalition, a minimum-winning coalition (Riker 1962), or even a "modestly oversized coalition" (Horowitz 2013, 290), Indonesian democracy was born with an all-encompassing party cartel. Backroom negotiations among all five major faction leaders (Wahid, Megawati, Amien Rais, Golkar's Akbar, and TNI head Wiranto) produced a cabinet that had to be expanded from twenty-five to thirty-five members to dissipate disputes over each group's share of the pie. Every single political group listed in Figure 4.2 gained a share of executive government power by claiming seats in the cabinet, as did two minuscule "mosquito" parties from the modernist-Islamic "Central Axis" that had gained only 1.5 percent (PK) and 2.8 percent (PBB) of the legislative seats. Ironically, *strenuous party-led mobilization along the regime and religious cleavages in the 1999 national election had produced a ruling coalition utterly devoid of clear convictions, or even leanings, on either the regime or religious divide.*

This cartelized party arrangement would be reinforced in 2000–2001 through the impeachment and removal from office of its erstwhile compromise president, Abdurrahman Wahid. When Wahid began chafing under the constraints of a cabinet of party nominees that he did not appoint and could not hope to control, he incrementally commenced purging ministers from major parties such as Golkar and PDI-P and packing executive ministries with his own personal loyalists (Slater 2004, 72–83). Perhaps unsurprisingly, this did not prove a winning strategy for a president enjoying the support of barely 10 percent of the legislature. Having coalesced across the regime and religious divides to elect Wahid in 1999, the full array of Indonesian parties came together again to force Wahid from office in 2001. Megawati thus ascended to the presidency and successfully urged the election of the leader of the Islamic/ancien regime PPP as her vice president. A cabinet comprised of all significant parties was again constructed under Megawati's leadership, with corrosive consequences for the leading parties' credibility as champions of reformist and religious blocs in Indonesian society.

THE COSTS OF CARTELIZATION: PARTY DISARTICULATION AND DEALIGNMENT

Having secured a plum posting for himself as speaker of Indonesia's parliament, and having secured for his Golkar party a handsome quiver of lucrative cabinet posts, Akbar Tandjung (2003) proudly proclaimed that Indonesian democracy had entered a "political moratorium." During the three years of Megawati's presidency (2001–2004), parties did precious little to mobilize or represent their core societal constituencies—much less build up broader political blocs. Confronting no meaningful organized party opposition, the ruling parties' energies became almost entirely devoted to Jakarta-centered struggles to carve up the state, rather than broader efforts to recruit, attract, and retain voters. Although the Megawati years were not entirely devoid of reformist gains (Crouch 2011), and undeniable accomplishments were made in promulgating a new democratic constitution (Horowitz 2013), these advances were typically a product of contentious pressure from civil-society groups rather than programmatic party commitments (Mietzner 2012). Of particular importance in this regard was the introduction of direct executive elections in 2002. Leading parties would pay a heavy electoral price—if not suffer a significant and inevitable loss of power—in the 2004 elections, as Indonesian voters enjoyed the right to elect their representatives and president directly for the first time.

The PDI-P would be the biggest loser in the April 2004 parliamentary election, seeing its vote share plummet from 33.8 percent to less than 18 percent. This astonishing result is worthy of a moment's reflection. It flies in the face, first, of any assumption that the power of incumbency is the key to party building in new democracies. The PDI-P had won a landslide in 1999 when it was out of power and still retained a powerful democratic reputation and image, then suffered a devastating setback in 2004 when it held the presidency and a collection of especially "wet" (that is, patronage-laden) cabinet ministries. The problem was not that Indonesians had ceased to identify with Sukarnoist nationalism, or with the reformist spirit on which the PDI-P initially rode to its massive 1999 electoral victory—it was that Megawati's collusive compact with ancien regime parties such as Golkar and Islamist parties such as PPP and PBB had sapped her imperative to perform diligently and effectively and damaged her hard-earned reformist and "Pancasilaist" credentials. In terms of the regime cleavage, Megawati's husband went so far as to admit, on the eve of the 2004 election, that PDI-P and Golkar had come to possess precisely the same platform (*Koran Tempo*, 2004). In terms of the religious cleavage, Ambardi nicely exposes the hypocrisy of parties talking the electoral talk without walking the coalitional walk on questions of religion and pluralism:

> Entering the 2004 election, two Islamic parties, PPP and PBB, had moved further to the right. They became more conservative, showed a higher degree of Islamism, and promoted the adoption of *syariah* or Islamic law for the constitution. They separated themselves from the pack. As a result, the ideological distance between the Islamic and the secular parties had increasingly widened. In spite of this fact, the secular parties embraced them in the coalition for presidential election, accommodated them in the cabinet, and embraced them in a parliamentary caucus as if there was no ideological disconformity between the Islamic and secular parties. (Ambardi 2008, 2)

The PDI-P's 2004 drubbing seems to affirm this article's argument that cleavage politics in democratic Indonesia is not simply about Islamism versus nationalism, as often surmised, but also the lingering (if limping) distinction between the politics of democratic reform versus the politics of authoritarian corruption, abuse of power, and unaccountability. It is a distinction that continues to resonate with voters, even as Indonesia's major parties have all failed to become reliable and recognizable proponents of deepened democratic reform. In short, the evident regime cleavage of the late 1990s has become disarticulated in the party system of the 2000s and 2010s.[9]

The same is true of the religious cleavage. By sharing power with nationalist parties such as PDI-P and pluralist Islamic parties such as PAN and PKB, even the most outspoken Islamic parties such as PPP and PBB have exposed themselves as more opportunistic than devout. Similarly, parties with nationalist and pluralist credentials and platforms have shown no compunction about sharing power with parties possessing quite alternative viewpoints, leaving voters without a clear religiously pluralist electoral option as well as a clear Islamist one (Buehler 2008).

Compounding the process of disarticulation is the fact that party cartels make it exceedingly difficult for alternative opposition parties to emerge from

Table 4.2. The data of dealignment: Parliamentary vote share for the "Big 5" parties, 1999–2009.

	1999	2004	2009
PDI-P	33.8	18.5	14.0
Golkar	22.5	21.6	14.5
PKB	12.6	10.6	4.9
PPP	10.7	8.2	5.3
PAN	7.1	6.4	6.0
TOTAL	86.7%	65.3%	44.7%

SOURCE: Slater 2014, 309.

scratch. In the absence of powerful competition, the five major parties from the 1999 election have been under extremely limited pressure to perform. And perform they have not—as suggested by the fact that all five parties suffered a decline in overall vote share in both the 2004 and 2009 parliamentary elections. After collectively winning over 86 percent of the national vote in 1999, Golkar, PDI-P, PKB, PAN, and PPP saw their share shrink to 65 percent in 2004 and 45 percent in 2009 (see Table 4.2).

Election results are always a complicated function of many factors, and much further research on Indonesian voting behavior will be necessary to determine the most powerful causal mechanisms through which dealignment since 2004 has occurred.[10] Yet the repeated electoral punishment of *all five* leading initial members of the party cartel is telling, and the signs of disarticulation are unmistakable. Even one of the most *aliran*-focused scholars of party–society linkages in Indonesia was forced to conclude, following a 2003 Asia Foundation survey, that "the link between parties and voters is loosening and that the rootedness in milieux is decreasing. . . . most Indonesians are unaware of differences among the political parties. Two-thirds of the voters (66 percent) say they do not know what differences exist among the parties or that there are none" (Ufen 2008, 29). According to a foremost scholar on Islamic politics in Indonesia, the 2009 election results "only solidify the fact that Islam is no longer an important factor in Indonesian (partisan) politics" (Effendy 2009b). The same can be said for religious pluralism and democratic reform—like Islam, vague virtues insipidly invoked by all parties, rather than robustly defended by some and denounced by others. Pronounced processes of political dealignment and disarticulation had thus reduced the originally workable Indonesian democratic party system to something of a shambles only a decade after democratization.

Of course this is not to say that disarticulation in Indonesia has been total. Some parties have intermittently made clear cleavage-based appeals that differentiate them from other parties on certain hot-button issues, such as a controversial antipornography law (Mietzner 2014). Nor is disarticulation irreversible. Since 2004, two new parties have made political headway by at least partly rearticulating what the initial big five parties have left disarticulated— or by making initial efforts at rebuilding the blocs that have been unbuilt. Yet even these emergent upstart parties have produced only weak attempts at articulation at best, thus confirming rather than disconfirming the overall trend toward disarticulation in the Indonesian party system.

The first is the Islamic party PKS, the successor to the PK, which won less than 2 percent of the vote in 1999 but was rewarded with a cabinet post regardless as a member of the Amien Rais–led Central Axis. After being left out of Megawati's reconstituted cartel cabinet in 2001, however, the PKS worked feverishly to mobilize voters and burnish its anticorruption credentials in the run-up to the 2004 vote. The hard work paid dividends, as the PKS leaped to 7.3 percent of the national vote, and even took first place in the capital city of Jakarta—the eternal epicenter of Indonesia's reformist electorate (Slater 2004, 62).

Yet, like its Islamic counterparts, PKS could not withstand the temptation to join the party cartel after the 2004 vote, accepting two cabinet posts under new president Susilo Bambang Yudhoyono (SBY). Also like its counterparts, the PKS saw its mobilizing thrust slacken and its electoral support soften. Although it snared a slightly larger total share in 2009 (7.8 percent) than in 2004, it lost badly in Jakarta, and saw its growth trajectory flattened precisely when many analysts expected it to steepen. Understandable voter confusion over whether to consider PKS a government party or an opposition party, and whether to support PKS for its expressed religious principles or to trust its claims not to wish to impose those principles on Indonesia's diverse society, have done the fledgling party no favors. As Liddle and Mujani summarized PKS's uncertain positioning on the eve of the 2009 elections:

> PKS's own intentions, however, are more ambiguous (or perhaps ambivalent, the product in part of internal party differences). While a self-declared dakwa (call, proselytizing for and preaching within Islam) party, PKS campaigned in 2004 not on Islamism but on a claim to be a "clean" (bersih) and "caring" (peduli) party. Party leaders fully recognize that most of their 2004

support came not from fellow Islamists but from voters who bought their secular good-governance promise. In the hundreds of regional executive elections (provincial and district/municipality) held between 2005 and 2008, PKS formed coalitions of convenience with a wide range of parties, including the Christian PDS.... Its 2009 parliamentary campaign themes are "clean, caring, and professional." (Liddle and Mujani 2009, 7)

Like the PDI-P before it, the PKS would have been better served by eschewing cabinet posts and building a clearer and more consistent "party brand" from the ranks of opposition (Lupu 2011). Instead, the PKS has found itself entangled in embarrassing corruption scandals and seemingly interminable controversies over whether SBY will kick its cadres out of his cabinet in reaction to its recurrent refusal to toe his government's line. This mixture of political opportunism and inconsistency has inevitably muddied the message—*any* message—that the PKS might want to send to the electorate about what it stands for and, equally importantly, what it stands firmly against. Like other Indonesian parties that have prioritized access to executive power over building ideological blocs with likeminded allies, the PKS has lost electoral ground after engaging in promiscuous power-sharing, slipping from 7.9 percent of the vote in 2009 to 6.8 percent in 2014.

The second new entrant aiming to rearticulate party–society linkages has been the party vehicle of President SBY—the Democratic Party, or PD. The party came to life in 2004 under the leadership of the retired general, who defeated the PDI-P's Megawati in a landslide in Indonesia's first-ever direct presidential election. (Incumbency again provided no advantage, given how little politicians such as Megawati have employed their authority to provide public goods and cultivate voter loyalty.) Having placed fifth with 7.5 percent of the national vote in the 2004 parliamentary elections, the PD skyrocketed in popularity in 2009, placing first with 20.8 percent of the vote, at the direct expense of fellow nationalist parties such as PDI-P and Golkar, which continued their steady electoral slides. Those parties' sinking power and shrinking popularity became even more painfully evident in the presidential elections of July 2009, when President SBY won more than 60 percent of the national vote in a three-cornered contest against PDI-P and Golkar nominees.

To some degree, SBY and his PD party succeeded in 2009 by rearticulating what had been disarticulated. Specifically, by presenting himself as a principled (if not exactly dogged) opponent of corruption and allowing more prosecutions and convictions of well-connected old-guard figures than Megawati had permitted or pushed in her tenure as president, SBY and the PD initially became broadly associated in the public mind with deepened political reform. This was not just rhetorical bluster, as prosecutions by Indonesia's Corruption Eradication Commission (KPK) skyrocketed from two in 2004 (the year of SBY's first electoral victory) to sixty-one in 2009, while prosecutions went from zero to thirty-nine in the same period (von Luebke 2011). Whereas the PDI-P suffered huge losses after generally abusing (and underusing) the power of presidential incumbency, SBY and his PD party made enormous gains between 2004 and 2009 by generally not abusing their power for corrupt purposes and by associating themselves in the public mind with an array of modest new welfare policies.

Yet the eruption of corruption scandals implicating PD leaders after the 2009 election virtually destroyed the reformist credentials that the party had only just begun to build. Its punishment in the 2014 polls was severe, slipping from 20.8 percent of the national vote to a mere 10.2 percent in 2014. The PD's effort to rearticulate what the PDI-P, PKB, and PAN have squandered on the reformist dimension was never a particularly strong one; and it appears in any event to have ended in profound failure. Hence, on the eve of the 2014 national elections, the reformist cleavage remained as disarticulated as the religious cleavage in Indonesian democratic politics.

CONCLUSION AND CODA

In their decade-plus of democracy, Indonesian voters have exhibited an eager willingness and a surprising capacity to punish the elite politicians who have largely ignored them. The unfortunate consequence of this fortunate trait is that Indonesia's party system has become destabilized before Indonesian democracy has had the opportunity to grow deep and strong social and historical roots. From a comparative perspective, this raises the specter that Indonesia's collusive, elitist, oligarchic democracy is structurally vulnerable to the kind of strong-armed, charismatic, populist challenges that have recently roiled and rocked so many other democratic polities—from the Thailand of Thaksin to the Peru of Fujimori, from the Venezuela of Chavez to the Italy of Belusconi, and from the Philippines of Estrada to the Bolivia of Morales (Slater 2004, 2013; Slater and Simmons 2013).

In fact, Indonesia is fortunate that such a destabilizing presidency is yet to occur (with the informative exception of Abdurrahman Wahid's quixotic and truncated unilateralist turn in 2000–2001). Indonesia's presidentialist electoral rules clearly raise the risk of a sudden shift toward "delegative democracy" (O'Donnell 1994) or, worse, destabilizing populism or even outright authoritarianism (Slater 2013). The outgoing president, SBY, has had the formal tools at his disposal to stop sharing power with everyone and start not sharing it at all. After his 2009 landslide reelection, SBY indeed put more executive power in his own party's hands and less in the maws of his coalition partners. As a creature of the party cartel from its very inception, however—SBY reportedly organized the "Ciganjur-Plus" meeting of reformist leaders with military commander Wiranto in early 1999 and served as a coordinating minister in both Wahid and Megawati's cabinets before becoming president himself—the outgoing president proved to be disinclined to rule through personal aggrandizement rather than the sturdier bedrock of formal political institutions and elite political allies.

It would seemingly take the rise of a president from outside the current, cartelized party coalition to undo entrenched practices of promiscuous power-sharing and reverse Indonesia's ongoing process of democratic disarticulation. As it happens, both candidates in the July 2014 presidential election—Jakarta Governor Joko Widodo (also known as Jokowi) from the PDI-P and former army general Prabowo Subianto from the emergent Gerindra party—have been outsiders to the national promiscuous power-sharing arrangements detailed in this chapter. Yet the electoral rules crafted by Indonesia's party elites make a full-fledged outsider challenge to the status quo nearly impossible, because presidential candidates must be nominated by parties holding at least 20 percent of parliamentary seats. Although Jokowi's PDI-P and Prabowo's Gerindra made the biggest gains in the 2014 parliamentary elections from their position outside the SBY government—PDI-P improving from 14.0 percent to 19.0 percent, and Gerindra shooting upward from 4.5 percent to 11.8 percent—neither could nominate their preferred presidential candidate without engaging in pre-election power-sharing deals. That ironically meant teaming up with parties that had been part of the SBY government, even though the very electoral success of PDI-P and Gerindra had been predicated on their noninvolvement in that same government's lackluster performance.

The clearest prospects for renewed political articulation thus do not hinge on the rise of any new majoritarian party. They rest in the potential election-induced bifurcation of the cartelized party system into ideologically defined blocs. On that front, the Jokowi-Prabowo faceoff presents both promise and danger. The promise is that Jokowi might prevail and build the kind of reformist and pluralist-nationalist bloc that failed to coalesce back in 1999. Because every conservative Islamic party has thus far aligned with Prabowo, the prospects for Indonesia's party coalitions to be shaped once again by principled disagreements over questions of religious purity and pluralism are somewhat strong. Prospects for a rejuvenated reformist bloc are somewhat weaker because Jokowi's initial presidential coalition already includes many figures with deep roots in the Suharto era, including ex-Golkar leader Jusuf Kalla as his vice-presidential running mate. Hence, although Jokowi's impressive track record as Jakarta governor promises the advent of a reformist *presidency*, his ascendancy would not necessarily amount to any building of a reformist *bloc*, just as the election and reelection of a president with relatively clean hands from 2004 through 2014 did not serve to rearticulate Indonesia's reform cleavage.

Unfortunately, the danger of a radical reversal of Indonesia's modest reform gains since 1998 seems greater than the promise of any major reformist advances. Jokowi's opponent, former General Prabowo Subianto, was once the son-in-law of former president Suharto and is the brother of one of Indonesia's richest men. Considering that he was discharged from his duties and fled into exile after Suharto's fall as a result of his units' role in the kidnapping and disappearance of democracy activists and the massive rapes of Chinese women that occurred in the New Order's dying days, Prabowo patently lacks the basic democratic commitments to be entrusted with presidential power. Equally worrisome, his presidential coalition embraces the most blatantly corrupt and stridently antipluralistic figures from Indonesia's incumbent ruling constellation. Rather than presenting the kind of bona fide outsider challenge in which a populist leverages genuine mass appeal to attack a ruling oligarchy, Prabowo is teaming up with the oligarchy's worst elements in a bid to gain unchallenged executive power for himself. Given the failure by Jokowi's PDI-P—still led by former promiscuous-power-sharer-in-chief Megawati—to assemble a clear reformist alternative bloc to Prabowo's, the election will be much less of a referendum on questions of democratic reform than any election involving a once-disgraced and forcibly ousted army general should ever be.

Herein lies the greatest danger and the most predictable byproduct of disarticulated democracy. Ironically, as the historical analysis here has shown,

Indonesia's social cleavages gained greater political expression under the authoritarian regimes of Dutch colonialism, Sukarno's Guided Democracy, and Suharto's New Order than they have thus far secured in the country's new era of procedurally democratic politics. It would be tragic in the extreme if another authoritarian strongman were given the opportunity to rebuild the political blocs that Indonesia's democratic elites have spent the past decade and a half unbuilding.

FIVE WEAK PARTY ARTICULATION AND DEVELOPMENT IN INDIA, 1991–2014

Manali Desai

RECENT WORK ASSESSING TWO DECADES of liberalization in India suggests that, although the post-1990s period has seen large numbers of people come out of poverty mainly due to the trickle-down effects of the market, more extreme forms of poverty and vulnerability, as well as deepening inequalities, remain immune to high economic growth (Deaton and Dreze 2002; Kohli 2012; Krishna 2004; Sen and Dreze 2013). This leaves millions hovering at the poverty line, vulnerable to the effects of structural, interlocking deprivations, even as social inequalities widen. The question is: Why has the post-1990s pattern of high economic growth not translated into a developmental transformation? Although the term developmentalism is used in different ways in the literature, often referring to a semi-authoritarian path of capitalist growth led by states (see Leftwich 1995), I use it more broadly to refer to a policy regime that combines a pattern of moderate to high economic growth with rapid removal of poverty. The pathways to such an outcome could be "from above," that is, through state coordinated capitalism as occurred in the Asian "miracles," or "from below" through the mobilization of broad social sectors, as seen in Costa Rica, Jamaica, and Kerala. In India, although market liberalization was a first step[1] toward enabling higher growth rates, these already-mentioned forms of developmentalism appear to be blocked. Instead the state appears to have become largely "pro-business," excluding the poor from meaningful redistribution, yet working against markets by favoring large corporate actors and mitigating competition (Kohli 2007). Despite the existence of a large literature on this topic it is remarkable that parties and party-movement relationships have been largely sidelined in explaining this pattern of growth.[2] As

I will go on to discuss, the role of parties tends to be subsumed under a more general and often vague reference to broader processes of democratization. This chapter will show that it is the *weakness* of party-led political articulations in India that best explains why a democratic solution to blocked developmentalism has not emerged.

Weak articulations are articulatory projects that fail to become hegemonic; they remain prone to instability, challenge, and potential incoherence and thus cannot push forward any kind of desired transformation. At a minimum, weak articulations are the product of parties that are either not integral in their orientation to politics or whose integral qualities are hindered by factors that are contingent to particular historical moments (either internal or external to the party) (see Introduction to this volume).[3] Weak articulations as discussed in this chapter are measured by unstable and fluid vote shares, rapid turnover in government, and, crucially, the fragmentation of the partisan loyalties of different constituencies across several parties. There are degrees of weakness among articulations, but the fundamental point is that they lack transformative power. What parties do, whether in or out of government, is a crucial part of the explanation of weak articulations. What is being presented here, however, is not a voluntaristic argument about parties. To the contrary, parties cannot always do what they want, and thus weak articulations are also produced in the context of structural constraints on parties, not least the global political economy. Nevertheless, parties are not merely passive actors in a constrained field—many of the parties discussed in this volume are able to evolve into substantially transformative agencies by articulating new constituencies of support.

India's market transition has been premised on the *disarticulation* of state-led (or Nehruvian) developmentalism, but it has not been replaced by an alternative articulatory project. Indeed, the party that framed the terms of Nehruvian developmentalism was itself responsible for undertaking the first steps to dismantle this legacy. The length that had to be traveled politically is measured by the fact that the two dominant political parties in India, namely the Congress and the Bharatiya Janata Party (BJP), have despite their differences moved toward a neoliberal consensus in spite of prior ideological commitments that opposed it. I use the term *neoliberal consensus* to include the kinds of policies that Kohli (2007) refers to as "probusiness," insofar as both parties have moved politically closer to large business houses and global capital, while gradually eroding the state's founding socialist commitments to equality and propoor policy regimes. The term, however, also signifies the turn away from ideas of national development that underpinned the state's rhetoric until the 1990s, devolving this responsibility to states instead by increasing their autonomy to seek investment and develop markets according to their specific areas of strength. This has in turn increased interstate inequalities and made poverty reduction more difficult unless the route is via market-based trickle-down mechanisms.[4]

There are two key puzzles this chapter is concerned with. First, why has such a clear political consensus for market liberalization not paved the way for a developmental state? Second, given unprecedented levels of democratization and consequent political fragmentation during this period, which includes the electoral ascendancy of lower-caste parties (former untouchables, or *dalits*, and Other Backward Castes, or OBC[5]) and high electoral participation (Corbridge and Harriss 1997; Hasan 2002; Jaffrelot 2003), why has there not been a greater redistributive thrust in state policy? In other words, why has mobilization "from below" not left a greater imprint on state policy?

The growth of a neoliberal consensus together with political fragmentation has been noted in other contexts such as Indonesia, where traditional cleavages based on religion and reformism have dissolved into multiple movements and issues (see Aspinall 2013). Dan Slater (Chapter 4 in this volume) argues that this dissolution is a product of party *dearticulation*—that is, a power-sharing collusion among the major parties that has developed with the disintegration of ideologically driven cleavages and blocs. Katz and Mair (2009, 754–755) have more generally linked party collusion to globalization, which, they argue, has placed new constraints on mass parties and undermined the relevance of the left-right divide. In an environment of depoliticization parties increasingly resemble one another, whereas the goals of politics become "self-referential, professional and technocratic" (ibid., 755). The cartelization thesis appears to fit the Indian case; yet, as I go on to discuss, the context in which the parties have grown toward an implicit collusion is defined less by depoliticization (which is better suited to explaining the European cases) than new, emerging forms of politicization. These forms of politicization have been mostly ethnic, that is, caste and religious, but equally important are the growth of nonparty movements among the poor. It is the attempted articulation of political constituencies in caste, religious, and secular propoor terms—"from above" and "from below"—that has marked the landscape of liberalization, and it is the failure of these articulations that best explains why developmentalism from above or below has (until now) eluded the state.

TOWARD LIBERALIZATION IN 1991

After a decade of hesitant and partially successful attempts to liberalize the economy during the 1980s, in 1991 the ruling Congress Party broke with its own socialist legacy and implemented the first major liberalization program in India. These reforms were similar to, if less sweeping than, the package of reforms undertaken in many countries during that period. The bulk of the reforms were in the areas of licensing and regulation, external and internal trade, foreign direct investment, currency exchange, and financialization. It is important to make a clear distinction between the reform package (economic policies), and the broader political transformation that had begun well before 1991.[6] The economic reforms represented an emerging neoliberal consensus among the technocratic and political elite, yet the political changes that preceded liberalization signified a distinct opening up of democratic possibilities and participatory capacity among subaltern classes. The latter, in other words, did not necessarily support a clear neoliberal consensus. The preceding Nehruvian model of development was underpinned by traditional patron–client relationships between the Congress Party and lower caste-class groups, with the Congress functioning as a classic catch-all party. The central administration of development funds and social welfare programs ensured a modicum of parity across and within states, which prevented rapid inequalities from emerging. The subsequent pattern of development after 1991 was, on the other hand, marked by relatively high economic growth, rapid privatization, and sharply rising middle-class prosperity, together with deepening inequality, high unemployment, and severe regional disparities in economic growth (Deaton and Dreze 2002; Mahendra Dev and Ravi 2007).

The most common explanation for the developmental stasis in India is the weakness of the state, specifically its weak autonomy, cohesion, and capacity (Bardhan 1999; Kohli 2004, 2007). The weak Indian state, Kohli (2004) argues, has failed to impose cohesion on its inherent class fragmentation and gain sufficient autonomy to push for a developmental strategy. It is only at certain exceptional—and brief-lived—moments such as the early months of Rajiv Gandhi's administration in 1985, when the Congress Party won a distinct majority, that technocratic reformers gained sudden autonomy and attempted to liberalize economic policy (Kohli 1989). This involved sudden freedom from "coalitional entanglements and interest group pressures" including the left parties, organized labor, and populist interests that directly opposed the market (ibid., 312). The underlying assumption here is that the state is too weak to disembed itself from populist "bottom-up" pressures to create and implement effective proliberalization policies. However, if this argument is correct, it is difficult to explain why probusiness liberalization has proceeded at all, given growing democratization and the unprecedented entry of the masses into formal politics and state structures (Kumar 2008).

If we examine the liberalization process—proliberalization policies were first introduced and then withdrawn in 1966, then reintroduced and partially retracted in 1985, and finally implemented in 1991—it is apparent that what was required for liberalization to succeed was a transformation in the prevailing political consensus *against* markets. We need to explain how and why the major Indian parties broke with existing ideological tendencies and made programmatic change possible, yet what it is about that process that also impeded a developmentalist orientation. To do this, it is important to look not only at what parties did once they won power (as Kohli rightly does), but also at what they did *to win* power just as they were in the process of embracing a new ideological direction. The articulation thesis is important because, in breaking with prior tradition, the two major parties—Congress and BJP—did more than simply reflect an underlying cleavage between pro- and antimarket coalitions (along an identifiable left–right axis). Instead, *they attempted to draw together different elite and subaltern sectors into coherent blocs that undercut any serious challenge to liberalization.*[7] The creation of these new blocs involved constructing "chains of equivalence" that linked growing and often different demands among emerging social sectors, in particular the urban middle classes and rural subordinate castes through a nominally common project. Thus the arrow of causality that I put forward here is from party articulation to class or ethnic formation, rather than arguing that party consensus on market reforms was driven by classes with preexisting interests (for example, the middle classes).

My central contention, in fact, is that these articulation projects are inherently unstable and have failed to become politically hegemonic because of the problem of "thin commitments," that is, frequent switching of partisan loyalties among voters and the consequent fragmentation of voting patterns among existing cleavages such as caste or religion. This form of fickle political allegiance reflects the hollowing out of traditional ideological patterns of voting along a "right versus left" axis such as they were defined in India, between pro-Nehruvian socialists (Congress) and antisocialist, probusiness Right (among others, the Jan Sangh, which preceded the formation of the BJP). Nehruvian socialism underpinned Congress dominance for several decades after Independence in 1945 and began to weaken only during the 1980s. Succeeding articulations have attempted to cut across this older division, on the one hand preserving a neoliberal consensus between parties, while on the other hand producing new political divisions that deemphasize class and redistribution. The Congress party's attempt to rekindle a Nehruvian socialist-lite program in 2004 and 2009, as I will discuss later, appears to have failed. The resulting political logic can be likened to a seesaw—moving back and forth between attempted projects "from above," such as liberalization, and popular (and populist) momentum "from below," such as through demands for social security or via mass protests such as those led by the anticorruption movement. Neither momentum is strong enough to win. Instead, contention between the elite and mass realms leads to concessions, compromise, and accommodation. It is this dynamic that prevents a developmental transformation.

MARKET REFORMS AND WEAK HEGEMONY: TOO MUCH DEMOCRACY?

In this section I argue that democratization has not significantly troubled the liberalization project in India and by implication the interparty consensus. Some authors have argued that a developmental transition in India is hindered by the rise of populist movements and parties that oppose markets, partly for ideological and partly for pragmatic reasons (Ahluwalia 2002; Bardhan 2005; Jenkins 1999; Suri 2004). Although this has resulted in a gradualist or incremental approach to market reforms over time, as Peter Hall (1993, 279) notes, a Kuhnian "paradigm break" from prior statist regimes becomes necessary. Unlike "first- and second-order reforms," which involve small shifts within the existing policy paradigm, "third-order" changes are more radical and require considerable electoral support to succeed.[8] In India it is commonly argued that electoral support for "third-order" change, primarily in the key, sensitive areas of labor reform, deregulation of land use for industrial growth, and privatization of public sector units, has not emerged (Jenkins 2004). Instead, although there is mixed evidence on this, voter surveys suggest that parties seeking to deepen liberalization reforms or associated with an overly "proreform" image are generally voted out of power (Suri 2004; Yadav 2004).

There are two problems with this argument: First, the two major parties, Congress and BJP, pushed reforms between 1999 and 2009, often surreptitiously enabling labor reform, land appropriation, and privatization by passing the mandate onto the regional states. If democratization were such an obstacle, it would be difficult to explain the steady deepening of liberalization since 1991 or the convergence of both major parties in the same policy direction.[9] Second, it is difficult to establish causality—we cannot be sure that parties are being voted out *because* they have implemented market reforms. Most reforms to date have not directly affected ordinary people in the way that severe structural adjustment programs have done elsewhere. Deregulation in general has had a positive impact on business and middle classes but not necessarily an adverse impact on the masses. The removal of agricultural tariffs and subsidies (in keeping with the WTO) has had a negative impact on farmers, and the withdrawal of the state via loans has directly affected this constituency, yet protests tend to be sporadic and fragmented. It is only reforms in insurance and pensions that have met with large-scale left party and trade union protest, and these have slowed down or delayed these reforms. Thus the relationship between the adoption of a liberalization reform agenda and a party's electoral chances (which is dependent on the level of democratization) is far from straightforward.

To situate the Indian case comparatively, it is useful to quantify the difference in the social base of market opposition between India and countries such as South Africa and Mexico by focusing on working-class organization. Workers in industrial sectors most likely to be affected by labor reforms and privatization constitute a key threat to market reforms. Yet trade union activity in the form of strikes and lockouts (two major forms of union protest) in India had been steadily declining well before the reforms began (Desai 2012). There is no clear causal relationship between working-class organization and liberalization, other than that a decline in the former has potentially enabled more radical reforms to emerge. Indeed, in light of this the hesitation to reform the Indian labor market is somewhat puzzling. Such reforms have been achieved in countries with historically higher levels of working-class organization, significantly in parts of Latin America such as Chile, Brazil, Nicaragua, Mexico, and Peru. Furthermore, two important measures of labor union strength—trade union density (number of union members as percentage of total workers) and union concentration (percentage of workers represented by the largest union confederations)—show that although in India union density is roughly 5.4 percent (1994 figure), in Mexico it is 32 percent, South Africa 25 percent, and Chile 35 percent. Likewise the index of concentration is 0.22 in India, which is less than the 0.4 threshold for effective pressure through the strength of the largest union federation as specified by Roberts (2002, 17). By way of comparison in South Africa it is 0.58. Furthermore, the formal organized sector itself constitutes a very small part of the economy; roughly 93 percent of India's workforce is employed in the informal, unorganized sector. Informal workers tend to be poorly organized and lack the means to oppose national-level state policies. Rather than participate in the political networks of urban middle class and "bourgeois" civil society, they tend to seek rights in the context of illegality, for example squatting on public land or for electricity connections in unregistered settlements, all of which are sought through parties in exchange for votes (Chatterjee 2008). Similarly, small farmers affected by land appropriation or WTO regulations lack collective representation in national political parties. The ongoing crisis of farmer suicides due to indebtedness suggests that there are few direct political means or strategies available to them.

In summary, the absence of a developmental thrust is not the result of a Polanyian double-movement of push-back against markets, that is, "too much" democracy. For, if there has been a rise in democratization in India, it has not for the most part been fought in the idiom of antimarket welfarism. Instead, ethnic idioms, primarily caste, have dominated these democratization movements, a factor that I attribute to articulatory projects that emerged during the 1990s. Without attention to articulation we cannot explain the weak effect of democratization on developmental outcomes in India.

CONSTRUCTING THE INTERPARTY CONSENSUS
BEFORE 1999

I now examine how the interparty consensus developed in the context of democratization, increasing pressure on the Congress party by the urban middle classes and competition from other parties, significantly the BJP. This is important for understanding their subsequent articulation projects, as the growth of a consensus shaped how interparty disagreements and differences were incorporated into these articulations in the absence of older left–right divisions. The alternative articulation approach outlined in this chapter suggests that liberalization was intended as a hegemonic project within the context of a growing political crisis, specifically a crisis of representation and governability (Kohli 1990) that had emerged during the 1980s.

In 1991, although the Congress won as a minority party within a coalition and implemented the first strident market reforms, it was actually a weak party. Its social base was crumbling, and the party's organizational reach had vastly diminished in rural and urban areas. This reflected an organizational malaise that was caused by Indira Gandhi's attempt to centralize authority around trusted and loyal ministers in the wake of what she perceived as an internal threat to her leadership. Although the BJP was gaining political ascendancy, it was almost a decade away from posing a real threat to the Congress Party and was in dire need of extending its social base beyond traders and small businesspeople. A third front led by the socialist-leaning Janata Party was attempting to pull the political agenda toward the left, but it suffered from inherent fragmentation of leadership and major ideological disagreements. Achieving consensus among the ruling elite was thus a lengthy process, given the institutional stakes held by various sections of the state and party elite in the Nehruvian regime.

The early 1990s saw the intensification of business lobbying of the Congress Party and a rise in their influence within the party. Given that leading industrialists had gained a greater degree of influence since the late 1970s (under Indira Gandhi), and under her son Rajiv Gandhi in 1985, we can argue that the state–business alliance had begun well before 1991. Yet a mandate for liberalization also quite fundamentally required a resolution of *intraparty* struggles. Historically the weak impetus for liberalization stemmed from the fact that the ruling Congress Party was split between prosocialist and proliberalization factions, with the former dominating the party decisively in matters of national policy. However, the prosocialist orientation of Indira Gandhi's administration and the Emergency had alienated significant sections of the urban middle classes, which had grown during the 1980s (ironically as a result of liberalization under Rajiv Gandhi). This became a critical constituency to be wooed and incorporated into new articulations, not merely because of their growing numbers but because they were a vocal sector that had increasingly gravitated towards anti-Congress populisms (Desai 2012).

The spectacular rise of the Hindu Right (Bharatiya Janata Party, or BJP) during the 1990s was in part based on a growing appeal to the politically alienated urban middle classes. Thus *interparty* competition between 1990 and 1996, when the proliberalization BJP formed its first, albeit short-lived, government, spurred an even stronger "proliberalization" orientation within the Congress Party. The global discursive break from etatism was eagerly appropriated by proliberalization reformers within the Congress Party and business interests who stood to gain from the opening up of markets. If too much freedom for capital was once decried as a solution for poverty, it was now seen within the Congress Party as the essential antidote to Nehruvian socialism and its weak record in reducing poverty (Sharma 2011, 136).

The convergence of global discourse with the emerging strength of the proliberalization faction within the Congress Party in 1991 enabled concerted action by sympathetic ministers, advisors, and economists with continuity across administrations. Most of these advisors had experience of working within or advising the World Bank and had a technocratic rather than political inclination; two key figures in the liberalization push of the 1990s, Montek Singh Ahluwalia and Manmohan Singh (until recently the prime minister), had worked in the Rajiv Gandhi administration. This autonomous action cannot be explained on the basis of the electoral popularity of the Congress Party (as Kohli 1989 argues for the 1985 reforms), given that a politically weakened Congress was forced to form a coalition as a minority party in 1991. Nor can it be explained indirectly as a product of "identity" or religious politics, which, according to Varshney (1998), motivated secular parties that would normally have opposed the reforms, to mobilize support for the Congress party as a means of creating an anti-BJP bloc within parliament. This hypothesis does not explain why the Congress, which had historically been hesitant about liberalization policies before 1991, acquired this sudden boldness for reform. Both explanations—state autonomy versus political expediency—pay insufficient attention to parties themselves and, in doing so, cannot explain how a weak party could undertake major market reforms that were at the same time limited in their developmental capacity.

BJP AND THE ARTICULATION OF NEOLIBERALISM, 1999–2004

It was not the Congress, however, but the BJP that was to perform the function of an integral party and take the transformation forward decisively. But, like the Congress Party, this process involved protracted intraparty struggles over the ideological orientation and programmatic direction of the party. By the 1990s the BJP had begun to put forward a major political alternative in the form of Hindu nationalism (Hindutva), which combined a strident anti-Nehruvian and antisocialist rhetoric. However, in the context of the Congress Party's first market reform bid, the BJP was forced to fuse its cultural national-ism with a proglobalization stance, combining two potentially contradictory stances that reflected its own intraparty divisions. The adherents of Swadeshi, that is, protectionism and antiglobalization, dominated the BJP, who argued instead for "internal" liberalization, that is, the dismantling of Nehuvian era state controls and regulation without opening up to international capital. This ideological fusion between liberalization and antiglobalization mapped onto middle-class anxieties about Western lifestyles and global aspirations, which were at once tantalizing and jarring to their inherent cultural conservatism. Despite such cultural ambivalence, the BJP's entry into the political field as a serious alternative to Congress succeeded in displacing old ideological polari-ties such as "socialism versus market" and "left versus right" from the political field. These were replaced by new polarities around religion and nationalism, which were constructed on the basis of new cross-caste articulations (which I subsequently discuss). Discursively, the term *reform* was reduced to quanti-fiable indicators such as GDP, industrial growth, dollar exchange rates, and the like; that is, there was a rapid neoliberalization of economic discourse. In part this involved removing the discursive conjoining of socialism and pov-erty removal (*"garibi hatao"*), and its replacement by nationalist and regional subnationalist preoccupations with economic growth rates.

The BJP won the 1999 elections with a thin majority, gaining a large pro-portion of the urban votes, while retaining a strong upper-caste bias in both rural and urban areas. Having formed a coalition government in 1998 that subsequently collapsed when a coalition partner pulled support, the BJP was forced into fresh elections in 1999. It is ironic that, although the Congress Party tried to correct its elite "proreform" image, which it understood as being responsible for its defeat in the 1996 national elections, the revival of the 1970s slogan *"garibi hatao"* ("remove poverty") did not lead it to electoral victory in 1998 or 1999.[10] The 1999 elections marked a point at which it became evident—or at least was interpreted through voting results—that voters were becoming less interested in the caste or identity of local party representatives but rather more concerned with "governance" issues, that is, the extent to which roads, schools, drinking water, lighting, and basic infrastructure and employment had been provided by elected members of parliament.[11] The democratization trends that had brought lower castes to the voting booth had given rise to a new assertive citizenship that seemed less preoccupied with traditional party distinctions and more concerned with the delivery of developmental goods. But the Congress was not viewed as a vehicle for these demands, and it had not made any serious attempts to articulate a popular front on this basis.

If voter discontent with "governance" was really the case, however, it was not reflected in the party manifesto of the BJP either. Instead, the dominant rhetorical thrust of its manifesto was nationalist, that is, aimed at projecting national strength in defence, and a strong economy and cultural foundation for such a nation.[12] This form of party branding was somewhat ambiguous on the question of globalization given that in 1998 the BJP was still attempting to combine its economic nationalism (*swadeshi*) with a commitment to liberalization.[13] To make matters more complicated, some of the BJP's coalition partners professed radical antimarket views; for instance, George Fernandes of the Samata Party caused a furor when he threatened to remove multinational companies from the country once in power. The BJP was forced to state that foreign investment would be allowed only in "essential areas" such as infrastructure and public sector units (Saxena 1998). As Bhaskar Roy reported in the *Times of India*:

> The BJP's election manifesto and the eight-page "National Agenda for Governance"—the policy blueprint of the Vajpayee government—contain much that is disquieting to foreign investors and governments alike. Leading members of the government have given free vent to their "swadeshi" biases and even the allegedly "liberal" finance minister, Mr. Yashwant Sinha, has sought to peddle the distinction between investment in "priority" and "non-priority" areas. Yet, it is clear that there will be no major departure from the existing economic trajectory. Liberalisation is a fact of life. No existing investor will be asked to leave and it is extremely unlikely that any foreign company arriving on India's shores with hard cash to invest will actually be turned away. (Roy 1998)

The decisive trajectory of liberalization set in motion by both parties contrasted with the internal disarray in ideological and policy inclinations within the BJP. Indeed, the collapse of the 1998 coalition and the BJP's slim electoral majority in 1999 revealed the essential *political* weakness of the BJP, which was forced to rely on parties with different ideological persuasions to form government. Seizing this moment, between 1998 and 1999 the BJP changed course on market reforms and undertook a strident neoliberal agenda, which included privatization in banking, insurance, disinvestment of public sector companies, special economic zones, and liberalization of trade in compliance with WTO regulations. In pushing forward with the reforms the BJP leadership, despite its strong ties to the parent organization Rashtriya Swayamsevak Sangh (RSS), deviated markedly from its aggressive and chauvinistic brand of Hindu nationalism, which emphasized economic nationalism and aversion to foreign capital. If the 1998 national agenda reflected ambivalence over economic nationalism *within* the BJP, by 1999 it was defeated in favor of a redefined Hindu nationalism with full support for market liberalization.[14]

The BJP's ideological shift during this crucial conjuncture cannot be explained merely as a reflection of the interest of its social base. Many small traders and businesses stood to lose from foreign investment; even large industrialists such as Rahul Bajaj supported a protectionist or *"swadeshi"* policy. On the other hand, sections of Indian business had strongly protested the BJP coalition partners' perceived antireform stance. Although undoubtedly pressure from the business lobby had an impact on the BJP's economic policy, the reinvention of Hindu nationalism as a "chain of equivalence" offers a more useful lens with which to view this critical conjuncture. This chain linked national pride, military strength,[15] and economic growth in an attempt at the symbolic formation of the middle class into which various class fractions and castes were integrated. The BJP's rise from the early 1990s to 1999, as has been argued, represented the blending of traditional caste and class differences and the formation of a new "social bloc . . . defined by an overlap of social and economic privileges" (Yadav, Kumar, and Heath 1999). Survey data obtained as part of the National Election Survey (NES) certainly show that in 1999 votes for the BJP rose as one went higher up the caste hierarchy and were even stronger when caste and class reinforced each other. Correspondingly, to garner votes from lower castes, the BJP had to rely on its coalition partners in different states. Clearly this articulation had a contagion effect on Congress voters—the same NES data also show, for example, that the percentage of Congress voters in 1996, 1998, and 1999 that supported the entry of foreign companies was higher than among BJP voters; although, significantly, there is a sharp decline between 1998 and 1999 in the number of BJP voters opposed to the entry of foreign companies (Kumar 2004, 1626). Putting these figures together we can see that by 1998 the BJP had begun to articulate a promarket stance to capture a larger share of the urban middle-class vote, while attempting to articulate a broader social bloc by employing a form of cultural nationalism. In subsequent years, as it set out to push forward its transformative project, the BJP sought to incorporate other classes and castes ranging from OBCs to *dalits* and tribals. Yet that project was to take much longer and not really be accomplished until 2014. For its 1999 campaign, the central articulating sign was "India Shining," inspired by the "feel-good factor" put forward by Thatcher's spin doctors. It was a metaphor of national resurgence imposed on the forms of "lack" expressed in demands emanating from the middle classes, for example, for greater prosperity, global connection, military strength, and cultural chauvinism. These demands had begun appearing during Congress rule as far back as the 1970s, but solutions to these demands had been very slow, mainly in the form of hesitant liberalization during the 1980s. What Laclau (2005, 74) calls an "internal frontier" had thus already begun to appear, but until now it had met with a hesitant response by the Congress Party. It was the BJP that gradually and decisively consolidated this frontier— without its direct articulatory project, it is unlikely that the Congress Party would have been able to reinvent itself as a party of the urban middle classes without losing much of its social base.

The BJP's late 1990s articulation was, however, unable to become hegemonic and gain stability. In constructing the binary of "us" versus "them," redefined Hindutva sought to oppose national minorities, primarily Muslims, from the political mainstream, while characterizing Congress-era secularism as a form of "appeasement." The use of violence against Muslims, and in some instances Christians, and a variety of other practices of mobilization certainly allowed the BJP to begin to extend its base among lower castes and tribal groups. Yet, the discursive chain of cultural nationalism linking the Kargil war,[16] nuclear prowess, and the foreign origins of Congress leader Sonia Gandhi failed to create a chain of equivalence between demands emanating from sectors outside the middle classes. Despite rising incomes (10.3 percent growth since 1993–1994) and an increasingly prosperous middle class, factors that were directly attributed to the BJP (Dash 2004), in 1999 the party and its allies lost assembly elections in four key states—Bihar, Orissa, Madhya Pradesh, and Haryana. Between 1999 and 2003 it also lost elections in Uttar Pradesh, Himachal Pradesh, Punjab (as part of coalition), and Uttarakhand (Yadav and Palshikar 2009, 59). The thin appeal of cultural nationalism as a politically hegemonic strategy was even recognized by the BJP-leaning newspaper *Times of India*, which suggested that "in many regions, the state of roads, drains and schools has become a more potent election issue than 'foreign intruders'" ("Leading from Below," 1999). As the article notes, "In some areas, people seem to boycott or at least prevent campaigning politicians from entering their villages and mohallas; elsewhere, however, sitting MPs find that once impregnable electoral fortresses are crumbling around them and that victory is no longer assured by the colour of the party flag or the qualities of a party leader" (ibid.).

The disjuncture between the BJPs's victory in the national election in 1999 and subsequent defeat in the state elections suggests, paraphrasing Laclau, that the BJP had failed at undertaking the crucial step of expanding the equivalential chain across national space.[17] If hegemony is "the operation of taking up, by a particularity, of an incommensurable signification" (Laclau 2005, 70), then the reinvented Hindu nationalism that combined neoliberalism with aggressive cultural nationalism failed to take on this universality. In specific regions, however, notably the western state of Gujarat, Hindu cultural nationalism succeeded in creating a chain of equivalence between dominant and subordinate classes, in part by offering the lower castes a symbolic register to express their demands in the absence of a countervailing discourse from the left or center. The Gujarat case is of some significance because Hindu nationalism enabled the articulation of dominant castes and sections of the subordinate castes (*dalits* and OBCs) by incorporating the latter into a quasi-developmental regime. This incorporation was possible because for historical reasons the lower castes had failed to develop alternative associational forms in Gujarat (Breman 2004), whereas in the northern states of Uttar Pradesh or Bihar, as well as in the southern states of Tamil Nadu or Andhra Pradesh, clear challenges to the BJP's cultural nationalism had developed among the lower castes and classes. Many commentators, in fact misread the BJP's ability to hold power for five years (1999–2004) as a sign of its hegemony over Indian politics. Thus the Congress Party's victory in the 2004 national elections came as a tremendous surprise to the most seasoned observers of Indian politics.

SECULAR GOVERNANCE AND CONGRESS ARTICULATION, 2004–2009

The 2004 victory of the Congress Party, after over a decade of organizational decline and decay, has rightly been described as a "critical juncture" (Hasan 2006). But what did this juncture signify? The general view is that Congress Party victory was owed to a groundswell of political support from the anti-reforms poor and represented a consolidation of the longer-term "silent revolution" of growing claims for political representation among the low-caste poor (Hasan 2006; Yadav 2004). However, the voting data show a more complex picture. Although the Congress Party has always garnered more support from the lower-caste poor particularly in rural areas, the crucial factor that led the Congress to victory in 2004 was the *shift in upper-caste votes from the BJP to the Congress and a major swing in OBC votes, which is a another constituency that had been wooed by the BJP since 1999*. As Yadav (2004, 5392) notes, the countertrend in 2004 is crucial: "The higher one goes up in the class hierarchy, the greater the swing against the NDA [the BJP coalition]." Using data from the National Election Surveys of 1999 and 2004, Yadav and his team calculated that the swing vote in 2004 among Hindu upper castes for the Congress and its allies was 6.8 percent and –6.5 percent for the BJP and its allies (Yadav 2004, 5390). Similarly, among Hindu peasant proprietors as well as the OBCs, the swing votes were 9.1 and 7.5 percent respectively for the Congress alliance, and –8.3 and –10.8 percent respectively for the BJP alliance. If we were to merely identify the Congress and BJP respectively as propoor and upper-caste leaning, these data would make little sense. They would make even less sense once we took into account the fact that the BJP had been in power since 1999 and put through market reforms that were ostensibly in the interest of the upper-caste elite. The Congress, on the other hand, was seeking to promote itself as a major force for liberalization but in terms framed as "inclusive growth." As Hasan (2006, 478) aptly noted: "The INC base in 2004 is largely among the poor, even more so than before, while its policies are, oddly enough, less pro-poor. When its support was more evenly distributed, it was more centrist than at present."

We can put these two contradictory outcomes together to suggest that the garnering of support from specific class–caste constituencies was, contrary to the claims made by various scholars, not necessarily related to a party's stance on market reforms. At one level this "sharing" of upper-caste, middle-class support between the BJP and Congress suggests that there is an inter-party consensus on major policies; on the other hand, it also demonstrates the weakness or instability of the articulations constructed by each party. Although on average the upper-caste vote leans more favorably toward the BJP, the swing during its most stable period in politics suggests that a cleavage-driven analysis of voting patterns can be misleading. Instead, it supports the articulation thesis—the articulations pursued by each party in competition with one another were in effect weak. They resulted in growing convergence on the market path but stalled any further developmental possibilities.

As Yadav (2004, 5384) noted, the 2004 mandate

> . . . marked the closure of a historical possibility that arose in the beginning of 1990s, the possibility of competitive politics providing space for exercise of substantial choices by ordinary citizens. . . . The changes in the structure of political competition opened greater number of options before the electorate without expanding or deepening the choice-set in terms of issues and policies available to the citizens. The five years prior to this election had confirmed a trend of convergence, a tendency for the major players in the party political arena to become like one another, and thus pushed out issues with transformative potential from the political agenda.

What this important passage suggests is that although prior to its victory in 2004 the Congress Party had begun to construct an alternative social bloc to that of the BJP, it did so without disturbing the promarket consensus. This new chain of equivalence was marked by a relative erosion of identitarian and communal claims and their normative link to economic growth as constructed by the BJP. At the same time it was marked by the closure of the "historical possibility" that arose during the critical juncture of democratization in the early 1990s, when caste-based insurgency and popular movements had threatened the survival of the Congress Party, and begun the "bottom-up" erosion of the legitimacy of Nehruvian socialism.

In its 2004 campaign the Congress Party drew on a secular "governance" discourse, centered on what they called "*aam admi*," or ordinary people's concerns. The ordinary person was a figure denuded of caste, ethnicity, religion, or region and instead primarily concerned with "bread and butter" issues of livelihood, security, and good governance. The ordinary Indian, in other words, was removed from a defensive cultural nationalist or identitarian position and situated in a collective situation of "nondefinition," that is, lacking a specific position in the social structure. Like the resurgent Hindu, "*aam admi*" is a classic populist construction. But, more to the point, this construction is neutral with regards to middle-class–oriented economic liberalization. The expansive definition of "ordinary people" potentially encompasses key concerns of the middle classes, namely anticorruption, "good governance," and upward mobility, while portraying it at the same time as a basically classless entity. Thus rather than construct a clear class or other kind of social cleavage, the Congress articulation constructed a political enemy, namely the BJP, on grounds of its poor record of governance. Statecraft came to be associated with good management of the economy and stability, and, although both parties professed an agenda of distributive justice, for the Congress it was linked to effective governance. Thus the consensus on market reforms was left untouched.

One could argue that the turn toward governance in Indian political rhetoric since 2004 confirms the "cartel party" thesis that in recent decades the essential differences between parties have been reduced to technical issues of efficient management and governance (Katz and Mair 2009, 756). The articulation thesis proposed here, however, better explains why it was Congress rather than the BJP that won the 2004 and 2009 elections. This is because it is the only available explanation for the puzzle of how the democratization and mobilization of the poor could be accommodated within a form of politics that left the market consensus more or less unchanged.[18]

The new Congress articulation of 2004 was not simply a return to the rainbow politics of the past. Instead it came out of a protracted process of negotiation with popular movements and organizations in which tactical support for the Congress would be rewarded with a range of social policies such as midday meal schemes, right to education, health, and other antipoverty schemes. The Congress in 2004, and with greater success in the 2009 election, drew many civil society, propoor activist organizations into the "growth inclusion" agenda by jointly designing comprehensive antipoverty programs such as the landmark National Rural Employment Guarantee Act (NREGA) and other rights-based policies such as the Jawaharlal Nehru Urban Renewal Mission, Right to Information, and education, health, and food security that some likened to an Indian New Deal. As Sonia Gandhi, one of the key backers of these policies, stated, the "INC remains a party of equity and growth" (Hasan 2006, 479); she was in turn responsible for insisting on a quasi-Nehruvian tilt to the Congress policy agenda. Nevertheless, we should not take this to suggest a diminished drive to liberalize the economy, for there was no real dissent within the party on the need for market liberalization.

The recent sweeping victory of the BJP in the national elections in 2014 reveals just how weak the Congress-led articulations of 2004 and 2009 were. The overt symptoms of malaise—slow social development (that is, weak development from below) with growing inequality, hesitant liberalization, and corruption scandals are in fact symptoms of an articulation that lacked the means to hold it together. The policy framework that informed the Congress articulation was one of increasing social sector budget allocations from India's burgeoning tax receipts. Yet the articulation led by the Congress Party was framed somewhat vaguely as *inclusion* of the masses in the "growth process," without a programmatic agenda for the transformation of class relations through land reforms, or the infrastructural investment necessary for an industrial strategy, or radical participatory structures as designed in Porto Allegre, for example, that would introduce budgetary participation and in turn participatory growth. In that sense the Congress failed to act as an integral party; its policy orientation remained firmly in the rubric of old-style Congress social programs aimed at shoring up its voter base. There was insufficient attention given to the delivery of these programs on the ground that would require a structural transformation in the state's relationships to local bureaucracies, and various interest groups such as civil servants that skimmed off these programs. Neither did the Congress governments undertake radical policies to boost domestic growth and demand. A critical indicator of the inability of growth to generate direct benefits was the level of employment, which by the government's own admission was been slow to rise. The unemployment rate which was 6.06 percent in 1993–1994 rose to 7.31 percent in 1999–2000, and further to 8.28 percent in 2004–2005, reducing to 6.60 in 2009–2010 (Government of India 2011, 6). The rural sector, where most poverty is concentrated, grew slowly, suffering from weak investment and lack of reforms to alter the unequal land ownership patterns and alleviate problems of endemic debt and poor credit. Thus the Congress party's attempt to create a propoor articulation without significantly transforming the probusiness political economy proved to be a contradiction that rendered it fundamentally weak and open to challenge.

REGIONAL DISPERSALS AND CHALLENGES

The national frame, under challenge in the process of market reform, may prove beneficial to many states that have distinct advantages in resources endowments and a supportive political framework. Yet in this section I argue that the regional dispersal of political authority is a third factor that links political articulation to weak developmentalism in India. In considering this argument it is worth reflecting on Gramsci's use of the term *hegemony* as political leadership of the national-popular will. Aside from the importance of a Jacobin force (party) that would impose unity on the scattered forces, the idea

Table 5.1. Share of vote by party in national elections, 1991–2009.

Party	1991	1996	1998	1999	2004	2009
Congress	36.3	28.8	25.8	28.3	26.6	28.5
BJP	20.1	20.3	25.6	23.8	22.2	18.8
JD	11.9	8.1	3.2	3.1	n/a	n/a
CPM	6.2	6.1	5.2	5.4	5.7	5.3

SOURCE: Data from the *Election Commission of India* reports for 1991, 1996, 1998, 1999, 2004 and 2009 (www.eci.nic.in).

of *national* space is crucial for this concept. The emergent articulations under the two Indian parties reflect not only the absence of such a leadership but a dispersed and differentiated concept of political space that reflects the inability of any political actors to construct and thereby represent the "national-popular will."

The critical juncture of the early 1990s, marked as it was by the liberalization push was equally characterized by a growing shift in the balance of power toward state-level political parties and configurations. The share of vote captured by national parties steadily declined, forcing them to enter into coalitions with smaller state-level parties (see Table 5.1). Conversely, between 1991 and 2009 the share of vote captured by state parties in national elections had nearly trebled from 13 percent to 32.6 percent.

This dispersal of authority from the national to state level had two implications. First, because the large state parties were primarily caste based, identity articulations and their primary interest in political alliances were a tactical rather than long-term developmental policy. Second, because they held the balance of power in parliament, the political authority required for a developmental transformation was weakened.

Although the emerging state party formations differed substantially from each other, whether as *dalit* (former untouchable) politics in Uttar Pradesh, lower-caste socialist articulations, or Hindu Right articulations, they shared a common interest in challenging the old Congress consensus-based politics in which lower castes and classes were incorporated into patron–client relations. Although scholars have largely emphasized the fact that such emerging caste or religion-based parties were primarily mobilizing on the basis of identities, the important element they shared in common was that the nature of the antagonisms—Other Backward Castes versus Brahminical Castes, Dalits versus OBCs, OBC plus *dalit* versus Brahmins, or Hindu versus Muslim—was segmented, competitive, and fluid. In Uttar Pradesh, the state that returns the largest number of seats in parliament, the *dalit* movement has undergone several transformations from radical movement to party to catch-all party in search of winning alliances that at times have included other castes (OBCs) and Brahmins (once the sworn enemy). Similar caste equations can be found in other states.

The movements that formed the basis of caste parties, once dubbed the "silent revolution" (Jaffrelot 2003) because of their major challenge to Brahminical domination and political power in the northern states, were a far cry from a Polanyian backlash against the market. The *dalit* Bahujan Samaj Party (BSP), in Uttar Pradesh, formed on the cusp of a mass *dalit* movement during the late 1980s, has embraced liberalization and positioned *dalit* emancipation through the concept of *dalit* capitalism (Lerche 1999). Instead of offering an alternative to the market consensus, what these parties have in common is a shared interest in opposing Congress or BJP dominance at the state level; thus coalition alliances are almost entirely tactical and based on elemental ideological commonalities (for example, opposition to Hindu nationalism). The segmented character of political community and the fluid, ever-shifting alliances and contingent formations that have resulted from the democratization process have thus prevented the rise of developmental coalitions of states and producers, in alliance with the bureaucracy. Instead, bureaucratic recruitment and functioning is determined through a caste-based rather than developmental logic. Despite attempts to form a Third Alliance at several junctures, the major state parties have rarely succeeded in overcoming their ideological differences and rivalries. Thus the conditions for top-down or horizontal developmental coalitions have not been met. One exception is the prosperous Hindu Right–dominated state of Gujarat, where the ideology of Hindu nationalism (and antagonism toward the common enemy of Muslims) facilitated a top-down coalition through the political absorption of subaltern castes into the project of liberalization. Lower castes, whether *dalits* or OBCs, have identified with Hindutva as a means to raise their status in a high-growth, consumerist society, despite the actual prospects for wage increases or stable employment declining in the post-1991 period (Hirway 1995, 2000). Although religion has provided the basis of the BJP articulation that underpins its developmentalist regime, this has also had the effect of undercutting the caste logic that determines state policy in other parts of India. In other words, rather than caste patronage, the spoils of industrial growth and wealth generation from the private sector are appropriated by the upper castes without needing to use the state as a form of patronage (at least to the extent found in other states where there is weak industrial growth). The case of Gujarat is, however, an exception—the norm is that of unstable and antidevelopmental articulations at the regional level (which in turn affect the national level).

The intense competition between parties feeds the rise of (and is fed by) what I call, adapting Mabel Berezin's (2009) use of the term, "thin" political commitments with fragile relationships among parties and cleavages. Although voter studies tend to map preexisting cleavages onto party affiliations, in reality votes by specific castes (the typical unit of voter studies) are often split across several parties. In other words, there are strong divisions *within* castes, which in turn do not constitute the core of any single party.[19] Election surveys show a great deal of fluidity in electoral support from different castes and communities toward particular leaders and parties. The State of the Nation survey (January 2006) revealed, for example, that, in each of the previous four to five elections, roughly 32 percent of the voters voted for different parties. In addition, there are a large number of floating or uncommitted votes at every election who could alter the fortunes of the leaders and candidates even after the election process begins. The National Election Survey 2004 showed that roughly one-third of the respondents chose their candidates or party a day or two before the day of polling or on the day of polling itself (Suri 2004). In a situation where a few percentage points in electoral support could make all the difference, the proportion of floating or undecided voters is not insignificant. In brief, both the division of partisan loyalties across castes, as well as the the centrality of caste and ethnic claims in political articulations at the state level, feed an intense process of competition and consequent instability in Indian politics. The increasing electoral power of caste parties and their importance until 2014 to the formation of parliament thus have direct effects on the kinds of policies that the state can pursue.

CONCLUSION

In this chapter I have discussed pathways and obstacles to developmentalism by bringing parties and their relationships to movements to the center of theoretical explanation. I argue that parties articulate a variety of sectors to create a "bloc" at different historical moments, and these blocs, which cut across dominant and subordinate sectors, can be compatible with market transitions. The articulating role of parties (or other state actors) includes more than mere reflection of preexisting interests—parties can create new interests and identities and build antagonisms on this basis in ways that do not simply reflect pro- or antimarket affiliations. In successful developmental cases such as South Korea, rather than parties it was the state in an authoritarian context that brought about such articulations, especially drawing the rural and urban middle sectors into a developmental bloc. In other cases, such as Costa Rica or even Brazil, a social democratic route to developmentalism was forged by left-of-center parties.

In the case of India, since the early 1990s the BJP and Congress party have created alternative articulations that have been unstable and antidevelopmental. The construction of popular antagonisms can be very fluid in situations where parties and cleavages have a weak connection, and old cleavage politics have disappeared. Although the left versus right distinction was historically weaker in India than in Latin America, for instance, the erosion of Nehruvian socialism has not been replaced by corresponding stable articulations. Neither religious nationalism nor reinvented Nehruvian liberalism has been able to forge a premise for a developmental order. In offering an analysis of a particular historical sequence—from initial reforms in 1991 through the democratization period until 2014—I have argued that what parties did (and failed to do) mattered crucially, indeed determined how the obstacles to developmentalism were shaped and reproduced. In the case of the BJP, Hindu nationalism has until now failed to universalize the multiple demands for welfare, development, employment, and upward mobility, in part because caste offers an alternative language and system of signification for these demands. Thus, in a number of states, except Gujarat, the BJP is confronted by lower-caste parties, or a state-level Congress party that has captured the lower-caste vote on the basis of these demands. It is only in 2014 that, on the basis of a BJP-led alternative articulatory strategy, a successful, explicitly anticaste, proyouth articulation may be emerging (based on the overwhelming vote and decimation of the Left parties and Congress). The Congress Party, on the other hand, is confronted with the regional fragmentation and balance of forces that were set in motion against its prior dominance, many of which took shape as caste-based parties. Its strategy of seeking alliances with nonparty organizations and movements in 2004 and 2009 was in all likelihood a reflection of its inability to form stable alliances with state parties. Its defeat in 2014 suggests that weak, traditional (that is, nonintegral) parties in India face uncertain futures in parliament, a situation that integral parties such as the current BJP can turn to its advantage to craft a hegemonic developmental strategy.

The fluidity of popular antagonisms implies that parties have more autonomy in crafting their base and formulating and implementing policy regimes post-1991, but this also means that they can be voted out suddenly and unexpectedly. Yet incrementalism (hesitant liberalization) cannot be understood any more in terms of the obstructing power of an antimarket coalition of social forces, that is, a coalition of forces who would be adversely affected by market penetration, as such a coalition if it exists is not particularly strong. Incrementalism reflects, rather, the limited horizons of policy making that arise from a situation of inherent volatility, one that is at least partly a product of the parties' own making such as organizational weakness, for example, intraparty factions and weak leadership. These political uncertainties and fragile articulations have in turn given rise to a modicum of autonomous space for neoliberal technocrats to pursue market reforms with support from key ministries. In more general terms, the irony of weak articulations is that they may produce the space for decisive action from above.

Hegemony and Democracy in Gramsci's
Prison Notebooks

Dylan Riley

THE ARTICULATION VIEW PRESENTED in the preceding chapters rests primarily on the theoretical foundations worked out by Antonio Gramsci, particularly in the *Prison Notebooks*. In this, the authors are part of a broader
neo-Gramscian current evident in political sociology (de Leon, Desai, and
Tuğal 2009; de Leon, Desai, and Tuğal, Introduction to this volume; Riley
2010; Tuğal 2009), political theory (Laclau and Mouffe 1985), international relations (Morton 2004, 125–127), and "sociological Marxism" (Burawoy 2003;
Wright 2010). This work has many merits, including an admirable attempt to
combine social structural analyses with a proper appreciation for the specific
autonomy of politics as a form of human activity. But in two key respects the
general theoretical position sketched out in the preceding chapters remains
ambiguous. In particular, it is not always clear in general terms what articulation means, nor is it entirely obvious how articulation is produced. As a result
of these ambiguities the authors never entirely clarify what the role of political
parties is in relation to articulation.

Some of this ambiguity, I will argue, can be cleared up with some careful
attention to Gramsci's original argument about hegemony. This is not to suggest that the Sardinian's work is a sacred text containing the answers to ongoing research problems. However, my thought is that a careful examination of
the basic Gramscian framework can provide a useful heuristic for the further
development of the articulation position.

The concept of hegemony has already generated a substantial, indeed overwhelming, body of scholarship. But most of it can be placed into one of two
positions. One interpretation views hegemony as a theory of revolutionary

dictatorship: a "Leninism" for the West (Galli della Loggia 1977, 69; Salvadori 1977, 40–41). These writers tend to be highly critical of the various attempts by the Partito Comunista Italiano (Italian Communist Party, PCI) to use Gramsci as a symbolic justification for the party's moderate postwar strategy. As Galli della Loggia (1977, 69) acerbically noted in the late seventies:

> That Antonio Gramsci's ideological convictions, and the political and strategic proposals that follow from them can be made consistent with, or at least adapted to, the schemes of contemporary parliamentary democracy is an idea that, despite the prodigious theoretical efforts made by the communist party in the last twenty years, shows itself to have little substance as soon as one reads or re-reads the texts with an open mind.

This interpretation of Gramsci, based on the notion of a revolutionary vanguard party, places him firmly in the political tradition of the Third International. The second position, currently and most vigorously expressed by the director of the Fondazione Istituto Gramsci (Gramsci Foundation Institute), Giuseppe Vacca, holds that "there is no hegemony without democracy" (1999, 24), a view that may be more familiar to social scientists from the work of Laclau and Mouffe (1985, 176), on whom the editors of this volume also draw in developing their concept of political articulation. Scholars who advocate this interpretation of Gramsci tend to present his *Prison Notebooks* as a sharp break with Lenin's ideas about the state and revolutionary strategy. According to this position, Gramsci is a theorist of radical democracy, not a Lenin for the West.

I am quite skeptical of both these readings of Gramsci. The first washes away his originality, transforming him from a highly original thinker into an orthodox Leninist. The second domesticizes a man who remained to the end of his life committed to the revolutionary overthrow of capitalism. A useful starting point for breaking with both these positions is Perry Anderson's article on the "Antinomies of Antonio Gramsci." Anderson points out that the concept of hegemony was extremely widespread in Russian Marxism (1976–1977, 17–18). But whereas in this debate it referred to an alliance between workers and peasants in which workers would play the leading role, Gramsci in the *Prison Notebooks* "now employed the concept of hegemony for a *differential analysis of the structures of bourgeois power in the West*" (20). From Anderson's perspective then, hegemony should be understood as an explanation for the operation of class rule in advanced capitalism, not an incipient theory of radical democracy. This is a crucial point and correctly identifies an important area of continuity and difference between Gramsci and Lenin. However, although Anderson's essay suggestively points to a way of reconciling the two meanings usually associated with hegemony, his claim that Gramsci's originality lies primarily in applying the concept to bourgeois power remains far too limited.

I would propose a slightly different interpretation from Anderson's, one that understands hegemony as a general form of political relationship potentially applicable to both revolutionary politics and advanced democracies.

GRAMSCI'S VIEW OF HEGEMONY

Hegemony, generally speaking, is the fusion of the particular interests of some social group with the general interests of some broader social group and at the limit with the general interest of society. This fusion is the basis for the broad alliance of social groups characteristic of effective political agency that the editors of this volume term *political articulation*; articulation thus means a process of the identification of particular with general interests. But Gramsci discusses two forms of hegemony, and their operation is quite different. One form of hegemony is primarily political, organizational, and cultural. The second form of hegemony is economic, or at least based on interests, and can only be fully understood in terms of class-specific terms.

I start with the first form of hegemony. Gramsci discusses this form in his analysis of the relations between the Moderates and the Party of Action in the Italian Risorgimento, which turns around the following question: Why did the more conservative liberal "Moderates" win out in their struggle against the more democratic "Action Party" in the struggles over Italian unification? Gramsci provides two somewhat different answers to this question. One refers to Italy's relatively low level of economic development and the international circumstances of the unification period (Gramsci 1971, 82–83; Gramsci 2007, 2032). But this is a relatively subordinate theme in Gramsci's argument, for he believes that "subjective rather than objective reasons" explain the victory of the Moderates (Gramsci 1971, 82; Gramsci 2007, 2032). The reason that the Moderates won out against the Party of Action is that they had close organizational ties to the Piedmontese bourgeois aristocracy, which in turn was the main social force for national unification. As Gramsci writes, "They were intellectuals and political organizers, and at the same time company bosses, rich farmers or estate managers, commercial and industrial entrepreneurs"

(Gramsci 1971, 60; Gramsci 2007, 2012). Gramsci says that they were the "organic intellectuals" of this group in the sense that they represented "'specializations' of partial aspects of the primitive activity" of the Piedmontese ruling class. Gramsci suggests that this gave the Moderates an organizational weight that the Party of Action lacked. As he puts the point, "the Moderates exercised a powerful attraction 'spontaneously,' on the whole mass of intellectuals of every degree who existed in the peninsula, in a 'diffused,' 'molecular' state, to provided for the requirements, however rudimentarily satisfied, of education and administration" (ibid.).

In contrast to the Moderates, the Party of Action lacked any strong organizational links to a specific social class. Rather, in the terminology of the note on intellectuals, we can understand the Party of Action as a group of traditional intellectuals, a stratum with few connections to any decisive historical class. Gramsci (1971, 63; 2007, 2014) describes this group as:

> ... steeped in the traditional rhetoric of Italian literature. It confused the cultural unity which existed in the peninsula—confined, however, to a very thin stratum of the population, and polluted by the Vatican's cosmopolitanism—with the political and territorial unity of the great popular masses, who were foreign to that cultural tradition and who, even supposing they knew of its existence, couldn't care less about it.

Being dispersed and delinked from any significant social class, this group turned out to be mobilizable into different class coalitions. The success of the Moderates lay in their ability to bring these traditional intellectuals, the Action Party, into a coalition with themselves in a subordinate position. The Moderates were able to do this not only because they were organic intellectuals but also because they were able to develop a concrete and realistic program for unifying Italy. The important analytic point here is that there is no fundamental economic reason why the Action Party could not have become a hegemonic force. Its weaknesses were instead primarily organizational and political. The hegemonic struggle, the struggle for articulation, was thus here primarily political and organizational.

Gramsci, however, uses the concept of hegemony in a second, and very different, sense in the *Prison Notebooks*. In this second sense hegemony means the ability to solidify hegemonic alliances by delivering concrete material advantages to subordinate groups. This form of hegemony emerges for the first time under capitalism. For, as Przeworski convincingly demonstrates,

Gramsci saw capitalist class interests as distinctively linked to the promotion of economic growth. Therefore, in capitalism, and only in capitalism, the private appropriation of surplus can appear as the precondition for long-term improvement in the material circumstances of direct producers. The claim of capitalist classes to represent the general interests therefore has a real economic foundation: It is not strictly political, organizational, or cultural. In contrast in economic systems in which the interests of surplus appropriators do not appear as the precondition for long-term improvement in the material circumstances of direct producers, hegemony will have a more cultural or ideological content. But even this second form of hegemony is politically mediated because, even if a ruling class has the capacity to provide tangible material benefits to the underlying population, whether it does so depends on political processes and is not itself economically determined.

So far I have suggested that Gramsci was working with at least two notions of hegemony. One was organizational and political and the second economic. Because they are so different, the two forms of hegemony do not at all imply one another. In fact there are many instances in which the establishment of political organizational hegemony might undermine economic hegemony. Indeed, this is precisely Gramsci's broader point about the Risorgimento.

It is worth noting that Gramsci's main empirical discussion of the development of hegemony, the emergence of the Italian state, is an instance of hegemonic failure—not success. The success of the Moderates in achieving political and organizational hegemony within the Italian bourgeoisie during the Risorgimento had negative consequences for the ability of the Italian bourgeoisie as a whole to establish economic hegemony after unification.

Because the Moderates won out in their struggle with the Party of Action, the transition to a capitalist society in Italy occurred as a passive revolution. As Gramsci (1971, 59; 2007, 2011) wrote:

> It was precisely the brilliant solution of these problems which made the Risorgimento possible, in the form in which it was achieved (and with its limitations)—as "revolution" without a "revolution," or as "passive revolution" to use an expression of Cuoco's in a slightly different sense from that which Cuoco intended.

The victory of the Moderates over the Party of Action meant that the Italian bourgeoisie never experienced a heroic period in which it led a popular coalition against feudalism. Rather, the older feudal aristocracy and the rising bourgeoisie formed a rough working coalition and established some elements of a capitalist society, without carrying out the basic political tasks of bourgeois democracy. The significance of the struggle between the Moderates and the Party of Action is that the victory of the Moderates opened up a path of modernization that politically weakened the Italian bourgeoisie in the long run.

What then, was the long-term consequence of the victory of the Moderates within the bourgeois coalition, for the nature of class relationships after the Risorgimento? The basic thrust of this argument is simple enough. Precisely because the Moderates win out in the struggle against the Party of Action, the Italian state coalesces after the Risorgimento in a nonhegemonic form.

As Gramsci says of the Italian bourgeoisie, "They aimed at stimulating the formations of an extensive and energetic ruling class, and they did not succeed at integrating the people into the framework of the new state" (Gramsci 1971, 90; Gramsci 2007, 2053–2054). They did not succeed because the basis of the program on which the Moderates could present themselves as the hegemonic fraction within the Italian bourgeoisie was basically incompatible with the interests of the peasantry (Gramsci 1971, 61; Gramsci 2007, 2012–2013).

During the political and social crisis of the late nineteenth century this incapacity emerged again as Italian political elites chose to base themselves on "a capitalist/worker industrial bloc, without universal suffrage, with tariff barriers, with the preservation of a highly centralized State (the expression of bourgeois dominations over the peasants, especially in the South and the Islands), and with a reformist policy on wage and trade union freedoms" (Gramsci 1995, 29). In sum, the political and organizational hegemony that Moderates achieved within the Italian bourgeoisie as a whole undermined the formation of a strong material or economic hegemony over the direct producers.

The contrast to this case of failed Italian hegemony is the successful French case. Gramsci discusses this in terms of the concept of Jacobinism. From Gramsci's perspective, the main point about France is that the Jacobins were able to maximize the "magnetic force" of the French bourgeoisie. They did so by converting the demands of the "Third Estate," which were initially the demands of a limited corporate group, into the most general possible form. Thus, the French Revolution, which began with a set of complaints on the part of group within the Old Regime, became the demand for a national assembly. This allowed the French bourgeoisie to form an alliance with the peasantry limited only by the outer bounds of the class interests of the bourgeoisie, but the merit of the Jacobins is that they pushed the bourgeoisie to the very limits of its hegemonic capacity (Gramsci 1971, 79; Gramsci 2007, 2029). It is important that the ability of the French Jacobins to establish this alliance was based on their revolutionary political program.

This reading of Gramsci resonates with much of the basic message of the essays in this volume, but it also provides a way of contextualizing their arguments more fully within the Marxian tradition to which Gramsci obviously belonged. I might summarize the argument by saying that, although fundamental economic interests fix the hegemonic capacity of any dominant class, whether or not that capacity will actually be translated into hegemony, or a form of political articulation, is almost an entirely political matter. Probably more analytic work and research need to be done to precisely identify the range of hegemonic possibilities open to specific groups. However, Gramsci's scheme has an important merit. It accords politics a central, but also quite precisely circumscribed, space in the construction of hegemony. I return to this point in the conclusion.

HEGEMONY AND DEMOCRACY

Having sketched both Gramsci's conception of hegemony and his explanation of it, I now turn to the issue of democracy. Democracy and hegemony are closely connected concepts, but the notion of hegemony is more fundamental. Hegemony, broadly, is the foundation of democracy, and the existence of a functioning democracy is a sure sign of a consolidated hegemony. My view is that Gramsci understands democracy as the form that class rule assumes after the establishment of a fully fledged hegemony as a consequence of a revolutionary break with the past. Because such a break is a precondition for hegemony in Gramsci's sense, it is also a precondition for a fully functioning democracy.

The relationship between democracy and hegemony is best understood by thinking through Gramsci's connection to Lenin. Gramsci shared with Lenin two important arguments about democracy, and there is no evidence that he ever wavered from these. First, democracy in capitalist society was possible only when the working class did not challenge the basic pillars of ruling class power, particularly private property. Thus, from Gramsci's perspective there is no way to institute socialism (a regime defined by a fundamental alternation in the property regime) democratically. Second, true democracy is incompatible with the state, because state power is by definition a violation of the rule of the people (Lenin 1975, 323). A radical democratization of society remained a goal for Gramsci, but representative democracy, as a state form, was an inadequate means to achieve it.

From Gramsci's perspective, revolutions must always pass through a crisis that typically leads to a period of Bonapartism or Caesarism, which "represents the fusion of an entire social class under a single leadership, which alone is held to be capable of solving an overriding problem of its existence and of fending off a mortal danger" (Gramsci 1971, 211; 2007, 1604). This is the aspect of Gramsci's thought that forms the basis of Salvadori's claim that Gramsci basically saw himself as supplementing Leninism, rather than replacing it with something fundamentally different (Salvadori 1977, 44). To summarize, for Gramsci the nature of politics depends above all on whether fundamental class issues are at stake. When a ruling class is stably in the saddle, politics is primarily a matter of consent, and democracy can function. During periods of political crisis when political movements with contending visions of the state arise, politics becomes more a matter of force, and democracy must recede.

PARTIES, CLASSES, AND REVOLUTION

Gramsci's argument suggests that the tasks of a revolutionary party differ dramatically from those of a postrevolutionary or prerevolutionary party. A revolutionary party must fuse all of the elements of a single social class around itself in preparation for a final seizure of state power. The strategy here is to ensure "that the members of a particular party find in the party all the satisfactions that they formerly found in a multiplicity of organizations" and that alternative organizations are either destroyed or incorporated into this new single party (Gramsci 1971, 265). But this moment of concentration cannot last if the new class is to establish hegemony. The single party must recede, leaving a realm of pluralistic competition within the structural framework of a new class structure, for consolidated hegemony requires political pluralism (Gramsci 1971, 265). Two thinkers, extraordinarily different from one another, and both of them very different from Gramsci himself, perhaps grasped this point better than the Sardinian himself: Rosa Luxemburg and Karl Kautsky.

Kautsky, in his much-reviled critique of the Russian Revolution, argued, "One and the same class interest can be represented in very different ways, by various tactical methods" (Kautsky 1964, 31). For him the Bolshevik's basic error consisted in conflating party with class in arguing that only they represented the interest of the proletariat: a claim that from Kautsky's perspective was demonstrably false. Luxemburg (2004, 305), who of course hated Kautsky's reformism, also argued that the articulation of class interests required political pluralism *within the class*. Gramsci is similar to both these thinkers in rejecting a general theory of the role of parties. "Ethical parties" or "totalitarian parties" emerge at the beginning of a period in which a class seeks to establish its hegemony. However, fully developed hegemony cannot rest on a single party with a heavy-handed ideology, because hegemony depends on pluralism and at least relative political freedom.

BUILDING BLOCS: POSSIBILITIES AND IMPOSSIBILITIES OF A NEO-GRAMSCIAN RESEARCH PROGRAM ON PARTIES

What light do these reflections shed on the fascinating and imaginative case studies in this volume? These chapters, taken together, have effectively put parties at the center of historically oriented social science where they rightly belong. Further, and more ambitiously, they have begun to sketch out an exciting neo-Gramscian research program. In this section of my chapter I want to touch on what I see as three basic areas in need of analytic clarification and empirical research drawing loosely on my understanding of Gramsci as previously presented.

The Question of Class

Given their focus on political parties, it is natural that questions of class analysis as such should recede somewhat in the earlier chapters. And yet a class analysis, as I hope to have showed in the preceding pages is central to the original Gramscian agenda and is presumed in many of the chapters in this book, particularly in those of de Leon, Eidlin, and Tuğal. Each of these essays in different ways addresses the problem of class formation or class alliances. De Leon shows, in a gripping analysis of politics in nineteenth-century Chicago, how Democrats and Republicans politically organized the working class in different ways. He relates the Haymarket uprising to the collapse of the Republican bloc, which had organized workers as independent men, who were both antislavery and antisocialist (the two being linked in a bizarre rhetorical construction) (de Leon, Chapter 1 in this volume). Tuğal uses class analysis in a somewhat different way by suggesting that the basic social groups available to the AKP in Turkey and the Muslim Brotherhood in Egypt were similar but that, whereas the AKP was able to unite them around a neoliberal and vaguely liberal democratic project, the Brotherhood was unable to do so partly because of its association with legalism (Tuğal, Chapter 3 in this volume). Eidlin (Chapter 2 in this volume) perhaps is the most explicit here, as his analysis bears on the political coalition of workers and farmers in the CCF.

However, despite its empirical centrality in these chapters, I would argue that class needs to be made much more analytically central to the entire project of neo-Gramscian political sociology as sketched out in these chapters. This is so as much for methodological as for theoretical reasons. The basic point of this research program is to emphasize the importance of politics in the constitution of social identities and more specifically to underline the role of political parties. And yet, to show that politics matters requires the idea of a prepolitical identity, that is, a social class or some equivalent, that *could* be organized in different ways. It is precisely the gap between what is politically possible and what actually occurred that shows the importance of politics. But of course the concept of different politically possible coalitions implies that there are some coalitions that are impossible. In effect, to show the importance of politics requires that its limits be carefully specified. This is the point that Laclau and Mouffe forget when they reduce hegemony to a contingent linguistic practice. Paradoxically their "politics is everything" perspective is methodologically equivalent to absolute determinism. What is needed to demonstrate the importance of politics is a gap between social identity and political expression. I have tried to suggest in the preceding pages that this is precisely what Gramsci's concept of hegemony is designed to do. Of course de Leon, Desai, and Tuğal distance themselves from post-Marxism by stressing that their concept of political articulation is an organizational, rather than linguistic, one. Yet they skate dangerously close to a self-defeating poststructuralism in arguing, "Neither class, nor religious communities, nor ethnic groups have self-reproducing logics that bind them together" (de Leon, Desai, and Tuğal, Introduction to this volume). To be clear, I believe that my own work, which is broadly in this tradition, has at times moved too close to a political determinism as well. In sum, in my view the neo-Gramscian program needs a firmer foundation in class analysis precisely so that it can show the importance of the political.

Hegemony: Incipient versus Consolidated

A second issue that emerges from these papers is how we should think about the relationship between what might be thought of as incipient and consolidated hegemony. I have already touched on this issue in the discussion of democracy. This point is relevant to all of the analyses but particularly in the chapters from Desai, Slater, and Tuğal. Desai's chapter focuses on the failure of either the BJP or Congress to articulate an effective political bloc. She argues that this is one reason for the relatively low degree of developmentalism on the subcontinent despite the weakness of organized labor (Desai, Chapter 5 in this volume). Slater's chapter is an analysis of why an initially highly structured party sphere disintegrated after Indonesia's transition to democracy. In an argument that reproduces virtually exactly Gramsci's analysis of the Italian political system of *trasformismo* Slater (Chapter 4 in this volume) attributes fragmentation to the cartelization of politics, itself the contingent outcome of a split ticket for the presidential candidate in the 1999 elections. Tuğal (Chapter 3 in this volume) also contrasts the hegemonic AKP with the nonhegemonic Muslim Brotherhood.

All three of these analyses assume a strict relationship between party strength and hegemony—or "articulation," in the preferred terminology of the editors. But this seems to me a perhaps strained generalization from a set of highly specific historical situations. Integral parties that, as the authors emphasize, "attempt to redefine institutional rules, refashion political . . . language, and redraw the map of the sociopolitical blocs" are likely to be associated not with established hegemony but with incipient or weak hegemony (de Leon et al., Introduction to this volume). When a social class is truly hegemonic, it does not require organization into a party. As Gramsci himself was aware, the most well-established capitalist classes never ruled through a single party but rather through a system of alternating political parties. By contrast in the truly exceptional periods in which a particular social class organizes itself in a single political party with a highly articulated worldview, one can be sure that it is *not fully* hegemonic. For example, this absence of hegemony was for Gramsci characteristic of both the Italian bourgeoisie and the Russian proletariat in the interwar period. It explained the partial convergence in the organizational form of the respective "integral" or "ethical" political parties of these two groups. In short, I think that the authors are right to emphasize the importance of integral parties in the construction of hegemony, but

I think it would be useful to distinguish the role of parties sharply from this under periods of established hegemony.

Socialism

One final issue I think is important to consider. It is useful to remember that the model of the integral party is some combination of Bolshevism and German Social Democracy. But this model has been gravely weakened by the neoliberal counterrevolution that began in 1989. The collapse of the Soviet Union did not just eliminate an economic alternative to capitalism; it also eliminated a political alternative, cadre organization (with the partial exception of the Muslim world, as Tuğal shows) (Therborn 2008, 58). Given the national focus of the chapters in this volume it is natural that the Soviet collapse and the triumph of liberalism on a world scale is not a central focus. Yet it intrudes particularly in Slater's and Desai's chapters. After all, one of the main differences between Indonesia's first experience with parliamentary democracy in the 1950s and the more recent period is the presence in the first of the Indonesian Communist Party, and its absence in the second period (Slater, Chapter 4 in this volume). Similarly Desai (Chapter 5 in this volume) speaks of the "global institutional and discursive break" that occurred in 1991. This raises two main analytic issues. First, of course, it points to the need for a more serious analysis of how global patterns of political transformation affect the formation of parties. Second, it suggests that the claim of the importance of the integral party form needs to be carefully historicized. The Owl of Minerva flies at dusk. Is it perhaps the case that de Leon, Desai, and Tuğal are coming to an analysis of the integral party form precisely as it passing out of existence as a living historical reality? If that is so, what will be the shape of Modern Prince in the twenty-first century? That perhaps is the central question facing the neo-Gramscian program going forward.

REFERENCE MATTER

NOTES

Introduction. Political Articulation: The Structured Creativity of Parties

1. Here we are inspired by Jacques Lacan's discussion of "interpellation," though our debts to and differences from his followers (who are mostly concentrated in the humanities) will be discussed elsewhere in order not to divert attention away from our social scientific interventions.

2. This list is not exhaustive. Chapter 3, on Turkey and Egypt, demonstrates that even a court case and naturalization of new lifestyles can be turned into means of articulation, but further research is necessary to conclude whether these are typical means of articulation.

3. The resulting "index of political predisposition" consisted of three variables—socioeconomic status, religion, and rural versus urban residence—which accounted for most of the variation in vote choice. They wrote, "A person thinks, politically, as he is, socially. Social characteristics determine political preference" (Lazarsfeld et al. [1944] 1948, 27).

4. This is a caricature too often employed against the sociological approach and is, in any case, unnecessary (see, for example, Przeworski and Sprague 1986, 7–8).

5. The freezing hypothesis has been refuted many times over by scholars and observers of neoconservative and environmental parties, among others.

6. For a more comprehensive review of the social psychological approach, see Bartels (2008), Carmines and Huckfledt (1996), and Converse (2006). The landmarks in the social psychological approach are Campbell et al. (1954), Campbell et al. (1960), Converse (1964, 1966) and Stokes (1963). More contemporary applications include Green et al. (2002), Miller and Shanks (1996), and Smith (1989).

7. In this context, one can also talk of relatively more optimistic and more pessimistic strands. For instance, while "moderation theory" (Kalyvas 1996; Schwedler 2006) is generally laudatory of the role of pragmatic parties in toning down the radical claims of movements (which allows them to be incorporated into democratic regimes), some recent revisionists have questioned whether such deradicalization necessarily brings about democratization (Tezcür 2010).

8. For an early precursor to this approach, which is actually closer to our position because of the centrality of the party for maintaining or even creating social order, see Huntington (1968).

9. Even though Orloff (1993) does emphasize the "training, organization, and ties to . . . groups" of *state officials* as a part of her theoretical framework, such characteristics of politicians are only discussed under the heading of "elites," rather than being distinctly conceptualized.

10. It should be noted that Steinmetz (1999) stands much closer to this contextualist perspective when compared to other sociologists of state formation.

11. This is reminiscent of Weber's argument in "Class, Status, Party" (1946, 180–194).

12. On this account, there is a tension between most of Przeworski's writing; for example, see Przeworski (1985, chapters 1, 4, and 5, especially pp. 152–156), where he assumes, based on rational choice theory, that workers' basic economic interests are not only knowable independently of politics but mathematically measurable and transparent to the workers themselves and his influential essay on the political making of identities (Przeworski 1985, chapter 2).

13. It should be noted that there is no one-way causation in any of these processes, all determined by multiple causes.

14. Despite these insights, parts of the *Prison Notebooks* also feature traditional Marxist assumptions about correspondence between parties' ideology and class base, as well as assumptions of a linear history, where parties shoulder certain roles in a teleological dialectic (for example, Gramsci [1929–1933] 1992, 320–322, and [1930–1932] 2007, 108).

15. For the articulation to become consolidated, "a certain identity needs to be picked up from the whole field differences, and made to embody [a] totalizing function." This is what Laclau means by a "privileged" identity (2005, 81). Likewise, some elements of the social should be excluded as not belonging to the people. Much of this draws on Althusser's (1969) analysis of the Russian Revolution, though Laclau introduces his own poststructural logic into what he borrows from this structural neo-Marxist predecessor.

16. Laclau (2005) differentiates between institutional and populist politics. In the first variety of politics, differences are dealt within the system; so, politics does not

advance beyond the first step. Only in populist politics is there a differentiation of society into two antagonistic blocs (79–83). We see this as a huge advance over Laclau and Mouffe's work in the 1980s, where they insisted that the logic of "two camps" was no longer applicable to Western societies. Some of our case studies provide empirical refutation of that claim.

17. Explanations are offered only in passing, such as "these signifiers acquire this articulating role according, *obviously*, to a contextual history" (Laclau 2005, 87, emphasis added); Laclau provides a few historical narratives to show how certain demands and identities become or fail to become articulators (for example, 90–93, 133–138). We hold that this allegedly "obvious" link should be problematized by breaking down such contextual histories into their constituent sociological elements.

18. There is a place for leaders in Laclau's (2005, 99–100) theoretical framework but only as functions of the discursive logic, rather than experts embedded in institutions and organizations.

19. Here, we are heeding Bob Jessop's call to integrate Laclau and Mouffe's useful insights without falling into their discourse-centrism (1982, 199–200, 210).

20. We thus seek to restore to the concept of articulation its full sociological potential. Even though we want to avoid, as much as Laclau, the dialectical-teleological assumptions in Gramsci, we insist that aspects of his historicism (analytical focus on the formation of institutions, intellectuals, politicians, and soldiers) should be a part of any analysis of articulation, in order not to lapse into Laclau and Mouffe's discourse-centrism. In our sociological take on political articulation, history is neither a teleological nor a purposeless process. It is a contingent process overdetermined by multiple causes, which can potentially go in all kinds of different directions (where many sectors, demands and identities are bound to remain at least partially isolated). However, there are collective wills that articulate disparate identities and give an overall direction to history. The purpose of history is created in the process.

21. Although the group lost control over the process in this case too, in many historical cases the loss of control fluctuates more broadly. In this regard, one can contrast the arguably more intense input of the working classes in Scandinavian social democratic parties to their relatively more quick loss of control over party bureaucrats in the English case.

22. We also take stock of Bourdieu's (pp. 13–14) recognition that such group making as "worldmaking" brings together with it new ways of using words, classifying concepts, and associating certain traits with certain groups, which are all parallel to Laclau and Mouffe's focus on the making of chains of equivalence.

23. Another lineage we would like to acknowledge is psychoanalytic and goes back to the work of Jacques Lacan, the first thinker to use the concept of articulation in a systematic way—not, however, in the constitution of society, but of the individual

"subject." Althusser then generalized this usage and paved the way for Laclau's approach.

24. Hegemony is frequently defined, drawing on Gramsci, as the acceptance of the interests of the dominant class as "general interest." What we further emphasize is that the making, sustenance, and naturalization of even the dominant class itself are a part of the process of articulation. Likewise, what scholars call "general" in this formulation is itself an articulated whole.

25. See Gramsci ([1931–1932] 2007, 209, 382) for similar remarks.

Chapter 1. The Political Origins of Working Class Formation in the United States

I would like to thank Fred Block, Lis Clemens, Manali Desai, and the anonymous reviewers of Stanford University Press for their instructive comments on previous drafts of this chapter.

1. Przeworski would later abandon the Marxist framework in favor of rational choice theory. See, for example, Przeworski 1991.

2. The Republicans deftly suppressed anti-immigrant elements in their midst so as to secure the support of the vast majority of German voters, while retaining a specifically anti-Catholic posture that alienated the Irish and other Catholics, but in doing so they further cemented their support among Protestants and secularists (see Bergquist 1971, 209, 215, 217–219, 221).

Chapter 2. Continuity or Change?

The author would like to thank Kim Voss, Dylan Riley, Julia Adams, Maria Akchurin, Elisabeth Clemens, Cedric de Leon, Fred Eidlin, Neil Fligstein, Chad Goldberg, Jeff Haydu, Richard Lachmann, Mara Loveman, Michael McCarthy, Erin McDonnell, James Naylor, Ann Orloff, Michael Schwartz, Dan Slater, Adam Slez, Cihan Tuğal, Margaret Weir, Nick Wilson, Erik Olin Wright, the participants in the UC Berkeley Center for Culture, Organizations, and Politics colloquium and the UC Berkeley Labor Transformations Working Group, as well as two anonymous reviewers at Stanford University Press for helpful comments on previous versions of this chapter.

Archival data for this project were collected over the course of fourteen months between September 2008 and November 2009. Archives visited include:

- Library and Archives Canada, Ottawa, Ontario
- Confédération des syndicats nationaux (CSN) Library, Montreal, Canada
- Wisconsin Historical Society, Madison, Wisconsin

1. Although the party was officially founded in 1933 with the adoption of the Regina Manifesto, the initial gathering was held in Calgary in 1932.

2. Here we see echoes of the U.S. case described in the previous chapter, where the Republican Party's failed articulation of workers created space for socialist challengers to articulate a new working-class political identity.

3. Although these organizations considered themselves national in scope, in reality most activity was limited to industrializing pockets of Ontario and Quebec.

Chapter 3. Religious Politics, Hegemony, and the Market Economy

1. Berna Turam (2004) has developed a similar perspective on civil society.

2. The term *legalistic* here is only meant to point out that the key agents of Islamic mobilization in Egypt focus relatively more on the legal code; it does not imply that they exclude illegal ways of operating. The use of this term should not bring to mind the legal versus illegal dichotomy: Legalistic Islam should be thought in terms of its difference from liberalized Islam.

3. One goal, then, should be to account for why such a party emerged in Turkey but not in Egypt. The two following sections will focus on the monopolization of political capital and the professionalization of politicians in accounting for this emergence but also point out the role played by intellectuals, the practices of rival sociopolitical projects, state formation, foundational moments in party and/or movement formation, and civic activity.

4. Important exceptions are liberal secular associations, which have also supported (liberalized) Islamic forces in the last ten years.

5. For the internal contradictions of this Owenite, yet still developmentalist, program, which led to serious problems for the Islamist party, see Buğra (2002).

6. Kemalism denotes a nationalist, rigid secularist and authoritarian political line in Turkey, as differentiated from the moderate secularist and less authoritarian center-right.

7. Note that "liberalized" does not denote "completely free and democratic" in this chapter. Goals and strategies of Turkish Islamism were "liberalized," but they were not consistently liberal. This liberalization should be taken contextually. In other words, Turkish Islamism could be called conservative in a Western context, but it was "liberalized" in comparison to its own past and to other major movements in the region. For example, creationism and antigay mobilization were becoming core aspects of Islamism in 2010, replacing proshariah and pro-Islamic state mobilization.

8. This purge (and other self-destructive moves on the part of CHP) was not a *necessary* condition for AKP success, but such moves *changed the balances in the game*: If the CHP had retained, yet updated, its integral orientations of the 1970s, the Islamic party would not have the same free ride as it did in the 2000s, even though there is no way to retrospectively predict whether it could still become the governing party.

9. See Zollner (2007) for the political roots of this moderation in a split within the Muslim Brotherhood in the 1960s.

10. Sadat's administration had paved the road for this decisive move by positing in the 1971 constitution that Islam has a primary role in legislation (Al-Awadi 2005, 37, 41).

11. Even the more pragmatic and business-oriented Islamic activists in poor quarters remain opposed to the state (Ismail 2006, 52–57).

12. See Tuğal (2012) for further analysis of political economic similarities and differences between the two cases. Some of the paragraphs here also draw on that article.

13. Despite these proclamations, when the military actually intervened to disperse the protesters in the Square, the Guidance Bureau criticized this action.

14. However, this does not mean that the Brotherhood was directly responsible for police violence: The Brotherhood did not seem to have control over the police, most of which were still Mubarak loyalists (see Ellis Goldberg, "Whatever Happened to Egypt's Democratic Transition?" March 3, 2013; available at www.jadaliyya.com/pages/index/10444/whatever-happened-to-egypts-democratic-transition).

15. Parts of this analysis are based on Khalil al-'Anani, "Halat al-Islamiyyin fi Masr ba'ad 'amayn 'ala al-Thawra,"; retrieved on January 28, 2013, from www.jadaliyya.com/pages/index/9823/.

16. For example, see "Mutashaddidun al-Islamiyyun Yattahimun Jabhat al-Inqadh bi Tabanni al-'unf Qabil Mudhaharat Siyasiyya al-Yawm," *al-Sharq al-Awsat*, February 15, 2013; "Mustashar al-Ri'asa al-Masriyya al-Maqal li al-Sharq al-Awsat: al-Ikhwan Yaghraqun . . . Hawwalna Inqadhhum wa Rafadu," *al-Sharq al-Awsat*, February 19, 2013.

17. For further analysis of the coup, see Tuğal (2014).

18. See Ellis Goldberg, "Whatever Happened to Egypt's Democratic Transition?"; and "Egypt's Political Crisis," *The Middle East Channel, Foreign Policy*, December 10, 2012.

19. I offer a more detailed analysis of how the Gezi Revolt and the AKP–Gülen fallout put liberal–conservative hegemony in question in the following two essays: "Occupy Gezi: The Limits of Turkey's Neoliberal Success," June 4. 2013; available at www.jadaliyya.com/pages/index/12009/occupy-gezi_the-limits-of-turkey%E2%80%99s-neoliberal-succ; and "Towards the End of a Dream? The Erdogan–Gulen Fallout and Islamic Liberalism's Descent," December 22. 2013; available at www.jadaliyya.com/pages/index/15693/towards-the-end-of-a-dream-the-erdogan-gulen-fallo.

20. The evidence regarding this contrast is too extensive to evaluate here. On top of the ethnographic and comparative-historical observations offered in this essay, the following can serve as entry points into the issue. For the spread of the work ethic among Turkish and Kurdish Muslims, see Tuğal (2009) and the European Stability Initiative "Islamic Calvinists: Change and Conservatism in Central Anatolia," September 19, 2005; available at (www.esiweb.org/pdf/esi_document_id_69.pdf). Bottom-up ethnographies in Egypt emphasize text- rather than work-oriented ethics

(Mahmood 2005). Moreover, even charitable associations in Turkey are now bent on turning people into hard-working Muslims (Can 2007). Although there are similar developments in Egypt (Atia 2012), they are secondary and subordinated to an orthodox understanding of charity (Tuğal 2013; also see Davis and Robertson 2012).

Chapter 4. Democratic Disarticulation and Its Dangers

1. The concept of a "cartel party" was first elaborated in the Western European context by Katz and Mair (1995). In their initial formulation, these authors implied that a cartel was one in which all significant parties shared executive power. Although they have explicitly relaxed this requirement in their recent reformulation (2009, 757), Indonesia's original cartel clearly met the stiffer standard of an arrangement in which all significant parties were in, and none was out. These authors' relaxed definition of a party cartel accords rather closely with my notion of promiscuous power-sharing, which in my usage may or may not amount to a full-blown party cartel. To be clear, then, Indonesia has experienced promiscuous power-sharing from 1999 to the present but had a full-blown party cartel in place only from 1999 to 2004.

2. The PNI was also initially quite strong among what Geertz (1976) termed the "*priyayi*" *aliran*, or the Javanese bureaucratic and aristocratic elite.

3. Convenient as it may sound to label this side of the religious cleavage "secular" rather than "nationalist," I consider this formulation to be importantly inaccurate. All Indonesians must believe in a single God under the Pancasila, hence secularism is not an option (Menchik 2014). The "Islamic-nationalist" distinction serves as an important "category of practice" (Brubaker 2006) among contemporary Indonesians, making it the best available update of Geertz's classic "*santri–abangan*" divide.

4. One might also term this the "communist–noncommunist cleavage," beause it channeled differences in ideology as well as class and because noncommunists transcended class boundaries. Yet the destruction of Indonesian communism had devastating effects on the class cleavage that have outlasted the Cold War, and this warrants special historical emphasis.

5. Specifically, the PNI received 22.3 percent of the vote, Masjumi 20.9 percent (but the exact same number of seats as PNI due to malapportionment), NU 18.4 percent, and PKI 16.4 percent.

6. All non-Golkar parties fared badly but not equally so. The NU gained similar support in 1971 as it had in 1955, whereas the PNI saw its support collapse as civil servants (especially) sided (as required) with Golkar.

7. This is not to say that Golkar is devoid of *aliran* leanings or roots in social cleavages. Scholars such as King (2003) portray Golkar as a descendent of Masyumi, given its particular strength in certain Muslim organizational circles, especially in regions off Java.

8. Precise positioning within each quadrant is more heuristic than systematic, but it should be relatively uncontroversial in which quadrant each party belongs. The hardest task is placing PAN and PKB, which could reasonably be put on either side of the Islamic–nationalist divide. The reason PKB is placed further to the nationalist side is that both the party's platform and the party leader's reputation were resolutely pluralistic, whereas PAN leader Amien Rais lacked Abdurrahman Wahid's established anti-Islamist credentials in nationalist quarters. Although Golkar leader B. J. Habibie was probably as mistrusted by many nationalists as Amien Rais, his position as party leader was far more tenuous, and Golkar's historical association with Pancasila should be weighted more heavily than Habibie's personal Islamic ties.

9. It is not the case that a regime cleavage inevitably dissipates on democratization. Anti–ancien regime sentiment has continued to shape voting behavior in parts of Latin America and Eastern Europe, for instance.

10. For instance, these poor electoral showings both reflect and exacerbate the fact that these parties are all suffering from ever-worsening internal discord. Political articulation requires that parties be *internally unified* enough and *externally differentiated* enough to mobilize distinctive constituencies in effective ways.

Chapter 5. Weak Party Articulation and Development in India, 1991–2014

1. Sridharan (1991, 1204) argues that even a credible center-left agenda would need to "combine deregulation and some privatization for growth and efficiency with a redefined rather than reduced role for the state. This role would be redirected toward skimming some of the gain from industry's growth and putting it into long-neglected, productivity-raising (and equalizing and empowering) investment in education, health, rural infrastructure, and minimum needs."

2. In one of the rare articles discussing the role of parties in development, Randall (2007) argues that in "non-Western" countries parties are generally weak because of weak institutionalization, poor funding prospects, and clientelism. Parties are, therefore, unlikely to be important to developmental transitions in multiparty democracies.

3. As I will discuss, the BJP is an integral party whose projects have failed for reasons to do with factors both internal and external; however, the 2014 electoral victory that occurred at the time of writing this chapter might suggest that it has overcome these obstacles and may be in a position to break the developmental block. However, this is for now purely speculation given the relatively short term that the BJP has held power at the time of writing this chapter. Nevertheless, the large and decisive mandate won by the BJP suggests that the nationalist articulation may have gained resurgence once more.

4. There are exceptions among the states; for example Tamil Nadu's parties have built on ethnic populism to ensure some parity in social development combined with

NOTES TO CHAPTER 5   197

high growth rates. Theoretically this path is available to other states; however, for a number of historical, geographical, and political reasons that cannot be investigated here, many states enter the market arena with preexisting disadvantages that shape their ability to use the market as a means of poverty reduction. Strong national state capacity is crucial for such inequalities to be addressed through, for example, budget allocations for social and welfare programs, changes to the legal framework in which states operate, and dictating the pace and content of liberalization.

5. Untouchability was abolished in 1949 under India's constitutional law, although it continues to be practiced across India. The official term *Scheduled Castes* has increasingly been replaced in popular use and within social movements with the term *dalit* (broken). Other Backward Castes (OBCs) is the official name given to castes who are ritually oppressed but were not considered untouchable.

6. The term *reform* signifies a value-free depoliticization of economic activity and the necessity of a progressive transformation from socialism to markets, even though many aspects of this policy shift have had progressive consequences.

7. A similar process of class dearticulation and the rise of complex coalitions has been noted in the case of Latin America, where class-based left–right cleavages have been replaced by nonclass articulations that, if not explicitly promarket, are not directly opposed to it (Roberts 2002, 2008).

8. "First and second order change can be seen as cases of normal 'policy-making,' namely of a process that adjusts policy without challenging the overall terms of a given policy paradigm, much like 'normal science.' Third order change, by contrast, is likely to reflect a very different process, marked by the radical changes in the overarching terms of the policy discourse associated with a paradigm shift" (Hall 1993, 279).

9. Yadav (2004) acknowledges the puzzle of this convergence in the context of popular antipathy toward reforms but does not explain it.

10. Askari Zaidi, "Congress revives 'garibi hatao' plank," *Times of India*, July 22, 1999.

11. "Leading from Below," *Times of India*, September 27, 1999.

12. The National Agenda of Governance, for example, lists National Security as the priority, under which "national reconstruction," "dynamic diplomacy," "federal harmony," "economic modernization," "secularism," "social justice," and "probity" are listed in that specific order. The election campaign in 1998 reflected a preoccupation with nationalist rhetoric and very little debate about the substance of market reforms.

13. As a BJP leader put it: "Swadeshi is as much a political as an economic slogan, which aims at making India strong. India cannot be strong without political stability and the ability to take strong decisions in a transparent manner. Only when deals are negotiated transparently and there is a government which has the necessary strength to ensure the implementation of these deals, the foreign investors will show interest in India. And it is only the BJP whose government can ensure all this." Furthermore, he

added: "We are not afraid of competition. We are only against one-sided competition that has been encouraged in the country over the last few years so as to favour multinationals. A BJP government will help the Indian industries to compete successfully against the multinationals. Otherwise, liberalisation will lead to India's deindustrialisation," he said, accusing the past government of "not negotiating deals with the investors but being dictated by them" (Nanda 1998).

14. In part this included the marginalization of economists who had promoted *swadeshi* (nationalist) economics.

15. The BJP was seen to have managed the Kargil War with Pakistan in a deft and authoritative manner by the urban electorate (Balakrishnan and Rao 1999).

16. This limited war between India and Pakistan occurred between May and July 1999 along the Line of Control over allegations that Pakistani soldiers had infiltrated the Indian border.

17. This appears to have been rectified in the 2014 elections, when the BJP won enough seats to form a government without entering into coalition agreements with major state parties. Although this would require more analysis, it would appear that the new chain of equivalence was constructed around the signifier of "development" rather than Hindu nationalism, even if the latter lurks implicitly in the party's agenda.

18. This does not necessarily imply that both parties are equally effective at implementing market reforms; arguably, in 2004 the Congress was slightly hampered by its coalition with the CPM (Communist Party of India [Marxist]), but in 2009 it was no longer part of the Congress coalition.

19. A few illustrative examples listed by Suri (2004) include the Kapus and OBCs, who are divided among themselves between the Congress and the TDP in Andhra Pradesh; the Lingayats between the Congress and the BJP in Karnataka; the non-Yadava OBCs between the four parties in the electoral arena in Uttar Pradesh; and the Marathas between the Shiv Sena and the National Congress Party.

REFERENCES

Abed-Kotob, Sana. 1995. "The Accommodationists Speak: Goals and Strategies of the Muslim Brotherhood of Egypt." *International Journal of Middle East Studies* 27: 321–339.

Abella, Irving M. 1973. *Nationalism, Communism and Canadian Labour: The CIO, the Communist Party and the Canadian Congress of Labour, 1935–1956.* Toronto: University of Toronto Press.

Abramson, Paul R., John H. Aldrich, and David W. Rohde. 2010. *Continuity and Change in the 2008 Elections.* Washington, DC: Congressional Quarterly Press.

Ahluwalia, Montek Singh. 2002. "Economic Reforms in India since 1991: Has Gradualism Worked? *Journal of Economic Perspectives* 16(3): 67–88.

Al-Awadi, Hesham. 2005. *In Pursuit of Legitimacy: The Muslim Brothers and Mubarak, 1982–2000.* London and New York: I. B. Tauris.

Althusser, Louis. 1969. "Contradiction and Overdetermination." In *For Marx*, by Louis Althusser, 87–128. London: Verso.

Ambardi, Kuskridho. 2008. "The Making of the Indonesian Multiparty System: A Cartelized Party System and Its Origins." PhD Dissertation, Department of Political Science, The Ohio State University.

Anderson, Frederick W. 1949. "Some Political Aspects of the Grain Growers' Movement, 1915–1935, with Particular Reference to Saskatchewan." Unpublished master's thesis. Saskatoon: University of Saskatchewan.

Anderson, Perry. 1976–1977. "The Antinomies of Antonio Gramsci." *New Left Review.* 100: 5–78.

———. 1980. *Arguments within English Marxism.* London: Verso.

———. 2010. "Two Revolutions." *New Left Review* 61: 59–96.

Archer, Keith. 1990. *Political Choices and Electoral Consequences: A Study of Organized Labour and the New Democratic Party.* Montreal: McGill-Queen's University Press.

Arjomand, Said A. 1988. *The Turban for the Crown: The Islamic Revolution in Iran.* Oxford, UK: Oxford University Press.

Arrighi, Giovanni. 1994. *The Long Twentieth Century: Money, Power, and the Origins of Our Times.* London: Verso.

Ashworth, John. 1983. *"Agrarians" & "Aristocrats": Party Political Ideology in the United States, 1837–1846.* London: Royal Historical Society; and Atlantic Highlands, NJ: Humanities Press.

Aspinall, Edward. 2005. *Opposing Suharto: Compromise, Resistance, and Regime Change in Indonesia.* Stanford, CA: Stanford University Press.

———. 2013. "A Nation in Fragments: Patronage and Neoliberalism in Contemporary Indonesia." *Critical Asian Studies* 45(1): 27–54.

Ates, Davut. 2005. "Economic Liberalization and Changes in Fundamentalism: The Case of Egypt." *Middle East Policy* 12: 133–144.

Atia, Mona. 2012. "'A Way to Paradise': Pious Neoliberalism, Islam, and Faith-Based Development." *Annals of the Association of American Geographers* 102(X): 1–20.

Baker, Raymond W. 1991. "Afraid for Islam: Egypt's Muslim Centrists between Pharaohs and Fundamentalists." *Daedalus* 120: 41–68.

Balakrishnan, K., and GVL Narasimha Rao. 1999. "BJP Has an Edge in Urban India." *Times of India*, July 17.

Bardhan, Pranab. 1999. *The Political Economic of Reform in India.* Oxford, UK: Oxford University Press.

———. 2005. "Nature of Opposition to Economic Reforms in India." *Economic and Political Weekly*, 4995–4998.

Barnes, Samuel H. 1960. "Canadian Trade Unions and the Cooperative Commonwealth Federation." *Papers of the Michigan Academy of Science, Arts, and Letters* XLV(1959 meeting): 251–264.

Bartels, Larry M. 2008. "The Study of Electoral Behavior." Unpublished paper. Retrieved on November 26, 2012, from www.princeton.edu/~bartels/electoral behavior.pdf.

Bartolini Stefano and Peter Mair. 1990. *Identity, Competition, Electoral Availability: The Stabilisation of European Electorates, 1885–1985.* Cambridge, UK: Cambridge University Press.

Bayat, Asef. 2007. *Making Islam Democratic: Social Movements and the Post-Islamist Turn.* Stanford, CA: Stanford University Press.

Baylouny, Anne Marie. 2004. "Democratic Inclusion: A Solution to Militancy in Islamist Movements?" *Strategic Insights* 3.

Beck, Paul Allen. 1974. "A Socialization Theory of Partisan Realignment." In *The Politics of Future Citizens: New Dimensions in the Political Socialization of Children*, edited by Richard G. Niemi, and associates, 199–219. San Francisco: Jossey-Bass Publishers.

Beinin, Joel. 2012. "What Have Workers Gained from Egypt's January 25 Revolution?" *The Middle East Channel, ForeignPolicy*, July 20, 2011.

Berelson, Bernard, Paul F. Lazarsfeld, and William McPhee. 1954. *Voting: A Study of Opinion Formation in a Presidential Campaign*. Chicago and London: University of Chicago Press.

Berezin, Mabel. 2009. *Illiberal Politics in Neoliberal Times: Culture, Security and Populism in the New Europe*. Cambridge, UK: Cambridge University Press.

Bergquist, James M. 1971. "People and Politics in Transition: The Illinois Germans, 1850–1860. In *Ethnic Voters and the Election of Lincoln*, edited by Frederick C. Luebke, 196–226. Lincoln: University of Nebraska Press.

Black, Duncan. [1958] 1963. *The Theory of Committees and Elections*. Cambridge, UK: Cambridge University Press.

Blau, Joseph L. 1954. *Social Theories of Jacksonian Democracy: Representative Writings of the Period, 1825–1850*. New York: The Liberal Arts Press.

Block, Fred. 1987. "The Ruling Class Does Not Rule: Notes on the Marxist Theory of the State." In *Revising State Theory: Essays in Politics and Postindustrialism*, by Fred Block, 51–68. Philadelphia: Temple University Press.

Bourdieu, Pierre. 1984. *Distinction: A Social Critique of the Judgment of Taste*. Cambridge, MA: Harvard University Press.

———. 1989. "Social Space and Symbolic Power." *Sociological Theory* 7: 14–25.

———. 1991a [1971]. "Genesis and Structure of the Religious Field." *Comparative Social Research* 13: 1–44.

———. 1991b. *Language and Symbolic Power*. Cambridge, UK: Polity.

Boydston, Jeanne. 1990. *Home and Work: Housework, Wages, and the Ideology of Labor in the Early Republic*. New York: Oxford University Press.

Brady, David W. 1988. *Critical Elections and Congressional Policy Making*. Stanford, CA: Stanford University Press.

Breman, Jan. 2004. *The Making and Unmaking of an Industrial Working Class*. Oxford, UK: Oxford University Press.

Brodie, M. Janine, and Jane Jenson. 1988. *Crisis, Challenge and Change: Party and Class in Canada Revisited*. Ottawa: Carleton University Press.

Bronstein, Jamie L. 1999. *Land Reform and Working-Class Experience in Britain and the United States, 1800–1862*. Stanford, CA: Stanford University Press.

Brubaker, Rogers. 2006. *Ethnicity without Groups*. Cambridge, MA: Harvard University Press.

Bruce, Peter G. 1989. "Political Parties and Labor Legislation in Canada and the US." *Industrial Relations: A Journal of Economy and Society* 28(2): 115–141.

Brym, Robert J. 1978. "Regional Social Structure and Agrarian Radicalism in Canada: Alberta, Saskatchewan, and New Brunswick." *Canadian Review of Sociology/ Revue canadienne de sociologie* 15(3): 339–351.

Buehler, Michael. 2008. "The Rise of Shari'a Bylaws in Indonesian Districts: An Indication for Changing Patterns of Power Accumulation and Political Corruption." *South East Asia Research* 16(2): 255–285.

Buğra, Ayşe. 2002. "Political Islam in Turkey in Historical Context: Strengths and Weaknesses." In *The Politics of Permanent Crisis: Class, Ideology and State in Turkey*, edited by Neşecan Balkan and Sungur Savran, 107–144. New York: Nova Science Publishers.

Burawoy, Michael, 2003. "For a Sociological Marxism: The Complementary Convergence of Antonio Gramsci and Karl Polanyi." *Politics and Society.* 31: 193–261.

Burnham, Walter Dean. 1970. *Critical Elections and the Mainsprings of American Politics.* New York: Norton.

Burstein, Paul. 1998. "Interest Organizations, Political Parties, and the Study of Democratic Politics." In *Social Movements and American Political Institutions*, edited by Anne N. Costain and Andrew S. McFarland, 39–56. Lanham, MD: Rowman & Littlefield.

Bush, Robin. 2009. *Nahdlatul Ulama and the Struggle for Power within Islam and Politics in Indonesia.* Singapore: ISEAS.

Calman, Alvin R. 1922. "Ledru-Rollin and the Second French Republic." *Studies in History, Economics and Public Law* 103 (2).

Camfield, David. 2002. "Class, Politics, and Social Change: the Remaking of the Working Class in 1940s Canada." Toronto: York University.

Campbell, Angus, Philip E. Converse, Warren E. Miller, and Donald E. Stokes. 1960. *The American Voter.* New York and London: Wiley.

Campbell, Angus, Gerald Gurin, and Warren E. Miller. 1954. *The Voter Decides.* Evanston, IL, and White Plains, NY: Row, Peterson and Company.

Can, Yasemin İpek. 2007. "Türkiye'de sivil toplumu yeniden düşünmek: Neo-liberal dönüşümler ve gönüllülük." *Toplum ve Bilim* 108: 88–128.

Canadian Congress of Labour. 1941. *Proceedings of the Second Annual Convention, September 8–12.* Hamilton, Ontario.

———. 1943. *Proceedings of the Fourth Annual Convention, September 13–19.* Montreal, Quebec.

———. 1946. *Proceedings of the Sixth Annual Convention, September 23–29.* Toronto, Ontario.

Caplan, Gerald L. 1963. "The Failure of Canadian Socialism: The Ontario Experience, 1932–1945." *Canadian Historical Review* 44(2): 93–121.

Card, David E., and Richard B. Freeman, eds. 1993. *Small Differences That Matter: Labor Markets and Income Maintenance in Canada and the United States.* Chicago: University of Chicago Press.

Çarkoğlu, Ali, and Binnaz Toprak. 2006. *Deği_en Türkiye'de Din, Toplum ve Siyaset.* Istanbul: TESEV.

Carmines, Edward G. and Robert Huckfeldt. 1996. "Political Behavior: An Overview." In *A New Handbook of Political Science*, edited by Robert E. Goodin and Hans-Dieter Klingemann, 223–254. Oxford, UK, and New York: Oxford University Press.

Carmines, Edward G., John P. McIver and James A. Stimson. 1987. "Unrealized Partisanship: A Theory of Dealignment." *Journal of Politics* 49 (2): 376–400.

Carmines, Edward G., and James A. Stimson. 1989. *Issue Evolution: Race and the Transformation of American Politics.* Princeton, NJ: Princeton University Press.

Chatterjee, Partha. 2008. "Democracy and Economic Transformation in India." *Economic and Political Weekly*, April 19.

Chhibber, Pradeep K., and Ken Kollman. 2004. *The Formation of National Party Systems: Federalism and Party Competition in Canada, Great Britain, India, and the United States.* Princeton, NJ: Princeton University Press.

Çınar, Alev. 2005. *Modernity, Islam and Secularism in Turkey: Bodies, Places and Time.* Minneapolis: University of Minnesota Press.

Cizre-Sakallıoğlu, Ümit. 1996. "Parameters and Strategies of Islam–State Interaction in Republican Turkey." *International Journal of Middle Eastern Studies* 28: 231–251.

Clemens, Elisabeth, and Debra Minkoff. 2004. "Beyond the Iron Law: Rethinking the Place of Organizations in Social Movement Research." In *The Blackwell Companion to Social Movements*, edited by David A. Snow, Sarah A. Soule and Hanspeter Kriesi, 155–170. UK. Oxford: Blackwell.

Cohn, Bernard S. 1987. "The Census, Social Structure and Objectification in South Asia," In *An Anthropologist among the Historians and Other Essays*, edited by Bernard S. Cohn, 224–254. Oxford, UK: Oxford University Press.

Converse, Philip E. 1964. "The Nature of Belief Systems in Mass Publics." In *Ideology and Discontent*, edited by David E. Apter, 206–261. Glencoe, IL: Free Press; and London: Collier Macmillan.

———. 1966. "The Concept of a Normal Vote." In *Elections and the Political Order*, edited by Angus Campbell, Philip E. Converse, Warren E. Miller, and Donald A. Stokes, 9–39. New York: Wiley.

———. 2006. "Researching Electoral Politics." *American Political Science Review* 100(4): 605–612.

Conway, John F. 1978. "Populism in the United States, Russia, and Canada: Explaining the Roots of Canada's Third Parties." *Canadian Journal of Political Science/Revue canadienne de science politique* 11(1): 100–124.

Cook, Ramsay. 1984. "Tillers and Toilers: The Rise and Fall of Populism in Canada in the 1890s." *Historical Papers/Communications historiques* 19(1): 1–20.

Corbridge, Stuart, and John Harriss. 2000. *Reinventing India.* Cambridge, UK: Polity Press.

Cornell, Saul. 1999. *The Other Founders: Anti-Federalism and the Dissenting Tradition in America, 1788–1828.* Chapel Hill: University of North Carolina Press.

Corrigan, Philip, and Derek Sayer. 1985. *The Great Arch: English State Formation as Cultural Revolution.* Oxford, UK: Blackwell.

Costain, Anne N., and Andrew S. McFarland. 1998. *Social Movements and American Political Institutions.* Lanham, MD: Rowman & Littlefield.

Cross, Michael S. 1974. *The Decline and Fall of a Good Idea: CCF–NDP Manifestoes, 1932 to 1969.* Toronto: New Hogtown Press.

Crouch, Harold. 2011. *Political Reform in Indonesia after Soeharto.* Singapore: ISEAS Press.

Dahrendorf, Ralf. 1959. *Class and Class Conflict in Industrial Society.* Stanford, CA: Stanford University Press.

Dash, Priya Ranjan. 2004. "National Income Set for a Big Jump." *Times of India*, February 10.

Davis, Nancy J., and Robert V. Robertson. 2012. *Claiming Society for God: Religious Movements and Social Welfare in Egypt, Israel, Italy, and the United States.* Bloomington: Indiana University Press

Deaton, Anton, and Jean Dreze. 2002. "Poverty and Inequality India: A Re-Examination." *Economic and Political Weekly*, September 7.

de Leon, Cedric. 2008. "'No Bourgeois Mass Party, No Democracy': The Missing Link in Barrington Moore's American Civil War." *Political Power and Social Theory* 19: 39–82.

———. 2011. "The More Things Change: A Gramscian Genealogy of Barack Obama's 'Post-Racial' Politics, 1932–2008." *Political Power and Social Theory* 22: 75–104.

———. 2014. *Party and Society: Reconstructing a Sociology of Democratic Party Politics.* Cambridge, UK: Polity.

de Leon, Cedric, Manali Desai, and Cihan Tuğal. 2009. "Political Articulation: Parties and the Constitution of Cleavages in the United States, India, and Turkey." *Sociological Theory* 27(3): 193–219.

Desai, Manali. 2012. "Parties and the Articulation of Neoliberalism: From 'the Emergency' to Reforms in India, 1975–1991." *Political Power and Social Theory* 23: 27–63.

Douglas, Stephen A. [1853] 1961. "To J. H. Crane, D. M. Johnson, and L. J. Eastin, Washington, December 17, 1853." In *The Letters of Stephen A. Douglas*, ed. Robert W. Johannsen, 268–271. Urbana: University of Illinois Press.

Downs, Anthony. 1957. *An Economic Theory of Democracy*. New York: Harper & Row.

Duverger, Maurice. 1954. *Political Parties, Their Organization and Activity in the Modern State*. London, New York, and Methuen, MA: Wiley.

Effendy, Bahtiar. 2009a. "In the Shadow of Pragmatism: The Politics of Coalition." *Jakarta Post*, May 1.

———. 2009b. "Islamic Parties Have Long Been at an Impasse." *Jakarta Post*, April 17.

Einhorn, Robin L. 1991. *Property Rules: Political Economy in Chicago, 1833–1872*. Chicago: University of Chicago Press.

el-Ghobashy, Mona. 2005. "The Metamorphosis of the Egyptian Muslim Brothers." *International Journal of Middle East Studies* 37: 373–395.

Enelow, James M., and Melvin J. Hinich. 1984. *The Spatial Theory of Voting: An Introduction*. Cambridge, UK: Cambridge University Press.

Erbakan, Necmettin. 1991. *Adil Ekonomik Düzen*. Ankara: Semih Ofset Matbaacılık.

Ertman, Thomas. 1997. *Birth of the Leviathan: Building States and Regimes in Medieval and Early Modern Europe*. Cambridge, UK: Cambridge University Press.

Esping-Andersen, Gøsta. 1990. *The Three Worlds of Welfare Capitalism*. Princeton, NJ: Princeton University Press.

Evans, Peter. 1979. *Dependent Development: The Alliance of Multinational, State, and Local Capital in Brazil*. Princeton, NJ: Princeton University Press.

———. 1995. *Embedded Autonomy: States and Industrial Transformation*. Princeton, NJ: Princeton University Press.

Evans, Peter, Dietrich Rueschemeyer, and Theda Skocpol (eds.). 1985. *Bringing the State Back In*. Cambridge, UK: Cambridge University Press.

Eyal, Yonatan. 2007. *The Young America Movement and the Transformation of the Democratic Party, 1828–1861*. New York: Cambridge University Press.

Fandy, Mamoun. 1994. "Egypt's Islamic Group: Regional Revenge?" *The Middle East Journal* 48: 607–625.

Ferry, Darren. 2004. "'Severing the Connections in a Complex Community': The Grange, the Patrons of Industry and the Construction/Contestation of a Late 19th-Century Agrarian Identity in Ontario." *Labour/Le Travail* 54: 9–47.

Finegold, Kenneth, and Theda Skocpol. 1995. *Party and State in America's New Deal*. Madison: University of Wisconsin Press.

Foner, Philip S. 1977. *The Great Labor Uprising of 1877*. New York: Monad Press.

Ford, Lacy K. Jr. 1988. *Origins of Southern Radicalism: The Southern Carolina Upcountry, 1800–1860*. New York: Oxford University Press.

Forsey, Eugene. 1958. "The Movement Towards Labour Unity in Canada: History and Implications." *The Canadian Journal of Economics and Political Science/Revue canadienne d'économique et de science politique* 24(1): 70–83.

Frank, Thomas. 2004. *What's the Matter with Kansas? How Conservatives Won the Heart of America*. New York: Metropolitan Books.

Franklin, Mark N. 1985. *The Decline of Class Voting in Britain: Changes in the Basis of Electoral Choice, 1964–1983*. Oxford, UK: Clarendon Press.

Fraser, Nancy, and Linda Gordon. 1994. "A Genealogy of Dependency: Tracing a Keyword of the U.S. Welfare State." *Signs* 19(2): 33–58.

Fraser, Steve, and Gary Gerstle. 1989. *The Rise and Fall of the New Deal Order, 1930–1980*. Princeton, NJ: Princeton University Press.

Fudge, Judy, and Eric Tucker. 2001. *Labour Bbefore the Law: The Regulation of Workers' Collective Action in Canada, 1900–1948*. Don Mills, Ontario: Oxford University Press.

Galenson, Walter. 1960. *The CIO Challenge to the AFL*. Cambridge, MA: Harvard University Press.

Galli della Loggia, Ernesto. 1977. "Le ceneri di Gramsci." In *Egemonia e democrazia. Gramsci e la questione comunista nel dibattito di Mondoperaio*, 69–91. Rome: Avanti!

Geertz, Clifford. 1976. *The Religion of Java*. Chicago: University of Chicago Press.

Gerteis, Joseph. 2003. "Populism, Race, and Political Interest in Virginia." *Social Science History* 27: 197–227.

———. 2007. *Class and the Color Line: Interracial Class Coalition in the Knights of Labor and the Populist Movement*. Durham, NC, and London: Duke University Press.

Ghadbian, Najib. 1997. *Democratization and the Islamist Challenge in the Arab World*. Boulder, CO: Westview Press.

Ghannam, Farha. 2002. *Remaking the Modern: Space, Relocation, and the Politics of Identity in a Global Cairo*. Berkeley: University of California Press.

Goldstone, Jack A. (ed). 2003. *States, Parties, and Social Movements*. Cambridge, UK: Cambridge University Press.

Goodwin, Jeff. 2001. *No Other Way Out: States and Revolutionary Movements, 1945–1991*. Cambridge, UK: Cambridge University Press.

Goodwin, Jeff, and James Jasper. 1999. "Caught in a Winding, Snarling Vine: The Structural Bias of Political Process Theory." *Sociological Forum* 14(1): 27–54.

Gorski, Philip. 2003. *The Disciplinary Revolution: Calvinism and the Rise of the State in Early Modern Europe*. Chicago: University of Chicago Press.

Government of India. Planning Commission. 2011. *Faster, Sustainable and More Inclusive Growth: An Approach to the Twelfth Five Year Plan*. New Delhi.

Gramsci, Antonio. 1921. "Parties and Masses." *L'Ordine Nuovo*, September 25, 1921, translated by Mark Camilleri. Retrieved on March 21, 2011, from www.marxists .org/archive/gramsci/1921/09/parties-masses.htm.

———. 1971. *Selections from the Prison Notebooks*, edited and translated by Quintin Hoare and Geoffrey Nowell Smith. New York: International Publishers.

———. 1992 [1929–1933]. *Prison Notebooks, Volume 1*. New York: Columbia University Press.

———. 2007 [1930–1932]. *Prison Notebooks, Volume 3*. New York: Columbia University Press.

Granatstein, J. L. 1967. "The York South By_Election of February 9, 1942: A Turning Point in Canadian Politics." *Canadian Historical Review* 48(2): 142–158.

Green, Donald, Bradley Palmquist, and Eric Schickler. 2002. *Partisan Hearts and Minds: Political Parties and the Social Identities of Voters*. New Haven, CT, and London: Yale University Press.

Green, James. 2006. *Death in the Haymarket: A Story of Chicago, the First Labor Movement and the Bombing that Divided Gilded Age America*. New York: Anchor Books.

Hafez, Mohammed M. 2003. *Why Muslims Rebel: Repression and Resistance in the Islamic World*. Boulder, CO: Lynne Rienner.

Hafez, Mohammed M., and Quintan Wiktorowicz. 2004. "Violence as Contention in the Egyptian Islamic Movement." In *Islamic Activism: A Social Movement Theory Approach*, edited by Q. Wiktorowicz, 61–88. Bloomington: Indiana University Press.

Hall, Peter. 1993. "Policy Paradigms, Social Learning and the State: The Case of Economic Policymaking in Britain." *Comparative Politics* 25(3): 275–296.

Hall, Peter A., and David W. Soskice. 2001. *Varieties of Capitalism: The Institutional Foundations of Comparative Advantage*. Oxford, UK, and New York: Oxford University Press.

Hall, Stuart. 1986. "On Postmodernism and Articulation." *The Journal of Communication Inquiry* 10(2): 45–60.

———. 1987. "Gramsci and Us." *Marxism Today* (June): 16–21.

Hansen, Thomas, and Finn Stepputat. 2001. *States of Imagination*. Durham, NC: Duke University Press.

Harnisch, Chris, and Quinn Mecham. 2009. "Democratic Ideology in Islamist Opposition? The Muslim Brotherhood's 'Civil State.'" *Middle Eastern Studies* 45: 189–205.

Hartz, Louis. 1964. *The Founding of New Societies; Studies in the History of the United States, Latin America, South Africa, Canada, and Australia*. New York: Harcourt.

Hasan, Zoya. 2000. "Representation and Redistribution: The New Lower Caste Politics in India." In *Transforming India: Social and Political Dynamics of Democracy*, edited by Francine Frankel, Zoya Hasan, Rajeev Bhargava, and Balveer Arora, 146–175. Oxford, UK: Oxford University Press.

———. 2002. *Parties and Party Politics in India*. Oxford, UK: Oxford University Press.

———. 2006. "Bridging a Growing Divide? Indian National Congress and Indian Democracy." *Contemporary South Asia* 4(15): 473–488.

Hefner, Robert W. 2000. *Civil Islam: Muslims and Democratization in Indonesia*. Princeton, NJ: Princeton University Press.

Heron, Craig. 1984. "Labourism and the Canadian Working Class." *Labour/Le Travail* 13 (Spring): 45–75.

———. 1996. *The Canadian Labour Movement: A Brief History*, 2nd ed. Toronto: James Lorimer & Co.

Herrera, Linda. 2001. "Downveiling: Gender and the Contest over Culture in Cairo." *Middle East Report* 31: 16–19.

Hewitt, Steven R. 1995. "'We Cannot Shoo These Men to Another Place': The On to Ottawa Trek in Toronto and Ottawa." *Past Imperfect* 4: 3–30.

Hirsch, Eric L. 1990. *Urban Revolt: Ethnic Politics in the Nineteenth-Century Chicago Labor Movement*. Berkeley: University of California Press.

Hirway, Indira. 1995. "Selective Development and Widening Disparities in Gujarat: An Overview." *Economic and Political Weekly* October 14–21: 2603–2618.

———. 2000. "Dynamics of Development in Gujarat: Some Lessons." *Economic and Political Weekly* August 26–September 2: 3106–3120.

Hoare, Quintin, and Geoffrey Nowell Smith. 1995. *The Southern Question*. Translation and Introduction by Pasquale Verdicchio. West Lafayette, IN: Bordighera.

———. 2007. *Quaderni del carcere*. Turin: Einaudi.

Holt, Michael F. 1999. *The Rise and Fall of the American Whig Party: Jacksonian Politics and the Onset of the Civil War*. Oxford and New York: Oxford University Press.

Horn, Michiel. 1980. *The League for Social Reconstruction: Intellectual Origins of the Democratic Left in Canada, 1930–1942*. Toronto: University of Toronto Press.

———. 1984. *The Great Depression of the 1930s in Canada*. Ottawa: Canadian Historical Association.

Horowitz, Donald L. 2013. *Constitutional Change and Democracy in Indonesia*. New York: Cambridge University Press.

Horowitz, Gad. 1968. *Canadian Labour in Politics*. Toronto: University of Toronto Press.

Hotelling, Harold. 1929. "Stability in Competition." *The Economic Journal* 39: 41–57.

Huber, Evelyne, Charles Ragin, and John D. Stephens. 1993. "Social Democracy, Christian Democracy, Constitutional Structure, and the Welfare State." *The American Journal of Sociology* 99(3): 711–749.

Hung, Ho-Fung. 2011. *Protest with Chinese Characteristics: Demonstrations, Riots, and Petitions in the Mid-Qing Dynasty*. New York: Columbia University Press.

Huntington, S. 1968. *Political Order in Changing Societies*. New Haven, CT: Yale University Press.

Huston, James L. 1987. *The Panic of 1857 and the Coming of the Civil War*. Baton Rouge and London: Louisiana State University Press.

Imai, Shin. 1981. "Deportation in the Depression." *Queen's Law Journal* 7: 66–94.

Inglehart, Ronald. 1990. *Culture Shift in Advanced Industrial Society*. Princeton, NJ: Princeton University Press.

Irvine, William. 1920. *The Farmers in Politics*. Toronto: McClelland and Stewart.

Ismail, Salwa. 1998. "Confronting the Other: Identity, Culture, Politics, and Conservative Islamism in Egypt." *International Journal of Middle East Studies* 30: 199–225.

———. 1999. "Religious 'Orthodoxy' as Public Morality: The State, Islamism and Cultural Politics in Egypt." *Critique: Critical Middle Eastern Studies* 8: 25–47.

———. 2006. *Political Life in Cairo's New Quarters: Encountering the Everyday State*. Minneapolis: University of Minnesota Press.

Jaffrelot, Christophe. 2003. *India's Silent Revolution: The Rise of the Lower Castes*. London: Hurst.

Jamieson, Stuart M. 1968. *Times of Trouble: Labour Unrest and Industrial Conflict in Canada, 1900–66*. Ottawa: Task Force on Labour Relations.

Jenkins, Rob. 1999. *Democratic Politics and Economic Reform in India*. Cambridge, UK: Cambridge University Press.

———. 2004. "Labor Policy and the Second Generation of Economic Reform in India." *India Review* 3(4): 333–363.

Jentz, John B. 1991. "Class and Politics in an Emerging Industrial City: Chicago in the 1860s and 1870s." *Journal of Urban History* 17: 227–263.

Jentz, John B., and Richard Schneirov. 2012. *Chicago in the Age of Capital: Class, Politics, and Democracy during the Civil War and Reconstruction*. Urbana: University of Illinois Press.

Jessop, Bob. 1982. *The Capitalist State: Marxist Theories and Methods*. New York: New York University Press.

———. 1990. *State Theory: Putting the Capitalist State in its Place*. Cambridge, UK: Polity.

Johnson, A. W., and Rosemary Proctor. 2004. *Dream No Little Dreams: A Biography of the Douglas Government of Saskatchewan, 1944–1961*. Toronto: University of Toronto Press.

Jones, Gareth Stedman. 1983. *Languages of Class: Studies in English Working Class History, 1832–1982*. Cambridge, UK, and New York: Cambridge University Press.

Kalyvas, Stathis N. 1996. *The Rise of Christian Democracy in Europe*. Ithaca, NY: Cornell University Press.

Katz, Richard S., and Peter Mair. 1995. "Changing Models of Party Organization and Party Democracy." *Party Politics* 1(1): 5–28.

——. 2009. "The Cartel Party Thesis: A Restatement." *Perspectives on Politics* 7(4) (December): 753–766.

Katznelson, Ira, and Aristide Zolberg. 1986. *Working-Class Formation: Nineteenth-Century Patterns in Western Europe and the United States*. Princeton, NJ: Princeton University Press.

Kaufman, Jason. 2009. *The Origins of Canadian and American Political Differences*. Cambridge, MA: Harvard University Press.

Kautsky, Karl. 1964. *The Dictatorship of the Proletariat*. Westport, CT: Westview Press.

Kealey, Gregory S. 1992. "State Repression of Labour and the Left in Canada, 1914–20: The Impact of the First World War." *Canadian Historical Review* 73(3): 281–314.

Kealey, Gregory S., and Bryan D. Palmer. 1982. *Dreaming of What Might Be the Knights of Labor in Ontario, 1880–1900*. Cambridge, UK, and New York: Cambridge University Press.

Kepel, Gilles. 1995. "Islamists versus the State in Egypt and Algeria." *Daedalus* 124: 109–127.

Kertzer, David, and Dominique Arel. 2002. "Census, Identity Formation, and Political Power." In *Census and Identity: The Politics of Race, Ethnicity, and Language in National Censuses*, edited by David Kertzer and Dominique Arel, 1–42. Cambridge, UK: Cambridge University Press.

Key, V. O. Jr. 1955. "A Theory of Critical Elections." *Journal of Politics* 17: 3–18.

——. 1959. "Secular Realignment and the Party System." *Journal of Politics* 21: 198–210.

——. [1961] 1964. *Public Opinion and American Democracy*. New York: Knopf.

——. 1966. *The Responsible Electorate: Rationality in Presidential Voting, 1936–1960*. Cambridge, MA: Belknap Press of Harvard University Press.

Kienle, Eberhard. 1998. "More Than a Response to Islamism: The Political Deliberalization of Egypt in the 1990s." *Middle East Journal* 52: 219–235.

King, Dwight Y. 2003. *Half-Hearted Reform: Electoral Institutions and the Struggle for Democracy in Indonesia*. Westport, CT: Praeger.

King, William Lyon Mackenzie. 1930. "Diary Entry, September 22, 1930." *Library and Archives Canada* MG26-J13 (September 22): 1–2.

——. 1943. "Diary Entry, August 4, 1943." *Library and Archives Canada* MG26-J13: 1–3.

Kitschelt, Herbert. 1989. *The Logic of Party Formation: Ecological Politics in Belgium and West Germany*. Ithaca, NY: Cornell University Press.

Knoke, David. 1976. *Change and Continuity in American Politics: The Social Bases of Political Parties*. Baltimore and London: Johns Hopkins University Press.

Koğacıoğlu, Dicle. 2004. "Progress, Unity, and Democracy: Dissolving Political Parties in Turkey." *Law & Society Review* 38: 433–462.

Kohli, Atul. 1989. "The Politics of Economic Liberalization in India." *World Development* 17(3): 305–328.

———. 1990. *Democracy and Discontent: India's Growing Crisis of Governability.* Cambridge, UK: Cambridge University Press.

———. 2004. *State-Directed Development: Political Power and Industrialization in the Global Periphery.* Cambridge, UK: Cambridge University Press.

———. 2007. "State, Business, and Economic Growth in India." *Studies in Comparative International Development* 42: 87–114.

———. 2012. *Poverty amid Plenty in the New India.* Cambridge, UK: Cambridge University Press.

Koran Tempo. 2004. "Taufik Kiemas: Golkar dan NU Punya Platform Sama Dengan PDIP." February 28.

Krishna, Anirudh. 2004. "Escaping Poverty and Becoming Poor: Who Gains, Who Loses, and Why?" *World Development* 32(1): 121–136.

Kumar, Sanjay. 2004. 'Impact of economic reforms on Indian electorate.' *Economic and Political Weekly*, April 17–23, 1621–1630.

Labour Canada. 1977. "Strikes and Lockouts in Canada." *Historical Statistics of Canada.* Ottawa: Author.

———. 1980. *Directory of Labour Organizations in Canada.* Ottawa: Labour Canada, Labour Data Branch.

Laclau, Ernesto. 1977. *Politics and Ideology in Marxist Theory: Capitalism, Fascism, Populism.* London: New Left Books.

———. 1990. *New Reflections on the Revolution of Our Time.* London: Verso.

———. 2000. "Constructing Universality." In *Contingency, Hegemony, Universality: Contemporary Dialogues on the Left*, edited by Judith Butler, Ernesto Laclau and Slavoj Žižek, 281–307. London: Verso.

———. 2005. *On Populist Reason.* London: Verso.

Laclau, Ernesto, and Chantal Mouffe. [1985] 2001. *Hegemony and Socialist Strategy: Towards a Radical Democratic Politics* (second edition). London and New York: Verso.

Lause, Mark A. 2005. *Young America: Land, Labor, and the Republican Community.* Urbana and Chicago: University of Illinois Press.

Lazarsfeld, Paul F., Bernard Berelson, and Hazel Gaudet. [1944] 1948. *The People's Choice: How the Voter Makes Up His Mind in a Presidential Campaign* (second edition). New York and London: Columbia University Press.

Leacy, F. H., M. C. Urquhart, and K. A. H. Buckley. 1983. *Historical Statistics of Canada.* Ottawa: Statistics Canada.

"Leading from Below." *Times of India*, 1999. September 27.

League for Social Reconstruction Research Committee. 1935. *Social Planning for Canada.* Toronto: T. Nelson & Sons Limited.

———. 1938. *Democracy Needs Socialism*. Toronto and New York: T. Nelson & Sons limited.

Leftwich, Adrian. 1995. "Bringing Politics Back In: Towards a Model of the Developmental State." *Journal of Developmental Studies* 31(3): 400–427.

Lenin, Vladimir I. [1902] 1973. *What Is to Be Done?* Peking: Foreign Languages Press.

———. 1975. *The Lenin Anthology*. Edited by Robert C. Tucker. New York: Norton.

Lerche, Jens. 1999. "Politics of the Poor: Agricultural Labourers and Political Transformations in Uttar Pradesh." *Journal of Peasant Studies* 26(2): 182–241.

Levine, Bruce. 1992. *The Spirit of 1848: German Immigrants, Labor Conflict, and the Coming of the Civil War*. Urbana and Chicago: University of Illinois Press.

Lewis, David. 1943. "Socialism across the Border: Canada's CCF." *The Antioch Review* 3(4): 470–482.

Lia, Brynjar. 1998. *The Society of the Muslim Brothers in Egypt: The Rise of an Islamic Mass Movement 1928–1942*. Reading, UK: Ithaca Press.

Liddle, R. William, and Saiful Mujani. 2000. "The Triumph of Leadership: Explaining the 1999 Indonesian Vote." Paper presented at annual meetings of the American Political Science Association, Washington, DC, August 31–September 3.

———. 2009. "Indonesian Democracy: From Transition to Consolidation." Paper presented at conference on "Democratic Consolidation," Columbia University, New York, April.

Lijphart, Arend. 1999. *Patterns of Democracy: Government Forms and Performance in Thirty-Six Countries*. New Haven, CT: Yale University Press.

Lipset, Seymour Martin. 1950. *Agrarian Socialism; The Coöperative Commonwealth Federation in Saskatchewan, a Study in Political Sociology*. Berkeley: University of California Press.

———. [1959] 1965. "Political Sociology." In *Sociology Today*, vol. I, edited by Robert K. Merton, Leonard Broom, and Leonard S. Cottrell Jr., 81–114. New York: Basic Books.

———. 1960. *Political Man: the Social Bases of Politics*. Garden City, NY: Doubleday.

———. 1986. Conclusion—North American Labor Movements: A Comparative Perspective. In Seymour Martin Lipset, ed., *Unions in Transition: Entering the Second Century*, pp. 421–452. San Francisco, CA: ICS Press, Institute for Contemporary Studies.

———. 1989. *Continental Divide: The Values and Institutions of the United States and Canada*. Toronto: Canadian-American Committee.

Lipset, Seymour Martin, and Gary W. Marks. 2000. *It Didn't Happen Here: Why Socialism Failed in the United States*. New York: W. W. Norton & Co.

Lipset, Seymour Martin, and Noah M. Meltz. 2004. *The Paradox of American Unionism: Why Americans Like Unions More Than Canadians Do, but Join Much Less*. Ithaca, NY: Cornell ILR Press.

Lipset, Seymour Martin, and Stein Rokkan. 1967. *Party Systems and Voter Alignments: Cross-National Perspectives.* New York: Free Press.

Lipset, Seymour Martin, Martin A. Trow, and James S. Coleman. 1956. *Union Democracy: The Internal Politics of the International Typographical Union.* New York: Free Press.

Logan, Harold A. 1948. *Trade Unions in Canada: Their Development and Functioning.* Toronto: Macmillan Co. of Canada.

Loveman, Mara. 2005. "The Modern State and the Primitive Accumulation of Symbolic Power," *American Journal of Sociology,* 110 (6): 1651–1683.

Lupu, Noam. 2011. "Party Brands in Crisis: Partisanship, Brand Dilution, and the Breakdown of Political Parties in Latin America." Ph.D. Dissertation, Department of Politics, Princeton University.

Luxemburg, Rosa. 2004. *The Rosa Luxemburg Reader.* New York: Monthly Review Press.

MacDowell, Laurel S. 1978. "The Formation of the Canadian Industrial Relations System Dduring World War Two." *Labour/Le Travail* 3: 175–196.

Madrid, Robin. 1999. "Islamic Students in the Indonesian Student Movement, 1998–1999: Forces for Moderation. *Bulletin of Concerned Asian Scholars* 31(3) (July–September): 17–32.

Mahendra Dev, S., and C. Ravi. 2007. "Poverty and Inequality: All-India and States, 1983–2005." *Economic and Political Weekly,* February 10, 509–521.

Mahmood, Saba. 2005. *Politics of Piety: The Islamic Revival and the Feminist Subject.* Princeton, NJ: Princeton University Press.

Mainwaring, Scott. 1998. "Party Systems in the Third Wave." *Journal of Democracy* 9(3): 67–81.

Maioni, Antonia. 1998. *Parting at the Crossroads: The Emergence of Health Insurance in the United States and Canada.* Princeton, N.J.: Princeton University Press.

Mamdani, Mahmood. 1996. *Citizen and Subject: Contemporary Africa and the Legacy of Late Colonialism.* Princeton, NJ: Princeton University Press.

Mann, Michael. 1986. The Sources of Social Power, Vol. 2. Cambridge, UK: Cambridge University Press.

Manza, Jeff, and Clem Brooks. 1999. *Social Cleavages and Political Change: Voter Alignments and U.S. Party Coalitions.* Oxford, UK, and New York: Oxford University Press.

Martin, Andrew W. 2007. "Organizational Structure, Authority and Protest: The Case of Union Organizing in the US, 1990–2001." *Social Forces,* 85(3): 1413–1435.

Marx, Anthony W. 1998. *Making Race and Nation: A Comparison of the United States, South Africa, and Brazil.* Cambridge, UK: Cambridge University Press.

Marx, Karl. [1852] 1992. "The Eighteenth Brumaire of Louis Bonaparte." In *Surveys from Exile: Political Writings* (Volume 2), by Karl Marx, 143–249. London: Penguin Books.

———. 1859 [1978]. Preface to *A Contribution to the Critique of Political Economy*. In *The Marx-Engels Reader* (Second Edition), edited by Robert C. Tucker, 3–6. New York and London: Norton.

Marx, Karl, and Frederick Engels. [1848] 1998. *The Communist Manifesto: A Modern Edition*. London and New York: Verso.

McAdam, Doug. 1982. *Political Process and the Development of Black Insurgency*. Chicago: University of Chicago Press.

McAdam, Doug, Sidney Tarrow, and Charles Tilly. 2001. *Dynamics of Contention*. New York: Cambridge University Press.

McAllister, Ian and Richard Rose. 1986. *Voters Begin to Choose: From Closed-Class to Open Elections in Britain*. London: Sage.

McCarthy, John D., and Mayer Zald. 1977. "Resource Mobilization and Social Movements: A Partial Theory." *American Journal of Sociology* 82: 1212–1241.

McConnell, W. H. 1971. "Some Comparisons of the Roosevelt and Bennett New Deals." *Osgoode Hall Law Journal* 9(2): 221–260.

McHenry, Dean E. 1949. "The Impact of the CCF on Canadian Parties and Groups." *The Journal of Politics* 11(2): 365–395.

———. 1950. *The Third Force in Canada; The Cooperative Commonwealth Federation, 1932–1948*. Berkeley: University of California Press.

McInnis, Peter S. 2002. *Harnessing Labour Confrontation: Shaping the Postwar Settlement in Canada, 1943–1950*. Toronto: University of Toronto Press.

McMath, Robert C. Jr. 1995. "Populism in Two Countries: Agrarian Protest in the Great Plains and Prairie Provinces." *Agricultural History* 69(4): 516–546.

McVey, Ruth T. 1970. "Nationalism, Islam, and Marxism: The Management of Ideological Conflict in Indonesia." In *Nationalism, Islam, and Marxism*, edited by Ruth T. McVey, 1–33. Ithaca, NY: Cornell Modern Indonesia Project.

Mehrez, Samia. 2001. "Take Them out of the Ball Game: Egypt's Cultural Players in Crisis." *Middle East Report* 31: 10–15.

Menchik, Jeremy. 2014. "Productive Intolerance: Godly Nationalism in Indonesia." *Comparative Studies in Society and History* 56(3) (July): 591–621.

Michels, Robert. [1911] 1962. *Political Parties: A Sociological Study of the Oligarchical Tendencies of Modern Democracy*. New York: Free Press.

Mietzner, Marcus. 2012. "Indonesia's Democratic Stagnation: Anti-Reformist Elites and Resilient Civil Society." *Democratization* 19(2): 209–229.

———. 2014. *Money, Power, and Ideology: Political Parties in Post-Authoritarian Indonesia*. Singapore: NUS Press.

Miliband, R. 1969. *The State in Capitalist Society*. London: Weidenfeld & Nicolson.

Miller, Donald L. 1996. *City of the Century: The Epic of Chicago and the Making of America*. New York: Simon & Schuster.

Miller, Warren E., and J. Merrill Shanks. 1996. *The New American Voter*. Cambridge, MA: Harvard University Press.

Mitchell, Richard P. 1969. *The Society of the Muslim Brothers*. London: Oxford University Press.

Mitchell, Timothy. 1999. "Society, Economy, and the State Effect." In *State/Culture: State-Formation after the Cultural Turn*, edited by George Steinmetz, 76–97. Ithaca, NY, and London: Cornell University Press.

Montgomery, David. [1967] 1981. *Beyond Equality: Labor and the Radical Republicans, 1862–1872*. Urbana and Chicago: University of Illinois Press.

Morrison, Michael A. 1997. *Slavery and the American West: The Eclipse of Manifest Destiny and the Coming of the Civil War*. Chapel Hill and London: University of North Carolina Press.

Morton, Adam David. 2004. *Unravelling Gramsci: Hegemony and Passive Revolution in the Global Political Economy*. Ann Arbor, MI: Pluto Press.

Morton, Desmond. 1986. *The New Democrats, 1961–1986: The Politics of Change*. Toronto: Copp Clark Pitman.

———. 2007. *Working People: An Illustrated History of the Canadian Labour Movement*, 5 ed. Montréal: McGill-Queen's University Press.

Morton, W. L. 1950. *The Progressive Party in Canada*. Toronto: University of Toronto Press.

Mosca, Gaetano. 1939. *The Ruling Class*. New York and London: McGraw Hill.

Moustafa, Tamir. 2003. "Law versus the State: The Judicialization of Politics in Egypt." *Law & Social Inquiry* 28: 883–930.

Mujani, Saiful, and R. William Liddle. 2010. "Personalities, Parties, and Voters." *Journal of Democracy* 21(2) (April): 35–49.

Nanda, Prakash. 1998. "BJP: Swadeshi Is Liberalisation with a Human Face." *Times of India*, January 30.

Naylor, James. 1993. "Politics and Class: The Character of 1930s Socialism in Canada." *Canadian Historical Association Meeting Presentation* (June): 1–38.

———. 2006. "Canadian Labour Politics and the British Model, 1920–50." In *Canada and the British World Culture, Migration, and Identity*, 288–308. Vancouver: UBC Press.

Nelson, Scott Reynolds, and Carol Sheriff. 2008. *A People at War: Civilians and Soldiers in America's Civil War, 1854–1877*. New York and Oxford: Oxford University Press.

Nie, Norman H., Sidney Verba, and John R. Petrocik. [1976] 1979. *The Changing American Voter* (enlarged edition). Cambridge, MA, and London: Harvard University Press.

Norton, Augustus (ed.) 1995–1996. *Civil Society in the Middle East*. Leiden and New York: Brill.

Oberschall, Anthony. 1973. *Social Conflict and Social Movements*. Englewood Cliffs, NJ: Prentice-Hall.

O'Donnell, Guillermo. 1994. "Delegative Democracy." *Journal of Democracy* 5(1): 55–69.

Officer, Lawrence H. 2009. *Two Centuries of Compensation for U.S. Production Workers in Manufacturing*. New York: Palgrave Macmillan.

Olson, Mancur. 1965. *The Logic of Collective Action; Public Goods and the Theory of Groups*. Cambridge, MA: Harvard University Press.

Omi, Michael, and Howard Winant. 1994. *Racial Formation in the United States: From the 1960s to the 1990s*. New York and London: Routledge.

Orloff, Ann, and Theda Skocpol. 1984. "Why Not Equal Protection? Explaining the Politics of Public Social Spending in Britain, 1900–1911 and the United States, 1880s–1920." *American Sociological Review* 49: 726–750.

Orloff, Ann S. 1993. *The Politics of Pensions: A Comparative Analysis of Britain, Canada, and the United States, 1880–1940*. Madison: University of Wisconsin Press.

Ostry, Bernard. 1960. "Conservatives, Liberals, and Labour in the 1870s." *Canadian Historical Review* 41(2): 93–127.

———. 1961. "Conservatives, Liberals, and Labour in the 1880s." *Canadian Journal of Economics and Political Science/Revue canadienne d'économique et de science politique* 27(2): 141–161.

Owram, Doug. 1986. *The Government Generation: Canadian Intellectuals and the State, 1900–1945*. Toronto: University of Toronto Press.

Özdalga, Elisabeth, and Sune Persson (eds.). *Civil Society, Democracy and the Muslim World: Papers Read at a Conference Held at the Swedish Research Institute in Istanbul 28–30 October, 1996* (Istanbul: Swedish Research Institute in Istanbul, 1997).

Palmer, Bryan D. 1983. *Working-Class Experience: The Rise and Reconstitution of Canadian Labour, 1800–1980*. Toronto and Boston: Butterworth.

Panebianco, Angelo. 1988. *Political Parties: Organization and Power*. Cambridge, UK: Cambridge University Press.

Pareto, Vilfredo. 1984. *The Transformation of Democracy*. New Brunswick, NJ: Transaction Books.

Parsons, Talcott. 1951. *The Social System*. Glencoe, IL: Free Press.

Penner, Norman. 1977. *The Canadian Left: A Critical Analysis*. Scarborough, Ontario: Prentice-Hall of Canada.

———. 1992. *From Protest to Power: Social Democracy in Canada 1900–Present*. Toronto: J. Lorimer.

Pentland, H. Clare. 1968. *A Study of the Changing Social, Economic, and Political Background of the Canadian System of Industrial Relations.* Ottawa: Task Force on Labour Relations, Privy Council Office.

Petryshyn, J. 1982. "Class Conflict and Civil Liberties: The Origins and Activities of the Canadian Labour Defense League, 1925–1940." *Labour/Le Travail* 10 (Autumn): 39–63.

Pierce, Bessie Louise. [1937] 2007. *A History of Chicago,* Volume I. Chicago and London: University of Chicago Press.

———. 1940. *A History of Chicago,* Volume II. Chicago and London: University of Chicago Press.

Piven, Frances F., and Richard A. Cloward. 1979. *Poor People's Movements: Why They Succeed, How They Fail.* New York: Vintage.

———. 2000. *Why Americans Still Don't Vote.* Boston: Beacon Press.

Poulantzas, Nicos. [1968] 1973. *Political Power and Social Classes.* London: Verso.

———. 1974. *Fascism and Dictatorship.* London: New Left Books.

Przeworski, Adam. 1977. "Proletariat into a Class: The Process of Class Formation from Karl Kautsky's *The Class Struggle* to Recent Controversies." *Politics and Society* 7: 343–401.

———. 1985. *Capitalism and Social Democracy.* Cambridge, UK, and New York: Cambridge University Press.

Przeworski, Adam, and John Sprague. 1986. *Paper Stones: A History of Electoral Socialism.* Chicago: University of Chicago Press.

Rahman, Maha Abdel. 2002. "The Politics of 'UnCivil' Society in Egypt." *Review of African Political Economy* 29: 21–36.

Randall, Vicky. 2007. "Political Parties and Democratic Developmental States." *Development Policy Review* 25(5): 633–652.

Redding, Kent. 2003. *Making Race, Making Power: North Carolina's Road to Disfranchisement.* Urbana and Chicago: University of Illinois Press.

Riker, William. 1962. *The Theory of Political Coalitions.* New Haven, CT: Yale University Press.

Riley, Dylan. 2010. *The Civic Foundations of Fascism in Europe: Italy, Spain, and Romania, 1870–1945.* Baltimore: Johns Hopkins University Press.

Roberts, Barbara. 1986. "Shovelling Out the 'Mutinous': Political Deportation From Canada Before 1936." *Labour/Le Travail* 18 (Fall): 77–110.

Roberts, Kenneth. 2002. "Social Inequalities without Class Cleavages in Latin America's Neoliberal Era." *Studies in Comparative International Development* 36(4): 3–33.

———. 2008. "The Mobilization of Opposition to Economic Liberalization." *Annual Review of Political Science* 11: 327–349.

Robertson, Andrew W. 2004. "Voting Rites and Voting Acts: Electioneering Ritual, 1790–1820." In *Beyond the Founders: New Approaches to the Political History of the Early American Republic*, edited by Jeffrey L. Pasley, Andrew W. Robertson, and David Waldstreicher, 57–78. Chapel Hill: University of North Carolina Press.

Robin, Martin. 1968. *Radical Politics and Canadian Labour, 1880–1930*. Kingston, Ontario: Industrial Relations Centre, Queen's University.

Roediger, David R. 1991. *The Wages of Whiteness: Race and the Making of the American Working Class*. New York: Verso.

Roy, Bhaskar. 1998. "BJP Should Keep Contentious Issues out of the CMP: Fernandes." *Times of India*, March 5.

Rueschemeyer, Dietrich. 2003. "Can One or a Few Cases Yield Theoretical Gains?" In *Comparative Historical Analysis in the Social Sciences*, edited by James Mahoney and Dietrich Rueschemeyer, 305–336. Cambridge, UK, and New York: Cambridge University Press.

Rutherford, Bruce K. 2008. *Egypt after Mubarak: Liberalism, Islam, and Democracy in the Arab World*. Princeton, NJ: Princeton University Press.

Salvadori, Massimo L. 1977. "Gramsci e il PCI: due concezioni dell'egemonia." In *Egemonia e democrazia. Gramsci e la questione comunista nel dibattito di Mondoperaio*, edited by Federico Coen, 33–68. Rome: Edizioni Avanti!

Sarıbay, Ali Yaşar. 1985. *Türkiye'de Modernleşme, Din, ve Parti Politikası: Milli Selâmet Partisi Örnek Olayı*. Istanbul: Alan.

Sartori, Giovanni. 1969. "From the Sociology of Politics to Political Sociology." In *Politics and the Social Sciences*, edited by Seymour Martin Lipset, 65–100. New York: Oxford University Press.

———. 1976. *Parties and Party Systems:A Framework for Analysis*. Cambridge, UK, and New York: Cambridge University Press.

Saxena, Anil. 1998. "BJP Modifies Agenda to Keep Allies Happy," *Times of India*, March 15.

Schedler, Andreas. 2013. *The Politics of Uncertainty: Sustaining and Subverting Electoral Authoritarianism*. Oxford, UK: Oxford University Press.

Schmitt, Carl. [1922] 2005. *Political Theology: Four Chapters on the Concept of Sovereignty*. Chicago: University of Chicago Press.

Schneirov, Richard. 1991. "Political Cultures and the Role of the State in Labor's Republic." *Labor History* 32: 376–400.

———. 1998. *Labor and Urban Politics: Class Conflict and the Origins of Modern Liberalism in Chicago, 1864–1897*. Urbana and Chicago: University of Illinois Press.

———. 2008. "Chicago's Great Upheaval of 1877: Class Polarization and Democratic Politics." In *The Great Strike of 1877*, edited by David O. Stowell, 76–104. Urbana and Chicago: University of Illinois Press.

Schneirov, Richard, and Thomas J. Suhrbur. 1988. *Union Brotherhood, Union Town: The History of the Carpenters' Union of Chicago, 1863–1987.* Carbondale and Edwardsville: Southern Illinois University Press.

Schwedler, Jillian. 2006. *Faith and Moderation: Islamist Parties in Jordan and Yemen.* New York: Cambridge University Press.

Sellers, Charles G. 1991. *The Market Revolution: Jacksonian America, 1815–1846.* New York: Oxford University Press.

Sen, Amartya and Jean Dreze. 2013. *An Uncertain Glory: India and Its Contradictions.* Princeton, NJ: Princeton University Press.

Sharma, Chanchal. 2011. "A Discursive Dominance Theory of Economic Reform Sustainability: The Case of India." *India Review* 10: 126–184.

Shefter, Martin. 1977. "Party and Patronage: Germany, England, and Italy." *Politics and Society* 7 (4): 403–451.

Shorbagy, Manar. 2007. "The Egyptian Movement for Change—Kefaya: Redefining Politics in Egypt." *Public Culture* 19: 175–196.

Singerman, Diane. 1995. *Avenues of Participation: Family, Politics, and Networks in Urban Quarters of Cairo.* Princeton, NJ: Princeton University Press.

Skocpol, Theda. 1979. *States and Social Revolutions.* Cambridge, UK: Cambridge University Press.

———. 1980. "Political Response to Capitalist Crisis: Neo-Marxist Theories of the State and the Case of the New Deal." *Political Sociology* 10: 155–201.

Skogan, Wesley G. 1976. *Time Series Data for Chicago, 1840–1973.* Ann Arbor, MI: Inter-university Consortium for Political and Social Research.

Slater, Dan. 2004. "Indonesia's Accountability Trap: Party Cartels and Presidential Power after Democratic Transition." *Indonesia* 78 (October): 61–92.

———. 2010. *Ordering Power: Contentious Politics and Authoritarian Leviathans in Southeast Asia.* New York: Cambridge University Press.

———. 2013. "Democratic Careening." *World Politics* 65(4) (October): 729–763.

———. 2014. "Unbuilding Blocs: Indonesia's Accountability Deficit in Historical Perspective." *Critical Asian Studies* 46(2) (June): 287–315.

Slater, Dan, and Erica Simmons. 2013. "Coping by Colluding: Political Uncertainty and Promiscuous Powersharing in Indonesia and Bolivia." *Comparative Political Studies* 46(11) (November): 1366–1393.

Smith, David E. 1975. *Prairie Liberalism: The Liberal Party in Saskatchewan, 1905–71.* Toronto: University of Toronto Press.

Smith, Eric R. A. N. 1989. *The Unchanging American Voter.* Berkeley: University of California Press.

Smithies, Arthur. 1941. "Optimum Location in Spatial Competition." *Journal of Political Economy* 49: 423–439.

Solberg, Carl E. 1987. *The Prairies and the Pampas: Agrarian Policy in Canada and Argentina, 1880–1930*. Stanford, CA: Stanford University Press.

Somers, Margaret R. 1997. "Deconstructing and Reconstructing Class Formation Theory: Narrativity, Relational Analysis and Social Theory." In *Reworking Class*, edited by John R. Hall, 73–105. Ithaca, NY: Cornell University Press.

Snow, David A., and Robert D. Benford. 1988. "Ideology, Frame Resonance, and Participant Mobilization." *International Social Movement Research* 1: 197–217.

Sridharan, E. 1991. "Leadership Time Horizons in India: The Impact of Economic Restructuring." *Economic and Political Weekly* 31(12): 1200–1213.

Stallybrass, Peter. 1990, "Marx and Heterogeneity: Thinking the Lumpenproletariat." *Representations* 31: 69–95.

Stark, Jan. 2005. "Beyond 'Terrorism' and 'State Hegemony': Assessing the Islamist Mainstream in Egypt and Malaysia." *Third World Quarterly* 26: 307–327.

Starr, Paul. 2004. *The Creation of the Media: Political Origins of Modern Communications*. New York: Basic Books.

Starrett, Gregory. 1998. *Putting Islam to Work: Education, Politics, and Religious Transformation in Egypt*. Berkeley: University of California Press.

Steinmetz, George. 1992. "Reflections on the Role of Social Narratives in Working-Class Formation: Narrative Theory in the Social Sciences." *Social Science History* 16: 489–516.

———. (ed.) 1999. State/Culture: State Formation after the Cultural Turn. Durham, NC: Duke University Press.

Stepan-Norris, Judith, and Maurice Zeitlin. 1989. "'Who Gets the Bird?' Or How Communists Won Trust and Power in America's Unions: The Relative Autonomy of Intraclass Political Struggles." *American Sociological Review* 54(4): 504–543.

Stokes, Donald E. 1963. "Spatial Models of Party Competition." *American Political Science Review* 57(2): 368–377.

Stokes, Martin. 1992. *The Arabesk Debate: Music and Musicians in Modern Turkey*. New York: Oxford University Press.

Sullivan, Denis J., and Sana Abed-Kotob. 1999. *Islam in Contemporary Egypt: Civil Society vs. the State*. Boulder, CO, and London: Lynne Rienner Publishers.

Sundquist, James L. 1983. *Dynamics of the Party System: Alignment and Realignment of Political Parties in the United States*. Washington, DC: The Brookings Institution.

Suri, K.C. 2004. "Economic Reforms and Election Results in India." *Economic and Political Weekly* 39(51): 5404–5411.

Tamam, Hossam. 2009. "Back to the Future." *Al-Ahram Weekly* 970.

———. 2010. *Tahawwulat al-Ikhwan al-Muslimin*. Cairo: Maktab Madbouly.

Tandjung, Akbar. 2003. *Moratorium Politik Menuju Rekonsiliasi Nasional*. Jakarta: Golkar Press.

Tarrow, S. 1998. *Power in Movement: Social Movements, Collective Action and Mass Politics in the Modern State.* Cambridge, UK: Cambridge University Press.

Tepe, Sultan. 2006. "A Pro-Islamic Party? Promises and Limits of Turkey's Justice and Development Party." In *The Emergence of a New Turkey: Democracy and the AK Parti,* edited by H. Yavuz, 107–135. Salt Lake City: University of Utah Press.

Tezcür, Murat. 2010. *Muslim Reformers in Iran and Turkey: The Paradox of Moderation.* Austin: University of Texas Press.

Therborn, Göran. 2008. *From Marxism to Post-Marxism?* London and New York: Verso.

Thompson, E. P. 1966. *The Making of the English Working Class.* New York: Vintage Books.

Thompson, John Herd, and Allen Seager. 1986. *Canada 1922–1939: Decades of Discord.* Toronto: McClelland and Stewart.

Thornton, J. Mills III. 1978. *Politics and Power in a Slave Society: Alabama, 1800–1860.* Baton Rouge: Louisiana State University Press.

Tilly, Charles. 1978. *From Mobilization to Revolution.* Reading, MA: Addison-Wesley.

Tuğal, Cihan. 2009. *Passive Revolution: Absorbing the Islamic Challenge to Capitalism.* Stanford, CA: Stanford University Press.

———. 2012. "Fight or Acquiesce? Religion and Political Process in Turkey's and Egypt's Neoliberalizations," *Development and Change* 43(1): 23–51.

———. 2013. "Contesting Benevolence: Market Orientations among Muslim Aid Providers in Egypt." *Qualitative Sociology* 36(2): 141–159.

———. 2014. "End of the Leaderless Revolution." *Berkeley Journal of Sociology* 58: 83–87.

Turam, Berna. 2004. "The Politics of Engagement between Islam and the Secular State: Ambivalences of 'Civil Society.'" *The British Journal of Sociology* 55: 259–281.

———. 2007. *Between Islam and the State: The Politics of Engagement.* Stanford, CA: Stanford University Press.

Ufen, Andreas. 2008. "From Aliran to Dealignment: Political Parties in Post-Suharto Indonesia." *South East Asia Research* 16(1): 5–41.

U.S. Census Office. 1840. *Sixth Census of the United States, 1840. Volume 3.* New York: N. Ross Pub.

———. 1883. *Compendium of the Tenth Census (June 1, 1880), Part II.* Washington, DC: Government Printing Office.

Vacca, Giuseppe. 1999. *Appuntamenti con Gramsci. Introduzione allo studio dei Quaderni del carcere.* Rome: Carocci.

Varshney, A. 1998. "Mass Politics or Elite Politics? India's Economic Reforms in Comparative Perspective." *Journal of Policy Reform* 2(4): 301–335.

Veugelers, Jack W. C. 1999. "A Challenge for Political Sociology: The Rise of Far Right Parties in Europe." *Current Sociology,* 47 (4): 78–100.

von Luebke, Christian. 2011. "Rules, Rulers, and Rigidities: The Mesopolitics of Reform in Post-Suharto Indonesia." Paper presented at the annual meetings of the Association for Asian Studies, Honolulu, March.

Voss, Kim, and Rachel Sherman. 2000. "Breaking the Iron Law of Oligarchy: Union Revitalization in the American Labor Movement." *American Journal of Sociology*, 106(2): 303–349.

Waterbury, John. 1983. *The Egypt of Nasser and Sadat: The Political Economy of Two Regimes*. Princeton, NJ: Princeton University Press.

Watson, Harry L. 1981. *Jacksonian Politics and Community Conflict: The Emergence of the Second American Party System in Cumberland County North Carolina*. Baton Rouge: Louisiana State University Press.

———. 1990. *Liberty and Power: The Politics of Jacksonian America*. New York: Hill and Wang.

Wattenberg, Ben J. 1995. *Values Matter Most: How Republicans or Democrats or a Third Party Can Win and Renew the American Way of Life*. New York: Free Press.

Weber, Max. [1922] 1968. *Economy and Society: An Outline of Interpretive Sociology*, edited by Guenther Roth and Claus Wittich. New York: Bedminster Press.

———. 1946. *From Max Weber: Essays in Sociology*. Edited and translated by H. H. Gerth and C. Wright Mills. New York: Oxford University Press.

Weiss, Meredith. 2006. *Protest and Possibilities: Civil Society and Coalitions for Political Change in Malaysia*. Stanford, CA: Stanford University Press.

Whitaker, Reg. 1977. *The Government Party: Organizing and Financing the Liberal Party of Canada, 1930–58*. Toronto: University of Toronto Press.

———. 1986. "Official Repression of Communism during World War II." *Labour/Le Travail* 17(Spring): 135–166.

White, Jenny. 2002. *Islamist Mobilization in Turkey: A Study in Vernacular Politics*. Seattle: University of Washington Press.

Wilensky, Harold L. 1974. *The Welfare State and Equality: Structural and Ideological Roots of Public Expenditures*. Berkeley: University of California Press.

Wilentz, Sean. 2005. *The Rise of American Democracy: Jefferson to Lincoln*. New York: Norton.

Wilson, Major L. 1974. *Space, Time and Freedom: The Quest for Nationality and the Irrepressible Conflict, 1815–1861*. Westport, CT: Greenwood Press.

Wright, Erik Olin. 1990. *The Debate on Classes*. London: Verso.

Wright, Erik Olin. 2010. *Envisioning Real Utopias*. New York: Verso.

Yadav, Yogendra. 2004. "The Elusive Mandate of 2004." *Economic and Political Weekly*, December 18.

Yadav, Yogendra, Sanjay Kumar, and Oliver Heath. 1999. "The BJP's New Social Bloc." *Frontline* 16 (23).

Yadav, Yogendra, and Suhas Palshikar. 2009. "Principal State Level Contests and Derivative National Choices: Electoral Trends in 2004-2009." *Economic and Political Weekly*. February 7, 55–62.

Young, Walter D. 1969. *The Anatomy of a Party: The National CCF, 1932–1961*. Toronto: University of Toronto Press.

———. 1976. "Ideology, Personality and the Origin of the CCF in British Columbia." *B.C. Studies* 32(Winter): 139–162.

Zahid, Mohammed, and Michael Medley. 2006. "Muslim Brotherhood in Egypt & Sudan." *Review of African Political Economy* 33: 693–708.

Zaidi, Askari. 1999. "Congress revives '*garibi hatao*' plank," *Times of India*, July 22.

Zeghal, Malika. 1999. "Religion and Politics in Egypt: The Ulema of Al-Azhar, Radical Islam, and the State (1952–94)." *International Journal of Middle East Studies* 31: 371–399.

Zollner, Barbara. 2007. "Prison Talk: The Muslim Brotherhood's Internal Struggle during Gamal Abdel Nasser's Persecution, 1954 to 1971." *International Journal*.

Zubaida, Sami. 1989. *Islam, the People and the State: Political Ideas and Movements in the Middle East*. London and New York: Routledge.

Zuberi, Dan. 2006. *Differences That Matter: Social Policy and the Working Poor in the United States and Canada*. Ithaca, NY: Cornell ILR Press.

CONTRIBUTORS

Cedric de Leon is Associate Professor of Sociology at Providence College. His research examines the ways in which political parties shape labor movements, democratic change, and class and racial identity. Cedric's work has appeared in *Sociological Theory, Political Power and Social Theory*, and *Studies in American Political Development*. His first book, *Party and Society* (Polity, 2014), remaps the field of democratic party politics to include sociology's classical and contemporary contributions. His second book, on the political origins of American "right to work" laws, is forthcoming from Cornell University Press. Cedric serves on the Council of the Comparative and Historical Sociology section of the American Sociological Association.

Manali Desai (PhD, University of California–Los Angeles) is Lecturer in the Sociology Department at the University of Cambridge. Her work encompasses the areas of state formation, political parties, social movements, development, ethnic violence, and postcolonial studies. Among her publications are *State Formation and Radical Democracy in India, 1860–1990* (Routledge, 2006) and *States of Trauma* (Zubaan, 2009), in addition to articles in the *American Journal of Sociology, Social Forces, Social Science History, Comparative Studies in Society* and *History, and Journal of Historical Sociology*, among others. She has received grants from the British Academy and Leverhulme Foundation for her research. She is currently working on a comparative study of the politics of liberalization, investigating the role of parties in embedding new institutions at the level of state policy as well as in society.

Barry Eidlin is an American Sociological Association-National Science Foundation Postdoctoral Fellow at the University of Wisconsin–Madison. He is a comparative historical sociologist interested in the study of class, politics, social movements, and institutional change. His work has appeared in *Labor History*, *Sociology Compass*, and *The Wiley-Blackwell Encyclopedia of Social and Political Movements*. The chapter in this volume is part of a larger research project that explains diverging trajectories of working-class organizational power in the United States and Canada over the course of the twentieth century. This research won the Thomas A. Kochan and Stephen R. Sleigh Best Dissertation Award from the Labor and Employment Relations Association and is currently being developed into a book manuscript.

Dylan Riley is Associate Professor of Sociology at the University of California, Berkeley. He is the author of *The Civic Foundations of Fascism in Europe: Italy, Spain, and Romania 1870–1945* (Johns Hopkins University Press, 2010). Further he has published articles in the *American Sociological Review*, *Comparative Sociology*, *Contemporary Sociology*, *Comparative Studies in Society and History*, *Social Science History*, *The Socio-Economic Review*, and the *New Left Review*. He is a council member of the Comparative and Historical Section of the ASA and a member of the editorial committee of the *New Left Review*.

Dan Slater is an Associate Professor in the Department of Political Science and Associate Member of the Department of Sociology at the University of Chicago. His published articles can be found in disciplinary journals such as the *American Journal of Political Science*, *American Journal of Sociology*, *Comparative Politics*, *Comparative Political Studies*, *International Organization*, *Journal of Democracy*, *Perspectives on Politics*, and *World Politics*. He has received four best-article awards from various organized sections of the American Political Science Association (APSA) and American Sociological Association (ASA). His first book, *Ordering Power: Contentious Politics and Authoritarian Leviathans in Southeast Asia* (Cambridge, 2010), was a finalist for the Asia Society's Bernard Schwartz Book Award and received an honorable mention for the Barrington Moore Book Award from the ASA's Comparative-Historical Section.

Cihan Tuğal is an Associate Professor of Sociology at the University of California, Berkeley. He works on mobilization, socioeconomic change, and the role of religion in sociopolitical projects. His research so far has focused on how the interaction between capitalist development, religion, and politics shapes everyday life, urban space, class relations, and national identity. His book *Passive Revolution: Absorbing the Islamic Challenge to Capitalism* was published in 2009 by Stanford University Press. His research has also been published in *Economy and Society, Theory and Society, Sociological Theory, Qualitative Sociology, New Left Review, Development and Change, Sociological Quarterly*, area journals, and edited volumes.

INDEX